EMBODIMENT, RELATION, COMMUNITY

EMBODIMENT, RELATION, COMMUNITY

A Continental Philosophy of Communication

GARNET C. BUTCHART

THE PENNSYLVANIA STATE UNIVERSITY PRESS | UNIVERSITY PARK, PENNSYLVANIA

Portions of the text appeared in earlier forms. Chapter 1 is a revised version of "The Uncertainty of Communication as Revealed by Psychoanalysis," by Garnet C. Butchart, *The Review of Communication* 13, no. 1 (2013), copyright © National Communication Association, reprinted by permission of Taylor & Francis Ltd., www.tandfonline.com on behalf of The National Communication Association. Chapter 5 is a revised version of "Touch, Communication, Community: Jean-Luc Nancy's Semiotic Phenomenology," *Metodo: International Studies in Phenomenology and Philosophy* 3, no. 1 (2015): 221–44.

Library of Congress Cataloging-in-Publication Data

Names: Butchart, Garnet, author.
Title: Embodiment, relation, community : a continental philosophy of communication / Garnet C. Butchart.
Description: University Park, Pennsylvania : The Pennsylvania State University Press, [2019] | Includes bibliographical references and index.
Summary: "Integrates the perspectives of Giorgio Agamben, Roberto Esposito, Jean-Luc Nancy, and Lacanian psychoanalysis to distinguish communication theory from the philosophy of communication"—Provided by publisher.
Identifiers: LCCN 2018043356 | ISBN 9780271083254 (cloth : alk. paper)
Subjects: LCSH: Communication—Philosophy.
Classification: LCC P90 .B88 2019 | DDC 302.201—dc23
LC record available at https://lccn.loc.gov/2018043356

Copyright © 2019 Garnet C. Butchart
All rights reserved
Printed in the United States of America
Published by The Pennsylvania State University Press,
University Park, PA 16802-1003

The Pennsylvania State University Press is a member of the Association of University Presses.

It is the policy of The Pennsylvania State University Press to use acid-free paper. Publications on uncoated stock satisfy the minimum requirements of American National Standard for Information Sciences—Permanence of Paper for Printed Library Material, ANSI Z39.48-1992.

CONTENTS

Acknowledgments | vii

Introduction | 1

1 The Wager of Communication (as Revealed by Psychoanalysis) | 23
2 The Ban of Language and Law of Communication | 42
3 Of Communication and-as Immunization | 66
4 Body as Index | 94
5 What Remains to Be Thought: Community, or *Being-With* | 116

Epilogue | 137

Notes | 143
Bibliography | 179
Index | 191

ACKNOWLEDGMENTS

Support for the research presented in this book came from many sources, for which I am grateful. Colleagues in the Department of Communication and Rhetorical Studies and the College of Liberal Arts at Duquesne University provided steady encouragement, particularly Ron Arnett and Janie Fritz, who believed in this project. A Paluse Faculty Research Grant awarded by the Center for the Catholic Faith and Culture at Duquesne University, a Presidential Scholarship Award from Duquesne University, and multiple Wimmer Family Foundation Faculty Research Grants from the College of Liberal Arts at Duquesne University provided generous financial support. Intellectually, Isaac Catt welcomed me into a community of scholars (Richard Lanigan, Frank Macke, Deborah Eicher-Catt, Andrew Smith) whose orientation to communication study shaped the idea development of this book. The language of its expression was cultivated through years of conversation with Briankle Chang. The monograph could not have been completed without the labor of teaching assistants, particularly Margaret Mullan, as well as Blake Plavchak, William Aungst, Fr. Maximilian Ofori, and Christopher Bondi. Dena Taub, Sophia Nagel, and Rachel Morrell provided excellent research assistance. Thanks, finally, to Julie Love.

Introduction

Consider the commonplace crime of uttering a forged instrument. According to the U.S. common law code, such an act constitutes a crime if it can be shown to have met three basic criteria: "[1] An instrument was forged; [2] the person uttering the instrument knew it to be forged; and [3] it was uttered with the intent to defraud."[1] The so-called instrument of this crime could be any number of false documents, such as a bank note, driver's permit, passport, diploma, contract, or similar. However, a critical distinction is drawn in the legal code between the act of forgery (the technical, or artistic act of falsifying a document) and the act of uttering it, of passing it off with the intent to defraud. Although forgery and uttering appear related, they are enshrined in law as separate and distinct acts for the reason that the same person need not commit them both. Forging a state-issued identification card, for example, is neither the same act nor the same crime as a minor uttering the instrument in an attempt to buy booze.

What is significant about the crime of uttering is the equivalence drawn in the American legal code between it and the act of publishing.[2] Although a document may have been forged, uttering it constitutes a formally distinct crime for the reason that this act makes actual a breach of law that had, prior to the instance of utterance, stood in suspension, a virtual infraction to come. The gulf between the act of falsifying a document and the fraudulent use of it explains the retention in modern American law of the archaic sense of uttering as publishing: a forged document is transformed into an instrument of crime the moment at which it is presented, instituted by an act of giving or sharing—an act of *communication*, commonly understood. Prior to that moment, a falsified document will have neither value within an economy of exchange nor any criminal significance to anyone participating within it. For there to be a crime, the silence of the document has to have been broken, such as by offering a false diploma as proof of qualification, cashing a check with a forged signature, submitting a fraudulent will and testament for probate, handing over a forged prescription to obtain medications, and so on.

On its face, uttering or intentionally communicating a false instrument appears to be a crime because it violates a code designed to protect the promissory value of a document by underwriting the authority of office carried by its seal or the identity of its signatory.[3] Because the legal code is in force to secure conditions for exchange, and for commerce, breaking its code appears to put the possibility of commonality and, above all else, community, at risk.[4] However, although the legal system enshrines the act of uttering as an offense—codifies it and thereby renders it significant within a broader system of social and economic value—it is in fact the logic of risk that serves as the reference point of its criminality. The decisive, criminal feature of the act of uttering a false instrument is the dialogue that leads to its utterance in the first place. With bogus document in hand, what must be assessed are the consequences, both the risks as well as the benefits, of passing it off—consequences of communication. On the one hand, there is gain to be gotten, such as the increase in freedom and pleasure that accompanies the riches of a forged check. On the other, there is the risk of loss, such as the loss of rights and freedom that may accompany an arrest and conviction. To be sure, although two or more agents may debate the pros and cons of uttering a forged document, the decision to do so rests only with a single agent, the one who actually brings him- or herself to action. The decision of whether to utter—that is, to communicate—can be made only after careful reflection, a period within which the bearer of the forged document will engage him- or herself in the only way possible: namely, in language or, more precisely, dialogue with what psychoanalysis calls discourse of the Other. To arrive at a point of action, the utterer must measure his or her intentions against the prevailing legal and moral conventions of the community, accept or reject the risk of a loss, and reach a verdict.

Like many acts of communication, the crime of uttering a false instrument can be understood as an act of recitation, a present act in reference to a previous moment. As we know from Alfred Schutz's phenomenology of communication, the person makes reference to a prior self in anticipation of a moment ahead of present time, when he or she will communicate.[5] The process of reciting, or calling back with a view to moving forward—thinking before acting—adds to what we know about communication as an experience of coming after oneself: the human *Dasein* is, by definition, *there*, not here, always ahead of itself, leaving the "self" to come after. With regard to the example of criminal communication, although the process of deciding whether to utter or not may be viewed as ethical, what in fact stirs the wrath of law is the dialogue, or recital, that precipitates action in one way or another.[6] The decision to utter presupposes a prior, conflicted activity of risk assessment in which the agent imagines him- or herself in at least two future scenarios: utter the document and benefit from fraud, or withhold it and avoid breaking the law. It is precisely in *decisio* (L. *decidere*, to separate, cutting off) that an agent of the crime attempts to resolve an internal conflict: one of his or her future selves must be amputated—repressed, blocked, or in some way silenced—so that the agent may move forward, communicate the instrument or not.

The agent in question is "an agent of the crime" because even if the uttering does not actually occur, the possibility of it must have been recited nevertheless (so-called premeditation). In that sense, because the person is in possession of a forged document, he or she seems already to be caught—caught, that is, between awareness that the document is forged and uncertainty about what to do with it. For whatever action the agent chooses to take, what is communicated by the hesitation prior to the action is the possibility of communication—the silent signal of a potential crime to come. To be sure, it is not a crime to possess a forged document.[7] But because the agent of the crime of uttering must be in communication (dialogue) within him- or herself in order for it to be committed, finding proof of the intent to defraud is not difficult: the utterer who utters stood as witness to his or her own potential crime before the event had come to pass. Perhaps this is why modern law has so few leniencies for an accused who, in his or her defense, pleads ignorance of the significance of his or her actions. In the act of communicating a forged instrument, communication has already occurred, and there can be no such thing as failure to communicate for the reason that communication, in this case, cannot not have taken place.

These observations, on a source of modern thinking about a permanent and enduring question of communication—namely, the impossibility of human noncommunication—serve as a premise for the research presented in this volume and indicate the sense in which it inquires into human communication as an experience that is embodied because loaded with the bond of community. As the research will demonstrate, that bond, which is a relation, binds one to another in and through, and is experienced as such by way of, communication. Before any meaningful rehearsal can be offered of how this is so, and why it matters, it will help to begin with an intellectual background of what is to follow.

To start, what is communication? The *Oxford English Dictionary* offers its answer by grouping nine definitions, or senses, of communication into three categories: (1) senses relating to affinity or association, (2) senses relating to imparting or transmitting something, and (3) senses relating to access. The primary sense of communication reads as follows: "Interpersonal contact, social interaction, association, intercourse," which, the *OED* states, is "hard to distinguish from" the sense in category two, the "transmission or exchange of information, knowledge, or ideas, by means of speech, writing, mechanical or electronic media, etc."[8] In his classic tracing of the meaning of *communication*, Raymond Williams confirms both senses from the fifteenth-century Latin *communicationem*, a noun of action derived from the past participle *communicare*, the root of which is *communis* (L. common). Hence the modern meaning of *communicate* as to impart, to make common. By the late fifteenth century, according to Williams, the *action* of communication (bringing forth, imparting, and sharing) had become the object "thus made common" by such action: *a* communication, such as a letter, brief, order, forged instrument, and so on.[9] This has remained the main usage of the term, with important additions in the late seventeenth century to the *means* of communication (such as roads, rail, and other lines or channels) as well as the twentieth-century extension to the *media* of sharing information and maintaining contact.

Since the beginning of formal academic inquiry into human speech and media of mass communication in the United States more than one hundred years ago, several theories, models, and histories have been developed by scholars across the social sciences and humanities in attempts to better understand the structure, function, processes, practices, content, goals, and outcomes of communication.[10] This book, however, brings a contemporary continental philosophical perspective to bear on thinking about the practices, goals, outcomes, and experiences of this human phenomenon. It dispenses with rehearsing modern theories of communication and instead enters directly into a program of thinking about how we can think about the practices, goals, outcomes, possibility, and experience of human communication from the bottom—its philosophical foundations. Akin to the founding question of continental philosophy pinpointed by Leonard Lawlor, namely, "the question of thinking: what is called or what calls for thinking,"[11] what founds contemporary continental philosophy of communication is a, or the, question of what calls for *its* thinking—that is, the raising of communication to a level, or drawing it into the "orbit,"[12] of philosophical investigation.

What calls for thinking about human communication, summarily put, is posed by the concrete, and at times mundane, experience of being human—which means, at the very least, to be embodied, to be in community, and for that reason, to be communicative. What, for example, is the relationship between language and human communication? How are human persons connected to one another and other beings in and by way of communication? What are the embodied implications—the living experience—of a community symbolic matrix? What is the relationship between conscious awareness/perception and the grammar, logic, and/or rhetoric of human expression? In a world defined by differences of perspective, human history, belief, values, and experiences, how is mutual understanding, to say nothing of moments of agreement, accomplished? What role does human communicating play in the possibility or impossibility of striving for, achieving, maintaining, and/or destroying such moments? Questions such as these, which circumscribe the root subject of continental philosophical thought (namely, what it means to be human) help raise communication—a condition of being human and a fundamental feature of its meaning—to a plane of visibility typically unseen from the perspective of one's own so-called natural (i.e., prereflective and disinterested) attitude toward being in the world.

The guiding themes addressed in the course of the present research—communication, embodiment, and community—are admittedly massive. However, the goal of the work is not to report on the points of strength and weakness of various currents of inquiry into those themes in the humanities and social sciences, which would be a monumental task. Instead, it is to contribute to critical and philosophical thinking about human embodiment, communication, and community by way of a contemporary continental philosophical orientation to these themes and their manifold points of intersection. The philosophical figures that are central to the approach taken in this book are Jean-Luc Nancy, Giorgio Agamben, Roberto Esposito, and Jacques Lacan. Each of these scholars can be read as, but certainly not reduced to, philosophers of relation, and for that reason fit comfortably together in a single volume. On their own, each offers perspective on relation as one of the most important founding conceptual points of entry into thinking about human embodied being, identity and difference, community, and the materiality of human expressive media. Together, the styles of philosophical thinking represented by Agamben, Esposito, Nancy, Lacan, and contemporary Lacanian psychoanalysis can be brought to bear on communication thinking to open it in new ways. However, the objective of this book is not to rehearse and report on the ideas of each thinker. Instead, the objective is to write, which is to think, along with the orientation of thinking invited by and exemplified in their work. Summarily put, the argument of this book is that doing so helps demonstrate what human communication inquiry can look like, and accomplish, in a contemporary continental philosophical key.

To develop this argument in a manageable trajectory, the present research addresses the following topical areas, which are also, admittedly, expansive: subjectivity, speech, and language; human communication and the impossibility of noncommunication; law, belonging, and exception; communication and-as immunization; bodily presence and dis-integration; and human community as *being-with*. Although there are several points at which the writing and thinking of Agamben, Esposito, Nancy, Lacan, and contemporary Lacanian psychoanalysis intersect, and many more points of connection that could be drawn, what is implicit in each philosopher's approach to the kind of questions signaled by the topical areas just listed is a critique of the humanist, metaphysical, and positivist orientation of modern philosophy. In particular, each scholar is concerned in some respect with the problem of the subject, an entity that is thought from the perspective of modern philosophy as preformed, pregiven, and largely autonomous in its actions. It is the critical questioning of that humanist subject that fundamentally qualifies the philosophical orientation of Agamben, Esposito, Nancy, and Lacan as "continental."[13]

Lacan, for instance, and all the psychoanalytic theory and research that followed his writings through the twentieth century, sets a course for radically undermining modern philosophy's image of a unified self by positing instead an incomplete and lacking subject, which is by definition constituted as such in its relation to—that is, its foundation in—language. For Nancy, whose early work is informed by Lacan, the question of what "comes after" the subject has occupied his entire career. In response, Nancy offers a postphenomenological and deconstructive focus on being, emphasizing in much of his thinking that human being is always a being-in-relation, not prior to or after language, for instance, but "right at" language, as he would say, and therefore cannot be thought of as preformed, nonindependent, and fully closed upon itself.[14] Next, Agamben has drawn on Nancy's concept of "abandoned being" in his writings on sovereign power—writings that bring to maturity his career interest in the philosophical insights into the speaking subject offered by structural linguistics.[15] For Agamben, human being is a speaking being that does not come prior to language but is already in it, before it, as one stands before the law in being called into it. For Esposito, a contemporary of both Agamben and Nancy, the themes of subjectivity, law, and language are addressed by way of a focus on biopolitics.[16] For Esposito, one of the critical strategies for identifying the limits of modern metaphysical thinking is to locate points of coincidence of seemingly opposed terms—such as community and immunity, life and death, and interiority and exteriority—so as to expose the points of closure around which discourses of identity and difference, self and other, domestic and foreigner, "us" and "them" have coalesced in the modern order, with sometimes catastrophic consequences.

If continental philosophy is, cursorily put, a mid-twentieth-century intellectual movement that emerged in challenge to the humanist subject of modern philosophy, emphasizing the importance of language as the basis of the subject's production and experience, then what is contemporary continental philosophy? One effective way to discern that category of scholarship, albeit perhaps too easily, is in terms of the career period of the philosophers working within it. Scholars such as Jean-Luc Marion, Alain Badiou, Jacques Rancière, Catherine Malabou, and others engage and extend the intellectual programs and commitments of the continental philosophers who preceded them, in particular, Martin Heidegger, Louis Althusser, Michel Foucault, Gilles Deleuze, Jacques Derrida, Jean-François Lyotard, and Maurice Merleau-Ponty. Among contemporary, that is, living continental philosophers working within the French, German, and Italian traditions (which is itself another category distinction—namely, geographical), the most prominent figures at the time of the present writing are Nancy, Agamben, and Esposito.

Another way to discern the category of contemporary continental philosophy is thematically, which in this case includes, but is not limited to, the critical-philosophical focus that most of these thinkers bring to the political, the ethical, the ontotheological, and most importantly, the material. As indicated in the brief sketch in the previous paragraph, what one may notice in the work of all the philosophers named there is a tension between what can loosely be called thought of the linguistic and thought of the material. I do not want to go so far as to say that this feature defines the "contemporary" of contemporary continental philosophy. However, the tension, or perhaps better to say the relation, between thought of the material and of the linguistic in the diverse attempts to work within it is undeniably a major characterizing feature of contemporary continental philosophy and what I am here calling a contemporary continental philosophical perspective.[17]

One way to view this tension is as a working-with or working-within the relation between two distinct intellectual traditions: on the one hand, the linguistic paradigm of poststructuralism, the defining communication feature of which is semiotics and, on the other hand, phenomenology, particularly its mid-twentieth-century existentialist movement. Usually these two traditions are classified as being more at odds with one another than complementary insofar as structural linguistics and semiotics name the study of the sign logic of a culture according to which the latter is organized, and phenomenology, broadly speaking, is a movement in thinking about the givenness of being, especially human being, in its meaningful relation to the world.[18] As Ian James persuasively argues, many of the thinkers that he groups into the category of "new French philosophy," which includes Nancy, exhibit not only an attempted "break," beginning in the 1970s, from the linguistic paradigm of structuralism and semiotics but also a decided response to what he calls "the demand that thought re-engage with the material world."[19] The intellectual "break" encountered in the work of the contemporary continental philosophers and philosophical perspectives with which the present research engages, however, should be read not as a clean cut but rather as thinking that exhibits combined remnants of both these traditions.

For instance, contemporary psychoanalytic theory, research, and practice continue to work with Lacan's founding merger of the Saussurean linguistic model with Hegelian and Heideggerian preoccupations with consciousness and the experience of such mundane human conditions as anxiety, dread, and awareness of death.[20] Next, throughout Agamben's recent writings on law, community, and immunity, one finds an explicit and highly innovative working with the relation between human language, subjectivity, and human embodied experience, an intellectual effort informed most notably by the linguistics of Émile Benveniste and the communication theory of Roman Jakobson. Next, although Esposito's writing does not draw explicitly from structuralist semiotics or phenomenology, it does, nevertheless, exemplify a contemporary program of deconstructive criticism, and one finds in it a heavy emphasis on language, particularly the importance of etymology to explain the impact on life of the biopolitical paradigm. Finally, although Nancy is probably the philosopher in this category who is most committed to breaking from his preceding generation's thinking, he has never neglected the importance of accounting for the problem and deficiencies of language, especially evident, as I will discuss, in his attempt to think about the lived experience of being-*with*.[21]

To be sure, there are several philosophers who could have been drawn on in the pages to follow, but are not, whose work helps define and exemplifies continental philosophy in its contemporary mode. As already mentioned, these philosophers include Marion, Badiou, Rancière, and Malabou, as well as François Laruelle, Bruno Latour, Slavoj Žižek, Bernard Stiegler, Maurizio Ferraris, Franco Berardi, Joseph Vogl, Peter Sloterdijk, and others. However, it is the thought of relation, and its attendant questions of human relationality, that links the thinkers upon which this book focuses and that underscores the potential of their combined perspectives to expand our understanding of human communication. Nancy, Esposito, Agamben, and Lacanian psychoanalysis fit together, and can be engaged with, because of the attention they pay to the materially binding intersection of language, subjectivity, and communication—that is, the phenomena and human experiences of embodied communication communities. Motifs characterizing their efforts in this respect include law, abandonment, threat and protection, exposure and contact, immunity and commonality, exception, *exscription*, *being-with*, nonbelonging, bodily dis-integration, and so on.

A rehearsal may now be offered of the direction this book takes in its engagement with the questions, concepts, insights, and style of inquiry represented by Agamben, Esposito, Nancy, and Lacanian psychoanalysis regarding what those questions, insights, and inquiry styles offer to a contemporary continental philosophy of human communication.

If Agamben, Nancy, and Esposito make efforts to reengage thought of the material world, then it is Lacan, and Lacanian psychoanalytic theory and practice, that is central to the linguistic paradigm within which these philosophers work in that regard. This book begins with Lacanian psychoanalysis not in an effort to explain the formative role of this tradition in the discursive turn in twentieth-century thought but rather to identify its general relevance for philosophical understanding of human communication. Briefly summarized, psychoanalysis approaches communication in terms of its faults and failures more so than its smooth functioning. As we know, communication is often experienced as miscommunication, misunderstanding, and indeterminacy in the slippage of meaning. Its goal may be misinformation and deception rather than truth-telling, and even intrusion rather than assistance. The outcome can range from confusion to disagreement to "outright interpersonal and intergroup conflict. Psychoanalysis reminds us of these basic characteristics by way of accounting for the relation of the human subject to language. According to the Lacanian tradition, language both enables and restricts human expression and perception, both figuring and disfiguring the speaking subject in its appropriation. It is a tradition that undermines the essentialism of modern communication theory's image of a rational, complete, and autonomous speaker-subject by showing how, to the contrary, human communicative agency is incomplete, formed in language rather than preformed prior to instances of intentional communication.

From the psychoanalytic point of view, *communication* is defined as the ability of a speaker-subject to "make known" his or her thoughts. Although this perspective takes recourse to positivist sender-receiver models, and theories, of information transfer, Lacanian psychoanalysis can be read to demonstrate that the content of human communication (thought itself) is not preformed but instead shaped in the process of communicating. It shows how words accumulate an emotional history in a subject's appropriation of language and how the significance of that history to the well-being of a subject—a lived and thereby material condition—can be accessed and perhaps even improved upon by way of communicating, which the psychoanalytic interview demonstrates is not always intentional. Slips of the tongue, words forgotten or spoken out of context, gestures, and tone of voice, for example, may betray the conscious intent of a speaker-subject as he or she beats around the bush of something guarded or as yet unsayable in conscious, intentional speech. What the subject says in the analytic conversation is nevertheless meaningful in terms of what the subject wants to say but cannot as yet find words: not all can be said. In its failures to fully represent the subject, language strings it along with its promise, but not guarantee, of better and perhaps even more "effective" communication.

In contrast to mechanical transfer models of human communication, which presuppose by not questioning an already existing, preformed sender-subject and measure communication effectiveness largely in terms of the overall clarity of transmission and success or failure of reception, the beginning chapter of this book puts that model and the certainty of human communication into question by summarizing how human self-identity is undermined by self-difference in language and how conscious communication is destabilized by unconscious discourse. The objective is to draw attention to human communication not merely as self-certainty in message transfer, which can be taken as the basic goal of modern communication theory, whether as a liberal arts skill or as an academic challenge for designing models to improve communication.[22] Rather, the objective of the chapter is to offer perspective on human communication as uncertainty and risk, as unintentional (in part), and as potentially destabilizing, a perspective that helps fortify the possibility and human experience of communication as properly philosophical themes for investigation.

As indicated by the above observations on the crime of uttering a false instrument, there persists in modern thinking about human communication the presupposition of the impossibility of noncommunication: that "one cannot *not* communicate." Although scholars of human communication will recognize this as one, if not the, classic axiom posited by Paul Watzlawick, Janet Beavin, and Donald Jackson in the mid-twentieth century,[23] it is the legacy impact of psychoanalysis on modern conceptions of the self (from which that Palo Alto group of psychotherapists drew) that helps explain the endurance of this presupposition in human communication thought. According to Lacanian psychoanalysis, language operates with a law-like function, which means that it brings structure to sense and meaning to experience in a way that organizes and regulates the order of a culture, its *nomos*. The second chapter of this book reenters the space of interpretation opened by the presupposition of the impossibility of noncommunication and proposes to rethink it in terms of the *ban* of language. I argue that this ban, the conception of which is developed in Nancy's early work, is semiotic, which means it is embodied: it is experienced as an injunction against noncommunication. In an effort to develop and support this argument, I turn to Agamben's writing on the relation between sovereign power and bare life.

Crucial to that perspective is the parallel Agamben draws between the logic of sovereign power and what he describes as the sovereignty of language. Language is sovereign, Agamben argues, for the reason that it operates according to a paradoxical logic of exclusive-inclusion. As I explain in the chapter, language as sovereign stands in relation to instances of its taking place in human speech by way of its withdrawal—that is, in a relation of exception to the rules according to which it makes human communication possible. The sovereign power of language is tied existentially to its speakers (*I, you, him, her, them*) by way of the very act of uttering these pronouns, speech acts that bind the speaker to the conventions of his or her communication community. It does so, according to the perspective Agamben offers, because every speech act must be understood not merely as an active human expression but also as an instance of the taking place of language, its sovereign power. In its standing back, or exception, to the rules of communication it establishes (grammar, logic, and rhetoric), language as sovereign suspends its normal signifying function and refers to itself—it refers, that is, to the potential for communication. In human speech, language the sovereign can be heard. Even in the void of communication (such as in silence, misunderstanding, noise, or what some might call babble) there is the potential for communication—and not only that, but also noncommunication is ruled out.

I explain how this is so by drawing on Agamben's discussion of "abandoned being," which for my purposes means that human being cannot *not* communicate because it is abandoned to and by language, remains at its mercy, and is left to its own expressive capacities, "excluded and also 'open to all, free.'"[24] Benveniste, whose classic essay "Subjectivity in Language" was written in clarifying response to Lacan, proves this important point: there is no human being that is not already a speaking being. Human being is abandoned to language, subject to it as the authority ordering a culture: as Benveniste says, subjectivity is manifest in language. Furthermore, one cannot not communicate because human being does not merely exist; it has to: it is thrown into being and it does not know why (Heidegger). Communication, I argue, is the mode and means through which human being makes sense of its experience of having-to-be, its ontological abandonment to language as sovereign and its injunction against noncommunication. What is left for thought to think, as I address in the final chapter, is this being, a being-*with*.

To be sure, although there is widespread agreement in modern human communication scholarship that the presupposition of the impossibility of noncommunication has the potential to close rather than open new perspective (i.e., human action, reduced to information, is not simply equivalent to communication), many traditions of inquiry in both the humanities and the social sciences nevertheless begin from the point of agreement that human social action is necessarily communicative.[25] My want to return to the space of interpretation opened by the presupposition of the impossibility of noncommunication is not motivated by a desire to rehearse worn out debates about it. To the contrary, an institutionally legitimized discourse on human communication presumes the existence of a background or history of concepts, claims, and theories that may have won neither complete agreement nor perfection in application. *One cannot not communicate* is an exemplar of the unfinished history of human communication study. The fact that this presupposition has not yet been determined to be either completely true or false by modern theories of communication indicates its continued relevance to the development of ongoing philosophical inquiry.[26]

That said, the goal of this book is, in part, to add contemporary philosophical perspective to the communication problematic indicated by that presupposition and explore intellectual resources that may inspire thinking that avoids the deadlock associated with its persistence in discipline-specific communication scholarship. Central to accomplishing that goal is the figure of *exclusive-inclusion*, a device that does the philosophical work for both Agamben and Esposito of challenging the rigidity of dichotomous thinking exemplified by conceptual pairings such as identity/difference, self/other, domestic/foreign, interiority/exteriority, and life/death—thinking that structures perception, and thereby judgment, of the value of each term. Both Agamben and Esposito's objective of blurring such conceptual distinctions is not to resolve the contradictions inherent to such pairings (whether theoretical, historical, and/or lived) but rather to demonstrate how a nondichotomous style of thinking, such as we see with deconstruction, can help expose their fault lines and, in so doing, broaden perspective on individuality and community, the commonality of human embodied being, and as I demonstrate philosophically, communication and the impossibility of noncommunication.

To be human is to exist communicatively, a constant task that demands awareness of human coexistence as we are "suspended in language" together.[27] As scholars of communication freely acknowledge, as would anyone who has had meaningful conversation, the sense we make of our perceptions of others' expressions always has the potential to differ from, and at times conflict with, their intentions. At the same time, to share a world with one another is to take up and engage its discourses, whether directly, by way of speaking them, or indirectly, such as in attempts to disavow them. Because we inhabit the sign systems we use to make sense of ourselves, others, and the world, having to be in communication means being exposed. How will my words and actions be perceived? Do I make sense? Will I be recognized? Abandonment to language requires critical employment of its resources: one cannot not communicate; therefore, one must communicate. The third chapter of this book approaches the human ontological condition of having-to-be in terms of its threat and protection from exposure to communication. It turns to the work of Esposito, whose style of thinking offers a pivot point of the philosophical perspective advanced in the book, so allow me here to offer a slightly more substantive preview.

Esposito deepens our understanding of human communication as it presents a threat to as well as protection from itself. On the one hand, communication may be understood as a threat to the individual and the community if we define it not only as affinity—that is, the breaking of individual boundaries in the exposure to community—but also as transfer of new, differing, competing, and/or misleading ideas or even offhanded comments and unwanted remarks. More complexly still, communication may be understood as a threat if we define it as dialogue, where engaged perspectives can sometimes result in disagreement and even deadlock rather than agreement and the accomplishment of common goals. Basic examples here include the threat of persuasion by contagious ideas, such as assumptions about what it means to be a part of or disqualified from community; the threat of conflict, such as in confrontations with expressions of different, institutionally more powerful, and/or antagonizing points of view; the threat to self-certainty in one's conscious anticipation of being misunderstood, dismissed, or perhaps simply ignored; the threat of alienation, for instance, for not saying the right thing or not saying enough; and even the threat of censorship for saying too much or for disagreeing outright. On the other hand, communication may be understood as protection for the individual and the community, as a mode and means through which individuality is opened in, and as the invitation to dialogue, affinity, and goal accomplishment, all of which can potentially close in instances when what is transmitted is not received or understood, is ignored, dismissed, or lost over time; when misunderstanding and conflict can occur because the same thing can be communicated in many different ways; or when dialogue is foreclosed and harmonious coexistence is compromised by prolonged disagreement. In each case, as well as others, the semiotic resources that enable and thereby threaten communication can also be employed to protect it, strengthening community by enriching individual members' interactions within it.[28]

The critical concept employed in support of this argument is *immunity*. For Esposito, immunity is the main conceptual point at which the lexicons of two modern, related discourses overlap: Western biomedical discourse about the human organism (life) and juridical-political discourse about human organizing (community). First, in the biomedical context, immunity refers to the system function that protects an organism from exposure to foreign/external elements that threaten its internal operational integrity. Immunization is the common practice of deliberately introducing a nonlethal amount of a threatening element, such as a virus, into an organism in order to stimulate the production of antibodies that protect against it.[29] Second, in the juridical-political discursive context, immunity is typically contrasted with community, where the former refers to being free from the obligation that binds individuals within the latter.[30] Together, these overlapping discourses and their material, legal-scientific effects constitute what Esposito calls a "biopolitical paradigm," a regime of modern thought and assessment of life, how it is lived, and what to do about the threat and protection of its individual and collective borders.

The chief concern among continental philosophers of biopolitics, particularly Agamben and Esposito—but also Nancy, as we will see—is the intersection of law with biology and the force of their combined political power regarding life.[31] The objective of these philosophers, in short, is to unconceal the extent to which discourses of immunity are entrenched in how we talk about and thereby perceive and evaluate life, and assess the need for individual as well as collective security. Practically, biopolitical philosophy challenges the logic informing the extreme, biopolitical practice of executing some members of a community who are no longer tolerated by other members of the community, a practice based on the belief of the latter that their identity and survival is compromised by the sheer existence of the former, a decision about the value of life made, and justified, on the basis of ideological assumptions about human biology—what it means to be human/nonhuman, male/female, outside/inside, and so on.

Crucially, the object of concern for Western biomedical and juridical-political discourses that grounds the biopolitical paradigm historically is the identity and protection of a body. The body is critical to the field, function, and political-philosophical significance of discourses of immunity because, Esposito tells us, in order for life (which is the essence of community and individuality) to be assessed and evaluated, it requires some kind of "organic representation binding it to reality."[32] Body is precisely this organic structure binding "life" (an abstraction) to reality—a material reality. It is the absolute terrain of biopolitics, whether it concerns the identity of an individual human person, with his or her phenomenological/lived-biological and semiotic/lived-communicative openings, or the bounded identity of a group, community, or state, the perceived survival and/or destruction of which—its health—is implicated in, or some might go so far as to say "threatened" by, the flow and meanings made of persons, materials, and ideas in a globalized world. For both, body is "the frontline, both symbolic and material, in life's battle against death."[33]

Without rehearsing the intricacies of his study of the politics of immunity, for my purposes, Esposito's perspective helps explain how global biopolitics today may be characterized by an increasingly unquestioned, and wholly modernist, presupposition about the importance of better defining and tightening borders—not only individual borders that secure one's sense of bodily integrity and, hence, identity but also, and especially, collective borders or so-called homelands that distinguish regional, ethnic, and racial identities. These borders, in a world of thinking that has swung increasingly to the conservative right, are imagined to be under greater threat from what is "outside" of and "foreign" to them and, according to that logic, therefore in need of increased measures to protect both public life and private existence. As Esposito puts it, in light of the taken-for-granted discourse of immunity that informs unreflective thinking about "who we are," there is widespread support today not only "for violent defense in the face of anything judged to be foreign" but also for efforts to dominate and turn its threat back on itself.[34]

Against the destructive impulses of the biopolitical paradigm, which in history's recent horrors have gone as far as animalizing the human person so as to justify ruling on which life is worth living and which isn't, Esposito offers an antiessentialist and antifoundational philosophical critique of immunitary logic. His goal in that precise sense—namely, as critique—is to examine the logic of immunity, expose and turn it against itself, and then draw out the various affirmative and productive qualities of the logic.[35] The outcome of Esposito's critical-philosophical exegesis, and its direct relevance to contemporary continental philosophy of communication, I argue, is an innovative understanding of immunity as not merely a logic for the protective closure of borders in an effort to shore up the individual and community but one according to which their openness may be explained, returned to, and with foresight, maintained. As I explain, it is because of a lack inherent to the self (chapters 1 and 2) and the community (chapter 3)—an interdependence of dis-integrated, co-appearing identities (chapters 4 and 5)—that both community and individual wholeness can be imagined and desired in the first place, albeit without the possibility of ever achieving any pure, undifferentiated state of unity.[36]

To draw out the significance of Esposito's critique of immunity for new perspective on human communication, the third chapter focuses carefully on his analysis of *munus*, the etymological and conceptual origin of the ideas of immunity, community, and communication, adding insight into the order and relation—that is, the coincidence rather than contradiction—of all three. I characterize communication as immunization, which may be understood to include the processes of learning (taking up, absorbing, and embodying) and employing (gearing into, expressing, and reworking) linguistic-material resources that may not only initiate and encourage human communication (transmission, self-expression, other-perception, and interpersonal and intergroup association) but also potentially threaten to stifle it, confuse it, and perhaps even shut it down. Communication as immunization may encourage negotiation and assist mutual understanding—for instance, in contexts of debate, deliberation, and decision-making—but cannot eliminate the threat of possible contagion of antagonism, misinformation, conflict, and even manipulation. This is because communication as immunization is the condition of the possibility for and regulation of each of these phenomena. Communication *and-as* immunization invites public expression, and even protest, but also protects private contemplation as well as tradition, complementing an individual's capacity for reflective attending and ability to be affected by, learn from, and integrate—to remain open to—the experiences of difference rather than to merely tolerate, or worse, disavow them.

What is described in chapter 2 regarding the impossibility of human noncommunication gains force as a question when considered from the perspective of the *munus*, where the ban and law, threat and protection, of human communication can be seen as the internal horizon for understanding one another. Akin to the *munus* function of community that impairs its members' capacity to identify as being not part of community, so too does the human capacity for language (the absorption of it over a lifetime) impair one's ability to stand outside of it. For the human person (a linguistic-semiotic materiality), there is no immunity, legal or medical, from the ontological givenness of communication. As speaking beings, we are in communication. We must communicate, and we are able to do so by way of the immunizing protection of discourses that can, in turn, threaten. With regard to community, where "the risk of conflict [is] inscribed at the very heart of community, consisting as it does in interaction, or better, in the equality of its members,"[37] communication also immunizes it, protects community from devolving into a threatened state of dislocation, disconnection, misunderstanding, and conflict. However, what can result there is a condition of overprotection. Overprotection from too much immunization of communication threatens the potential for ongoing and open communication by way of closing identity borders, containing and curbing differences of viewpoint, expression, and interpretation in an effort to turn inward and away from one another. Such a condition, such as in an era of heightened, even paranoid, security consciousness, calls for a protective response from communication as immunization itself, what Esposito calls *autoimmunization*. Here we find the affirmative quality of immunity that his critique reveals: immunizing protection against too much protection by communication's immune system can help protect border openings as invitations to the common, the different, and the community.

The philosopher most invested in asserting the openness of embodied being, whether the body of that being is human-individual or community, is Nancy. In his book *Corpus*, Nancy moves away from the twentieth-century linguistic paradigm's vocabulary of signs and instead demonstrates a style of thinking about embodied being in terms of its indices. A body is not merely an integrated and unified identity, he tells us, but is in fact a collection, a corpus of parts, sensations, functions, masses, and magnitudes. Nancy's interest in indexing a body's points of entry and exit, its zones and functions, exemplifies the contemporary movement of continental philosophy from questions of language and subjectivity toward a more decided engagement with the material world. *Corpus* is a major text in Nancy's mature philosophical reflections in this regard, and it can be read as a guide for thinking about the relation of bodies and the insights offered by that perspective into community. Thinking of a body as relation, or what he calls a "singular plurality" (an opening of openings to new configurations and connections—that is, to communities), in turn broadens our perspective on communication: *community* is a sign of that which is lived meaningfully, in part, by way of shared values that define it and may be unwritten but are nevertheless embodied and practiced in transmission, in communication.

Chapter 4 argues that a body is an index of coexistence. To explain how this is so, and why it matters, the discussion engages Nancy's analysis of the Latin phrase *hoc est enim corpus meum*, "this is my body," which can be read in at least two ways: first, as a critique of the metaphysics of presence, a question of the "this is" of that phrase, and second, following from this critique and demonstrating its implications, as a question of what is one's own: What is and what can be called properly "my body"? To question the property of one's own body in this way undermines humanist notions of bodily integrity and wholeness, which work to establish a correspondence between body and self-identity that is often assumed and not questioned.

Although it may seem odd to question the self-certainty of identity linked to the sense one has of a body—for if there is anything that is truly proper or one's own, it must be one's body—Nancy's objective is to emphasize the fact that there are *bodies*, and not one body, such as the functionally ideal body represented in Western medical discourse, or a universally ideal and pure body of bodies—a "community." Despite the categories into which we place bodies and through which they are made meaningful, a body is nevertheless fluid in both senses of that term: its internal functions can disrupt and betray the "external" or conscious sense of identity, whether that identity is individual or collective, thereby demonstrating that the experience of a body, a singular existence, is always plural. Questioning modern suppositions about bodily wholeness and integrity (integration *and* dis-integration) helps confirm *every body* as a body in relation, a body that is ontologically communicative (both expressive and perceptive).

The final chapter of this book sharpens the discussion of Nancy's philosophy of relationality as a distinct philosophy of communication. It focuses on the concept of *being-with*, which Nancy claims is a sign of what remains to be thought of existence—namely, the future of our coexistence. In his effort to talk about coexistence without recourse to terms such as "identity," "presence," "containment," or "community," Nancy employs terms such as "open," "exposure," "unworking," "inoperable," and "touch." Chapter 5 engages Nancy's thinking by way of a description, reduction, and interpretation of the term *being-with* and in so doing outlines the parallels in thinking between Nancy's philosophical program and communication research in what is called semiotic phenomenology. Semiotic phenomenology is an appropriate descriptor of Nancy's philosophy, I argue, for the reason that his goal is to interrogate the limits of what can be thought about shared existence and develop a vocabulary for thinking that broadens its horizon. I offer a sketch of Nancy's relational ontology, focusing in particular on what I call his three-step semiotic phenomenological analysis of being-with as primary to being human and prior to thinking about what it means to be in embodied contact, communication, and/or community.

To summarize briefly, *being-with* refers first to the basic human awareness of living in a world with others. To better understand the phenomenology of human coexistence, Nancy opts for this term rather than "community" for the reason that *being-with* directly calls to attention the experienced world as shared, which means a world divided. In sharing, Nancy tells us, bodies remain separate, and distributed, even in moments of contact and togetherness. Second, *being-with* names a key feature of the active experiencing of the world. Although the signifier *being-with* has links to Heidegger's vocabulary (*Mitsein*), for Nancy, it indicates the conscious experience, or embodied sense, of communication. *Being-with* calls attention to the fact that one can only say "I" within the context of other beings. Being aware of one's being-with others is experienced (expressed and perceived empirically) in the semiotic materiality of contact and communication, which is lived as reversible. Nancy's attention to the phenomenon of touch, which includes both contact and separation, broadens how we can think about the boundary logic of communication—"communication" not as immediacy, or identity fusion, but by way of withdrawal, at the limits of the boundaries that open a context and therefore the possibility for human communicating. Third, *being-with* is understood as a sign representing a new perception of our common condition, what Nancy calls a shared *task* for thinking. A key concept in the third step of his analysis is *Mitdasein* (being-with-there), which draws attention to the fact of human embodied exposure. We are self-exposed, and *being-with* adds to our awareness of this condition as a challenge to protect the *with* as fundamental to the meanings and/or, perhaps, dreams of our being human together.

Although the dream quality of a sign such as "community" won't dissolve under philosophical analysis, the advantage of a term like *being-with* (or, *we*) over "community" is that it invites thinking about the disturbances and distances that are always part of community. It allows space for thinking about the fact of beings that are part of community, willingly or not, simply by virtue of *being there* (being exposed) in a world shared with others. *Being-with* calls attention not only to the boundary logic of inclusion and exclusion but also to the estrangement, marginality, and separation of those beings who, for whatever reason, may not be able, willing, or even interested in reciprocity, intimacy, and/or mutual exchange—ideals of community that are often presupposed in thinking about its uniformity over and above its dislocations. Just as communication involves the possibility of ambiguity and uncertainty, so too is being-together necessarily hesitant and tentative, whether actually, in public or private, or virtually, as we may be in various "imagined" communication communities.

Having rehearsed the direction and scope of this book's argument—namely, that when taken together, the perspectives of Agamben, Esposito, Nancy, and Lacanian psychoanalysis considerably expand philosophical inquiry into human communication—it is worth reiterating that the chapters to follow are not rote reportage on the ideas of each of these figures. There are many volumes that offer thorough accounts of the perspectives of Agamben, Esposito, Nancy, Lacan, and current Lacanian psychoanalysis, and even more—and more massive—volumes devoted to defining and contextualizing continental philosophy.[38] That said, I want to end here by adding a few more words to help situate the present research within its general intellectual-disciplinary context. I will do so by quoting Simon Glendinning's rather perfect definition of continental philosophy as "the defining 'not-part' of analytic philosophy . . . an 'incorporation'; where something is constructed and retained 'within' but *as* an excluded outside, *as* a foreign body which is impossible to assimilate."[39]

The scope and feel of Glendinning's definition, especially the "not-part," is highly apropos to the contemporary continental philosophy of communication presented in this book because, although the topics addressed in it are at the dead center of communication inquiry as a modern academic field of human study, the perspective on those topics developed throughout this book is nevertheless somewhat afield from, but not outright alien to, the majority perspective that dominates and largely defines human communication study in the Anglo-American mainstream tradition: namely, more a social scientific than a humanistic perspective, stimulating scholarly output that is empirically grounded and positivistic more often than qualitative, literary, and philosophical in style and scope. Just what the contours and limits of the philosophy of communication represented in the work of this volume are is a question that, like the one regarding Glendinning's definition of continental philosophy, cannot yet be fully answered. Philosophy of communication is indeterminate at present, outside, marginal and, as of late, unincorporated by mainstream North American human communication inquiry.[40]

From the point of view of institutional legitimacy, it may at some point become necessary to refine the interdisciplinary boundaries of what philosophy of communication is and what it is not. On the one hand, for example, it is interpretive inquiry into human communication questions about language (How does language bring structure to sense? How is language different from communication? How does meaning-making occur? Why is human communication possible?), human consciousness (How do we become aware of our lived environments? How is that awareness experienced? Why is that experience embodied?), expressive media (What can a phenomenology of communications media reveal about the epochal orientation of a culture?), and difference and identity (How are signs valued? How do we experience those values? What is the impact of others' expressions on one's self-perceptions?). On the other hand, philosophy of communication is not, for example, analytic philosophy of mind or language, cognitive or generative linguistics, or cybernetics, systems theory, or classic information theory, and certainly not "anything goes."

Nevertheless, for now, I think the question of what philosophy of communication is and what it is not should remain open and left out in the open as an invitation to thinking—an invitation not for thinking about what is the question of thinking (that's continental philosophy) but what calls for thinking today about human communication (that's continental philosophy of communication). The opening or outside that is this question offers intellectual space for thinking about what human communication inquiry allows us to think, and therefore to perceive and express, about human embodied being and what that labor of thinking—that is, philosophy rather than theory of communication—can offer for future inquiry.

CHAPTER 1

The Wager of Communication (as Revealed by Psychoanalysis)

This beginning chapter enters into contemporary continental philosophy of human communication by way of a basic review of Jacques Lacan's perspective on language. Put simply, what Lacan reminds us about language is that it is not self-evident, not all can be said in conscious discourse, and therefore, although human communication may be possible, it is itself never fully guaranteed, certain, or completely stable. This uncertainty revealed by psychoanalysis helps deepen our understanding of communication as a possibility rather than a guaranteed outcome of human expression, demonstrating how self-identity is neither pregiven nor prior to language but shaped and even destabilized within it. The objective of the present discussion is to specify the relevance to communication inquiry of the Lacanian psychoanalytic perspective on the role language plays in the formation of the human communicative subject.

Psychoanalysis is important to contemporary continental philosophy of communication to the extent that it helps challenge humanist conceptions of communication as an outcome of expressive exchange between agents whose identities are presupposed to be fully contained, undivided, and self-certain. This is what Briankle G. Chang calls the "subjectivist metaphysical thesis" of modern theory of communication, wherein the speaker-subject is preformed and communication appears as both a challenge and a means to transcend its inner privacy and personal solitude.[1] The humanist-theoretical perspective on communication is not unfamiliar. It presupposes, for instance, that human communication is coterminous with expression, that communication is one-way rather than reversible, that all behavior is information, that communication is reducible to messages, that communication is equivalent to understanding, that either communication succeeds or it fails, and so on.

As we shall see, although the language of Lacanian psychoanalysis is informed by such humanist and positivist suppositions about communication, a critical review of its main tenets demonstrates that psychoanalytic theory is in fact consistent with, and offers a ready point of entry into, a contemporary continental perspective on the instability and contingency of communication. In the context of the psychoanalytic interview, *communication* is defined as an outcome of exchange in which a patient learns to recognize the impact of language on his or her emotional history and, in so doing, attempts to sharpen his or her skill in speaking about emotional suffering—to communicate "successfully" rather than remain helpless in articulating the cause of suffering. Despite its recourse to classic information theory's sender-receiver vocabulary, however, Lacanian psychoanalysis can be read as a challenge to suppositions about both the certainty of communication (its success or failure) and the pregiven status of the communicative subject. It reveals, in short, how communication can be understood as an embodied experience of the signs, codes, and contexts of expression that shape self-identity and have the irreducible potential to undermine a person's employment of them, thereby undermining the theoretical foundation of humanism's preformed expressive agent.[2]

Discourse of the Other: A Vast Material Apparatus

I begin with a distinction that runs throughout Lacan's major works.[3] I draw it out not as a line to be crossed, as if it were a barrier, but as an opening for examination of the role played by language and communication in the formation of the self. The distinction is classically drawn between two so-called functions of language.[4] One is communicative; the other is structural. The difference between these two functions may be shown as follows: On the one hand, language is understood as a medium for the transportation and exchange of information. In this sense, its communicative function is as a vehicle or instrument that makes possible the activity of encoding, transmitting, receiving, and decoding of information, from low level binary to complex high level. On the other hand, language is also understood as a system of representation. As a network of finite symbols governed by recursive rules that specify the relation of symbols with one another and their meaning,[5] this system functions, as Anthony Wilden puts it, "to bring structure to the representation of reality, for where there is no structure, there is no sense."[6] Taking these two functions together, we see that language helps not only name phenomena in the world but also classify them into different categories. In short, language brings order to sense perception via a web of meanings delivered in words and sentences that are generated according to rules and, in doing so, endows the lived human world with concrete, psychical/conceptual reality.

This basic distinction between the two functions of language helps us see how language (the sphere of the semantic) is relatively insignificant on its own. It is only in its use—that is, as discourses (the sphere of the semiotic) developed over time by people interacting with one another—that a sign system can bring order, sense, and meaning to the world. "For unlike a language," Wilden famously explains, "a discourse has a subject and subject matter."[7] Yet as we know, if language is "a culturally organized system that must be learned from the parents and in the family to obtain entrance into social life,"[8] then using it will never be straightforward and without consequences. This is because not all discourses are valued equally. Only those that prevail in a society, derived from its principal social and economic relations, Wilden tells us, will "form the ground of what the dominant members of society accept as true and false, legal and illegal, legitimate and illegitimate."[9] The experience of entering into social life may lead to significant emotional suffering, for some people at least, because what the culture wants or demands may be, at times, at odds with what the person wants or thinks he or she wants. It may even be at odds with whomever the person believes him- or herself to be.

The capacity of language to enable and thereby to constrain ways of seeing, knowing, and judging explains its cultural significance as what Lacan calls "discourse of the Other." Simply put, the Other is not a person. It is a locus of symbolic authority identified with the structure of language (a structure governed by the logic of difference), and the order of culture (also called the Symbolic, a historical realm governed by law-like conventions), and the unconscious.[10] Discourse of the Other is a vast, material apparatus of values, beliefs, and meanings that flows into a person from others and stitches everyone into the fabric of culture—"stitches" us together, that is, by virtue of our use of language and thereby our implication in the discourses we speak.

For the present discussion, the import of this basic psychoanalytic principle cannot be overstated. The unconscious is *nothing but* discourse of the Other, Lacan insists.[11] It is "a discourse which *dispossesses* us of our imaginary sense of self-completeness."[12] As I will discuss, language is critical to the psychic life of the person not only as a medium for expression but also as embodied discourse, a system of representation that reveals a subject in its use.

But first, in order to explain how a subject is revealed by language in its use, I must identify a third function of language: its metacommunicative function. The metacommunication of language may be identified as the presence or experience of language beside itself, beyond the meaning of words and sentences. This "beyond" is no mystical realm; it is the province of context, to be sure. More specifically, it is the province of the concrete sense impression made by the signifier. Beyond meanings that may be evoked by it, a signifier may be audible in its articulation (e.g., phonemes that distinguish it), it may be visible in its inscription (e.g., graphemes that constitute its identity), and it may even be disturbing in its embodied experience (e.g., the alienating encounter of an unfamiliar or unwelcomed word, in text or conversation). What is shown by the audibility, visibility, and effect of signifiers is that language not only names things and brings meaning to lived experience but also announces itself as language.[13] The presence of any signifier carries with it, as its backdrop, the entire signifying system of which it is a representative element. The phenomenality of the signifier, seen from this perspective, helps us understand how the metacommunicative function of language is to communicate communicability—to declare, by the rupture of the linguistic act, that in language there is at minimum the possibility for communication. In its use, language speaks—it speaks itself.[14]

This point may seem trivial for humanities scholars today, at least for the reason that theories of metacommunication have long underpinned the social scientific study of human communication.[15] However, with regard to Lacanian psychoanalytic theory and the technique of its application, particularly in the contemporary current,[16] the importance of its insights into this metacommunicative function of language should not be taken lightly. For, although language may be a medium and vehicle for the activity of communicating—the transport of ideas, the cocreation of meaning, the expression of experiences, the interpretation of expressions, and so on—it is precisely because language communicates *itself* that a pathway is opened to the psychic life (i.e., the embodied history) of a person. Psychoanalytic theory and practice show that the conscious control a person has over his or her intentions in language can be undermined, at times, by language's metacommunicative function. Because the unconscious is a repository of discourse of the Other, it is via language—that is, self-expression in signs—that a person's emotional past may be exposed.

In the clinical setting of psychoanalysis, the communicative, structural, and metacommunicative functions of language together play the key role. There, it is accepted both in theory and in practice that in the cognitive acquisition of language (the process of learning to speak to others, being spoken to, and being spoken about by others), a person absorbs and internalizes an entire system of meaning. As a child, the person absorbs words that have been used to label his or her intentions, demands, and wishes in the process of building complex maps of meaning; however, as an adult, that person may be encouraged in the context of analytic therapy to attend to key words or phrases spoken as points of focus that might bring those maps of meaning to conscious awareness so that they may be explored and perhaps even reconfigured.[17] A course of psychoanalysis may, for example, uncover the failed dreams of the parent as they recur to the speech of the child who, even in adulthood, suffers a burden of fulfilling those wishes as if they were his or her own (for example, one's career choices). In those cases, as well as others, one of the goals of psychoanalysis is to help a patient listen to how he or she speaks—listen, that is, for how he or she uses language in order to communicate.

Later, I discuss how *communication*, defined in this context as an outcome of speaking so as to be heard and understood, is taken for granted in the language of psychoanalytic theory. But for now, let me pursue the background of Lacanian psychoanalytic theory a little further, specifically as it offers insight into how a person may step back from him- or herself with a view to developing an awareness of the extent to which his or her speech is a product not simply of individual creative agency but also of a shared system of representation, a product of discourse of the Other.

Meaning to Say: Talking to Hear Oneself Speak

The challenge for a patient as well as the psychoanalyst is to listen for the system of beliefs, principles, and values that structures concretely a patient's relations with others and shapes his or her actions, self-perceptions, and communication patterns. To meet this challenge, what an analyst must do is highlight, underscore, and insert "inverted commas" into the text of a patient's speech—to *punctuate* the significance of what has been said during the course of analysis in order to draw explicit attention to it.[18] In this way, the psychoanalyst serves the role of editor, a figure who has the ability to help a patient "articulate verbally his or her emotional experience"[19] and, in so doing, ease his or her emotional suffering by way of talking about it.

The editor function is essential to psychoanalytic practice because what a patient says in that context may not always be the same as what he or she means to say. As with daily conversation (for instance, the contextual differences between the content and relational aspects of a statement), the meaning intended by the speech of a patient through his or her selection of words combined into sentences may differ from the meaning that may be made of those words and sentences and the manner in which they are expressed.[20] One thing said may be another thing heard. Metaphor, sarcasm, and humor used to evade sensitive topics, for instance, or to imply them indirectly, as well as the repetition of words, the substitution of names, pauses in speech, and slips of the tongue, all of which can often go unnoticed by the patient him- or herself, may communicate something beyond, or altogether different from, what a patient consciously intends to express. As Richard Kearney explains, it is "in the *faults* of communication rather than its *fitness* that unconscious discourse is revealed."[21] Because words in a patient's vocabulary have undergone a "long developmental history of emotional accumulation of meaning,"[22] the main purpose of the psychoanalyst-editor is to help a patient draw out, unravel, and ideally decode the key parts of what a patient says in analysis and how he or she wishes to be heard. Talking and listening in psychoanalysis is, in short, discourse en route to self-understanding the significance of unconscious language to conscious perceptions of phenomenal experiences.

That being said, it is important for the purposes of the present discussion to point out that the objective of intervening into a patient's speech in the context of psychoanalysis is not only to draw attention to his or her patterns of communication but also, and crucially, to draw attention to the fact that the psychoanalyst can do no more than assist the patient in the process of locating and making sense of the psychic-symbolic source of his or her emotional suffering. The analyst may direct a course of analysis. However, the work of interpretation must fall, in large part, on the patient.[23] This shift is decisive in psychoanalytic treatment, and as we shall see, it marks an important point of broadening contemporary understanding of human communication beyond information-theoretic suppositions of its success or failure. For the "talking cure" to have a long-term impact on a patient's awareness of meanings made of past experience, part of the authority to interpret, or to "author," what is said in the course of analysis must be drawn away from the analyst (a figure who, like the parent, is perceived to have all answers to all questions) and must be assumed by the patient. Therein lies the paradox of the psychoanalytic enterprise: a patient hires someone to help, but ends up doing most of the work him- or herself.

What should come as no surprise is how this shift in authority from an analyst trained to listen to a patient encouraged to listen to, and for, him- or herself is dictated by the very structure of communicating in the psychoanalyst's consulting room. Although I will not discuss the significance the relative positions of patient and psychoanalyst in the consulting room has to communication—whether each is seated facing one another or whether the patient is classically lying on a daybed and the analyst is seated perpendicular to the patient and outside of his or her field of vision[24]—I will say that contrary to what might be expected from this interpersonal dyad, the analyst does not function simply as the receiver of a patient's speech. Rather, the analyst functions as its transmitter, a mechanism through which the speech of a patient is encoded into signals for delivery back to him or her. The analyst assumes the role of transmitter because when a patient speaks in analysis, it is the Other that may be heard—heard by the analyst, that is, but not yet by the patient, who misrecognizes its discourse as if it were simply his or her own.[25] To be sure, psychoanalysts today do not simply assume the clichéd position of a silent, detached observer, like an owl in the room. Instead, treatment is pursued through mutual sharing of experience between the analyst and patient over a long period of time so that trust may be developed, a mutual bond may be established, and meaningful dialogue may take place.[26]

Psychoanalytic treatment seeks, in part, to address the patient's lack of awareness of the discourses of the Other (the prevailing beliefs, attitudes, and values of a culture, community, and/or family) by transforming the patient into a receiver of his or her own speech. Like the voice piece of a telephone handset, the psychoanalyst mediates communication between the patient's ear and what comes out of the patient's mouth. As editor-transmitter, the analyst points to and leads in highlighting what may be significant parts of a patient's speech, such as when metaphor is used to beat around the bush of a heavily guarded secret, or when slips of the tongue appear to indicate conflict between the meaning of a word and a speaker's intent in using it, or when pauses in speech or repetitive associations mark the place of a memory too painful to put into words—and so on. This is done so that the patient might recognize for him- or herself those parts of speech that conflict with, and thereby unsettle, the conscious intent with which the patient believes he or she had expressed them in the first place. To be sure, any speaker will have the capacity to receive his or her own speech as long as he or she is able to hear the sound of his or her own voice. But this is elemental. Possessing the auditory capacity to hear one's voice may be insufficient to recognize the significance of what is being spoken, and how it has been said over a lifetime, to one's emotional history.[27]

That said, the point to grasp about the analytic interview is that a patient speaks before an analyst who is trained to listen clinically so that the significant parts of what comes out of the patient's mouth (i.e., signals from the Other sent to the self about its relationships to others) may be encoded as new interpretations and sent back to their source of verbal articulation—sent back, that is, to the patient him- or herself. As Lacan explains, "The subject's own speech is a message to him, first of all, because it is produced in the Other's locus. It originates in that locus and is worded as such not only because his demand is submitted to the Other's code, but because his demand is dated by this Other's locus (and even time)."[28] With effort, a patient-sender may become a consciously aware receiver of such "messages" because the source and destination of communication in the psychoanalytic setting are one and the same. The role of the analyst-editor may be to draw attention to how a patient speaks and thereby lead the patient in the direction of a different self-perception; however, it is a patient's awareness of the meanings made of his or her past experiences that must be cultivated by the process of talking in analysis. Communication in the psychoanalytic context is, in short, communication within oneself.

This point is crucial. Communication occurs in psychoanalysis, if ever, as speech awareness—a process, on the part of the patient, of reflective attending to what is spoken, what has been said, and what meanings might have been made of experiences shaped by vocabulary of the Other announced in the patient's speech.[29] In the context of analysis, communication therefore is not merely the act of speaking (transmission, reporting) about personal experience, or parroting statements, or narrating a carefully curated fantasy—a performance in speaking accompanied by gestures, breathing patterns, twitches, and so on that, we are told, are loaded with information and, thereby, communication. Communication can also be said to occur when the stability of self-sending (expression) is in fact shaken, disturbed, and dismantled rather than affirmed by the very words used to make meaning of a patient's experience—that is, when the consistency of one's so-called personal narrative, which functions as support of the perspective one has of oneself, is called into question by the sheer telling of its tale.[30]

Although Lacanian psychoanalytic theory, especially in its classical sense, adheres to the sender-receiver language of information theory, its contemporary practice works to reveal how the theoretically pregiven, rational, and self-sustaining locus of information transmission (i.e., the subject of communication) is neither as stable nor as certain as a mechanical sender-receiver model of communication would have us believe. *Communication* in psychoanalysis is not merely that which is achieved through the "making-known of the thoughts of a speaker to another speaker."[31] It inheres in awareness of the signifiers of expression (i.e., their embodied, lived experience) arrived at through a process of identification. It draws out and attends to the lived-historical importance, to the patient, of what is said by him or her during the analytic interview, in order to bring about a transformative effect—to jolt the patient, as it were, in his or her confrontation with the signifiers of psychic suffering revealed in the spoken and audible register of language in use. Strange but true, communication in psychoanalysis is a semiotic phenomenological experience that *may* occur in the process of a patient talking in order to hear him- or herself speak.

Voice, or a Message Returned in an Inverted Form

Consider the injunction, "find your voice." This injunction makes sense for the reason that voice, whether written or spoken, is an alienating phenomenon. It comes from oneself, but also it goes from oneself. "It *goes* as it comes," Jean-Luc Nancy says.[32] One's voice—in particular, one's speech—is at once a coming and a going. As Steven Connor puts it in *Dumbstruck*, "What I say goes."[33] We experience our voice as particularly alienating whenever we hear the sound of it played back to us from its recording. "That's not me!" we often say. The disturbance to the sense of oneself that is caused by the experience of hearing one's voice—which is to say, the experience of listening to oneself speak—is not limited to disembodied recordings. This experience also occurs in routine communication settings, such as when we recite in mind something we plan to say before coming out with it, or when something we say returns to us from others who have been persuaded, or perhaps contaminated, by our words.[34]

The experience of hearing the words of others recur to the speech of the self is central to Lacanian psychoanalytic theory, research, and practice. As is well known, Lacan's reading of Freud's biological model of psychosexual development integrates the phenomenology of Heidegger (the idea that language is the house of being, that human "consciousness exists in language and it is granted reality because language is articulated in *voice*"[35]) with the structural linguistics of Ferdinand de Saussure. But it is in the connection between these two traditions that Lacan can be read as offering a picture of human communication that contrasts significantly with information theory—a picture of communication as a reversible relation. Its clearest articulation is found in Lacan's famous dictum: "Human language is like a communication where the sender receives his own message back from the receiver in an inverted form."[36] Unpacking this formula will tell us a lot about voice/speaking and listening as a reversible relation of communication.

First, the sender receives his own message: As previously discussed, the aim of Lacanian psychoanalysis is not merely to encourage patients to speak openly about themselves or others but to lead them to recognize how they speak by listening for (to listen attentively, F. *écouter*) signifiers of the desires of others that shape self-perceptions.[37] In this sense, we understand a "message" sent in the psychoanalytic conversation as the sender's own: it is a message spoken to be heard not only by the analyst but also, and most importantly, by the patient who utters it. As I stated above, communication in psychoanalysis occurs when the stability of self-sending is disturbed by reflective attending (thinking as listening) to the words used by a patient to make meaning of his or her lived experience.

Second, the message comes back from the receiver: Communication in psychoanalysis is neither a mutual nor an equal exchange, and certainly not an exchange between equals. Patients speak, and analysts listen. That is, to reiterate, the analyst listens for what the patient cannot yet hear, let alone put into words: namely, discourse of the Other that shapes the speech of the self. The analyst recites or transmits back to a patient the words spoken before the analyst, the goal of which is for the patient to hear (F. *entendre*) his or her words through the channel of the analyst's voice.[38] Although a receiver in the context of psychoanalysis can be said to be the same as a sender, what cannot be said is whether the patient will in fact hear what he or she has been led to listen for in the long conversation of analysis. I return to this point later.

Third, the message is received in an inverted form: The reversible relation between speaking and listening reveals a complex issue, indicated by the final phrase in Lacan's dictum regarding the form of the message received. The form of a message is the patient's speech, its rhetoric. The message form is not merely an auditory signal (a signifier); it is also a mental image (a signified) evoked by the utterance, or voicing, of the former. The form of the message is, as such, a sign, a particular combination of signifier and signified delivered in speech. Its rhetoric is the how of its delivery.[39] The fact that Lacan chooses the term *inverted* leads us to believe that he takes Saussure at his word: namely, that a signifier makes an acoustic impression.[40] Words are felt. To explain, two points need to be made here.

First, the form of the message to be received (an image delivered in speech—what Saussure calls an "acoustic image") is a critical component of communication as a reversible relation through which the patient perceives, or sees, him- or herself. A message (the patient's self-expression) arrives to his or her conscious awareness as a picture—it is received by the so-called mind's eye. It is thereby "inverted" according to the laws of refraction. Note the primacy of the visual, even in discourse about speech and listening. However, and second, what the analyst is trained to do is help the patient listen for what he or she cannot or will not say—listen, that is, to how the image is delivered, its rhetoric, and thereby return to the patient what remains unspoken in all that has been said in a given exchange. As John Muller and William Richardson explain, the objective is to turn unconscious discourse into conscious speech: "The good listener resonates with what is unconscious in the speaker's conscious communication, and his or her response thus consists in returning to the speaker (by way of 'inverting' and making the unconscious conscious) what was left unsaid in what the speaker said."[41]

I have been referring to speech, speaking, and the words of the patient. Before moving forward, it is crucial to draw out the significance of these terms by attending to the distinction between what Jonathan Culler calls "the purely relational and abstract" units of a language and their "physical realizations."[42] To do so, we must attend to the distinction between their form and substance. In his discussion of the arbitrary nature of the sign, Culler identifies a subtle but critical insight upon which Saussure insists: namely, neither the sounds produced in language nor the concepts they evoke (mental images) are linguistic units. Instead, he explains, "The linguistic unit is form rather than substance."[43] The form of a linguistic unit remains unaffected by the substance of its expression. For example, a sloppily handwritten "a" or a clearly typewritten "a" are of no consequence to the a-ness of the letter "a." Its value within a linguistic system remains unchanged by how that "a" is expressed. Similarly, slurred speech, or dialects, while perhaps difficult to understand, will affect not at all the ideal form of the uttered words—they remain purely relational and abstract.

Returning to the patient in analysis, the substance of his or her words actually spoken in the way they are spoken has no effect on the form of the linguistic units themselves. This is why, in order for the "talking cure" to have any impact on the conscious life of the patient, the form of the message returned in analysis must be "ideal": that is, it must return to the patient, by way of the analyst, stripped of the substance of its expression, coming back as signs exposed as part of the linguistic apparatus that brings structure and meaning to experience. The form of the message is "ideal" in its return to the patient insofar as it belongs to, or has its origin in, *la langue*, what Bruce Fink calls a "*hoard* deposited by the practice of speech in speakers who belong to the same community, a grammatical system which, to all intents and purposes, exists in the minds of each speaker."[44] A message in analysis comes back as ideal to the extent that its punctuation by the analyst (how it is said) makes audible the imprint of the values, beliefs, and attitudes of the language community inhabited by the patient.

In the context of the psychoanalytic interview, the patient learns to listen for what he or she wants to say, even if he or she lacks the words at the time, and learns to listen for the possible meanings of what he or she does say, albeit in the words of a language system that is never exclusively his or her own. Communication in that reversible relation occurs, takes place, whenever the community discourse is felt—when its voice resonates, especially in its power to disturb the sense a patient has of him- or herself and/or whomever he or she wishes to be.[45]

Talking to Hear the Other Speak

Thus far, I have shown that Lacanian psychoanalysis, in its clinical application, can be understood as a recursive mode of talk therapy. It is an interaction that opens a circuit wherein a patient has the opportunity not only to examine words used in speech with others, about others and oneself, but also to better understand and perhaps come to terms with the unique impact of that vocabulary on his or her emotional past. Because the patient is positioned both as speaker and as listener, as sender as well as receiver of his or her speech, communication in psychoanalysis unfolds not only between patient and analyst but also, and necessarily, within the patient for the reason that "only the patient has the key to open the meanings of his or her communications, fears, and desires."[46] To move the discussion forward, it is important to note how any clinical enterprise that asks patients to talk in order to hear themselves speak would rest upon unsteady ground. Why would anyone agree to such an interaction—and pay for it, too?

Sigmund Freud anticipated skepticism of this kind as early as 1890, in an essay where he addresses the potential for resistance to the method of talk therapy. "A layman will no doubt find it hard to understand how pathological disorders of the body and mind can be eliminated by 'mere' words," Freud says. "He will feel that he is being asked to believe in magic. And he will not be so very wrong, for the words we use in our everyday speech are nothing other than watered-down magic."[47] Words are like magic, perhaps, because the experience of being human is impacted concretely by them, the solitude of suffering may be transcended through their use in conversation, and analysis of linguistic metacommunication may disclose how the psyche is a substance of history, or a knot in the web of culture, rather than a cabinet of mysterious forces. That being said, it is precisely the paradox of paying to speak freely that makes psychoanalysis a destabilizing enterprise, a clinical method of treating emotional suffering with conversation designed intentionally to unsettle the autonomy of the self, to challenge what Freud calls the "autocratic nature of personalities"[48] and dissolve its psychic formations.

Consider the price of a course of psychoanalytic treatment. It obtains from two major costs: an acquisition cost and, to borrow from the language of economics, a psychic cost. First and foremost, a patient must pay the cost of communication. That is, a fee must be paid for the opportunity to talk, be listened to, and learn to hear oneself speak—to listen for unconscious discourse that undermines conscious speech. The second cost of psychoanalysis is one's self-image. Simply put, a patient must give it up. But this cost is paid not merely in an exchange of one self-image for another that has been made over through ego boosting and restoration (albeit cosmetic) of the certainty with which a patient expresses his or her "self." To the contrary, psychoanalysis is the task of dismantling and unbinding, a mode of mental therapy that "facilitates alienation from a self-image that encapsulates the subject."[49] It is an enterprise designed, in many cases, to lead a patient to discover, through the process of speaking in analysis, that he or she is always, in part, separate from and thereby different from the image of self to which he or she has been fastened, an image that is, by definition, imaginary, sustained by discourse of the Other.

To explain, allow me to summarize Lacan's theory of the mirror phase of identification. According to Lacan, the mirror phase of identification is the brief period in human development when an infant develops a self-image based on the appearance of its body as it is reflected upon a surface, such as a mirror, or the facial expression of a caregiver, where the infant understands that the caregiver's smile is intended for him or her—just as he or she recognizes his or her reflection as him or her and not another person. This image, of a unified body in control of its surroundings, comes into view and is perceived by the infant child in stark contrast to the disunity, helplessness, and lack of motor coordination that characterizes the child's conscious experience of its physical body. The primary experience of lack of coordination, bodily disunity, and helplessness contrasted with the image of a unified, complete, and controllable body (what is typically called "misrecognition" for the reason that the body perceived is not "me"; it is an image of me) creates a permanent gulf, lack, or fracture in the child's psyche. It establishes a differential relation of the child to him- or herself as another. What we typically call our identity is constituted in a disturbing and irresolvable difference within oneself.

The emotional significance of the differences within the self deepens after completion of the mirror phase, particularly in the later phases of language acquisition, when the child learns to say "I," a signifier. In order to say "I," the child must learn to recognize him- or herself as a subject first and foremost of the family discourse, a subject that becomes an object in communication with and about the child. This passage from reality to representation (from singular being into the realm of plurality, of society) means that the child learns to refer to him- or herself as an object-signifier in the vocabulary of the family. Referring to oneself in that way (for instance, as *he, she, I,* or a proper name) amounts to finding a place for oneself in the order of the entire culture by "losing oneself in language."[50]

The psychic implications of being subject to language—that is, learning to speak and being articulated by and into words—are profound and enduring. As Christian Lundberg summarizes, "The subject is simultaneously produced and disfigured in its unavoidable insertion into the space of the Symbolic."[51] In its recourse to a language system that is never fully its own, the subject forever seeks to live up to the internalized demands placed upon it to be something that is not it—a signifying image circulated in the discourse of others. On this point, Lacan's theorem that "a signifier represents a subject for another signifier" is relevant.[52] It means that words cannot fully represent a subject. They represent it poorly; hence more and more words are required. Signifiers string us along in the promise they offer not only of representation but also of more effective communication and thus improved understanding. Words may fail the subject, but the attempt to communicate succeeds their failure to capture everything.

The mirror phase of identification provides a solid theoretical backdrop against which we may better understand how what is at stake in psychoanalytic treatment is relevant to human communication inquiry: namely, transformation of the self into a subject. What is specifically at stake is the transformation of a self—one that may not yet recognize and appreciate the implications of the cultural discourses that sustain it—to a subject that, in the conscious experience of communicating, will have learned to recognize the significance of those discourses to the structure and meaning of the experiences according to which he or she has organized and lived his or her life. "The point [of a course of psychoanalysis]," Lacan says, "is not to know whether I speak of myself in a way that conforms to what I am, but rather to know whether, when I speak of myself, I am the same as the self of whom I speak."[53] This psychic cost—of "losing oneself" in language—can be revealed gradually over time in what Ana-Maria Rizzuto calls the "prolonged speech event" of psychoanalysis, a long conversation with the analyst who "continuously attends to the patient as *the subject of* his or her own words."[54] The objective of this conversation is to depose the patient of the illusion that his or her beliefs, words, and self-perceptions are entirely of his or her own authoring. Its aim is thereby to cast lingering doubt on the certainty with which the person talks about him- or herself, others, and his or her place in the world, ultimately cultivating an awareness of one's limited communicative agency in being subject to language and the discourses of a community. In short, psychoanalysis tries to demonstrate that the self is subject to its history and not the master of it.[55]

The Wager of Communication, or Faith in Analysis

Crucial to the procedure through which a self may come to recognize its self-division is the transaction with which psychoanalysis begins: namely, submission to analysis. Undertaking a course of psychoanalysis constitutes an initial, albeit critical, conversion from a patient to an analysand, or to use the contemporary term, a *client*—a subject par excellence. Both terms, *analysand* and *client*, indicate active participation and, thereby, self-alienation of the patient-subject in the process of treatment. No one can be forced into analysis. Instead, because treatment inheres in willing conversation, a client must subject him- or herself to it, must arrive to therapy of his or her own will, must give in to speaking freely before the analyst, and must pay for it, too—pay one cost, that is, for the opportunity to pay a second. As Ghyslain Levy explains, "Payment frees the analysand from the danger of the analyst's repeating the kind of abuse to which the analysand has already been subjected in life. It is a mechanism . . . that saves the patient, in the transference, from acting out and paying in pounds of flesh and with the coin of suffering."[56] At the risk of giving up money as well as parts of the lived, emotional history attached to one's self-image, the losses to be incurred in psychoanalytic treatment are, nevertheless, rewarded by the promise of something to be gained—not a cure itself but the chance of a cure.[57] This point is key.

The client of psychoanalysis pays for the opportunity to step outside of his or her "self" in order to better understand the web of words within which that self, and the client's perception of it, have been historically structured and, ideally, with this recognition, to "achieve the psychic changes required to have a freer emotional life."[58] Taking this chance, the client may, in fact, win with his or her loss. On the one hand, the paying client may win—that is, may ease his or her emotional suffering—by having lost the self-image that at first could not be seen or heard in the Other's discourse: he or she may win by losing a lost self. However, on the other hand, this is a win that can be had only at the price of a further and more substantial loss. The client pays dearly for the opportunity to develop his or her conscious awareness of the fact that the so-called lost self—that seemingly complete, unified, and wholly independent entity prior to the mirror phase of identification—was in fact never there in the first place. The "self" is always divided from itself, dependent on the material network of discourses that sustain it. Psychoanalysis reveals that a self is a subject forged over time by language in its use.[59]

Should a client reach that point of awareness, at which the speaking or announcement of one's desire can be heard, then the objective of analysis will have been met and the course of therapy will be terminated shortly thereafter. Lacan describes this objective as follows:

> The point to which analysis leads, the end point of the dialectic of existential recognition is—*You are this*. In practice, this ideal is never reached. The ideal of analysis is not complete self-mastery, the absence of passion. It is to render the subject capable of sustaining the analytic dialogue, to speak neither too early, nor too late.[60]

As suggested by this important passage, once a course of psychoanalysis has drawn to a close, there is no guarantee of any long-term improvement to the analytic client's well-being. This is widely understood as the main controversial feature of the psychoanalytic enterprise. Namely, it is gauged not by rigid empirical standards but rather, and only, by the effects it produces—conscious effects that are felt because they are embodied but nevertheless difficult to put into words.[61] For that reason, any empirical evidence that psychoanalysis actually works can be found only in a patient's "faith in testimony"[62] that years of paying top dollar for someone to listen while the subject talks to hear the Other speak has yielded positive emotional results.

Although analytic interpretation of the source of an emotional problem that brings a client to psychoanalysis remains the essential means of treatment, it is not as if the client must accept the interpretation as true in order for the work of analysis to have an effect. As I have explained, the long-term work of interpretation falls on the client, and for that reason, what is of prime importance to psychoanalysis—indeed, what it relies on for its legitimacy—is that the client benefit from at least something that transpired in the experience of talking and listening. Something must move the client toward different self-perceptions. This is not to imply that a different perception of self will resolve the differences within oneself. Rather, it means that one might become better aware of the fundamentally incomplete and open condition of self-identity.

On this agreement—regarding the scope and limits of psychoanalytic treatment, its costs, its risks, and its promise of only a chance to benefit from the experience of communication—Lacan is explicit: "Since it is to the patient's account that we must transfer this understanding," he says, "we shall involve him with us in a wager, a wager that we understand their meaning, and then wait for a return that makes us both winners."[63] Here, Lacan does not hesitate. At the outset of psychoanalysis, and despite its price, there is no guarantee that successful or effective communication—between client and analyst, and through it, within the client—will ever occur.

Psychoanalysis and Philosophy of Communication: Not All Can Be Said

Allow me to conclude by letting Lacan have a say. In 1973, Lacan appeared on television to deliver a lecture on the topic of psychoanalysis, and he began with the following: "I always speak the truth." He then added, after a dramatic hesitation, "Not the whole truth, because there's no way to say it all. Saying it all is literally impossible: Words fail."[64] This statement could be taken to mean that one cannot express everything; that is, there are phenomena and experiences of them for which there is not adequate language nor time for their articulation.[65] This is certainly true. However, the more crucial point made by the statement "there's no way to say it all" arrives, or is intimated, by way of its assertion: namely, the possibility of communication *can* be communicated. Or better, the *possibility* of communication can be communicated. It is a possibility that appears by asserting itself in the statement "There's no way to say it all." The "all" that Lacan says cannot be said has been said, literally. In addition to that, what amounts to a *not* in his statement ("there's no way to say it all" is another way to say "not all can be said") isn't a simple negation. It too carries with it an affirmative assertion. It is a *not* that, as a boundary, establishes the possibility, if not a wager, for future communication.[66] The *not* communicates in spite of Lacan's hesitation before the failure of (putting the relation established by the *not* into) words. "Not all" speaks. Even in the void of communication (the *not all* that can be heard as spoken) there is communication. Lacan neither minces words nor lies.

Three basic, psychoanalytic insights into language that are relevant to contemporary continental philosophy of communication have been reviewed here. First, language of the self is discourse of the Other. The prevailing values, beliefs, and attitudes of a culture are circulated in a system of signs—words, gestures, images, and codes—that arrive to us from other people, unifying us into a social formation, a "community." Membership in such a culture or community requires that the person find him- or herself in language, which means appropriating its rules. Speaking the discourse of others, and being spoken by it, can be both an affirming and an unsettling experience.

Second, oneself is another. In the passage from reality to representation in communication, the person is divided between the experience of embodiment and the meanings attributed to his or her self-image. For Lacanian psychoanalysis, self-image, or self-identity, is imaginary and symbolic, sustained by discourse of the Other. Self-difference, the permanent mark of subjectivity in language, disturbs the coherence and complete fulfillment of self-identity. The self has agency, and is expressive, but it is also subject to the meanings made by others' perceptions of its expressions.

Third, communication is never certain. It is made possible by language, but it is a possibility that is nonassured, often compromised by language *use*. Although on the surface "communication is tied to the transfer of a content (in the speaker's mind) through a medium (the speech, functioning as an intimation) to another location (becoming a content of the hearer's mind),"[67] conscious speech can be unsettled by unconscious discourse. The content of human communication is not preformed but shaped in language—that is, a shared medium of communication through which private thoughts find public expression. Human communication is part of a process of the formulation of meaning and not merely its transfer. In psychoanalysis, human communication, the long process of making known the thoughts of a speaker, may be achieved when the sphere of self-identity is fractured by awareness of self-difference.[68]

Lacanian psychoanalysis reminds us why human communication is not a *fait accompli*. As a theory of the formation of the subject in alienating relation to itself in language—which stands in contrast to, and even undermines, modern communication theory's subjectivist metaphysical thesis of a pregiven subject—Lacanian psychoanalytic theory and practice offers insight into human communication as it begins "in an absence of certitude . . . as speculation—or, better, as *conjecture*."[69] In particular, Lacanian psychoanalysis underscores the main trouble with language: namely, that it is not self-evident, does not reveal everything, and not all can be put into words. The main insight of this intellectual tradition, and its primary value to understanding human communication from a contemporary continental philosophical perspective, is that one can never be as assured in self-expression as one may wish to be. There is always risk.

What is certain, however, is that the risk, uncertainty, or wager of human communication revealed by psychoanalysis is slightly unsettling. Psychoanalysis is a long, but not uncontested, intellectual tradition, reminding us how human communication is not merely the transport of information but the basis and the potential for exposure that remains primary to living with one another as we learn to live with ourselves. We have the means for self-expression and other-perception, but are we understood? Do we understand others? How well? What is this *I* to which we all cling? Is human noncommunication, the topic of the next chapter, possible?

Questioning the limits of expression by attending to what thoughts, values, and ideas are properly one's own, and the words used to give them meaning, invites the possibility of a shift in self-perspective, where one may feel, in some respects, difference from oneself and thereby openness to others as common to the experience of human communicating.

CHAPTER 2

The Ban of Language and Law of Communication

The legacy impact of Lacanian psychoanalysis on modern conceptions of the self explains, at least philosophically, in part, the persistence in modern communication thinking of the presupposition that human communication cannot *not* take place. As discussed in the previous chapter, psychoanalysis, in its hermeneutic approach to speech and language, reminds us why human communication is uncertain rather than stable, characterized by its faults rather than by its smooth functioning.[1] It shows how language is a resource common to all but the property of no one, and how some of the words we use may carry a private, emotional history accumulated over time, one that has the power to destabilize the subject in its conscious attempts to communicate. It shows how the subject of communication is not pregiven or preformed but rather constituted by a lack in identity that may be worked through, but never overcome, in communication. Despite occupying the attention of structural-linguistic and psychoanalytic-inspired scholarship throughout the twentieth century, however, further attention can be paid by contemporary philosophy of communication to the more general problematic, raised by psychoanalysis, of the authority and force of language in human communication. How does language enjoin people to communicate? How are words affective? What determines the limits to or flexibility of what signs mean? Is human being always communicative? Is noncommunication possible?

To be sure, the authority and force of language in human communication certainly have not been overlooked by philosophy of communication scholarship. To the contrary, groundwork examining it has been established, for example, by psychoanalytic-informed communication studies, deconstruction-informed discourse studies, semiotic phenomenologies of human embodiment, and so on.[2] In addition to these research currents, questions regarding the authority of language have long been signaled for human communication theorists by the Palo Alto group of psychotherapy's classic axiom, "one cannot not communicate," itself an outcome of behavioral research announced in the 1960s, which nevertheless endures as a presupposition of modern thinking, both academic and nonacademic, about human communication.[3]

In the contexts of human communication study, particularly in Anglo-American contexts, the presupposition that one cannot not communicate often strikes a negative chord. It implies, in some sense, that we are under the burden of some kind of surveillance and thereby are less expressively free as communicating agents than we may imagine ourselves to be. Even the tone of the presupposition feels restrictive. On its surface, and at first blush, "one cannot not communicate" comes across not only as prohibitive but also, perhaps, as personally condemning, as though we are just not able to *not* communicate, even if we tried, say, by not speaking or writing, by not making sense or refusing to, by blocking all points of contact, and so on. This axiom seems a direct affront to the values we hold about the modern subject (the individual) in its rights, power, and personal freedom. However, as negative as the impressions left by this presupposition of modern thought may be, they can be somewhat eased and new philosophical inquiry can be invited once not being able to not communicate is considered to be a productive and protective, even fortifying, human condition. That is the perspective developed over the course of the present chapter and the next.

New reflection on the impossibility of human noncommunication resituates this classic presupposition as a prime entry point for contemporary philosophical perspective on human community, communication, and embodiment. Discussion of it in this chapter is therefore neither communication theoretic (semantics, pragmatics) nor social scientific. Dispensing with seesaw theory debates about the Palo Alto group axiom, the objective here is to reopen the space of interpreting the presupposition of the impossibility of noncommunication with perspective offered by the work of Giorgio Agamben. A contemporary of Roberto Esposito and Jean-Luc Nancy, and a major figure in critical theory and philosophy of biopolitics, Agamben is best known for his three volumes *Homo Sacer*, *State of Exception*, and *Remnants of Auschwitz*, which together mark the high point of his scholarly program examining the concepts of sovereignty, law, and life. Agamben is relevant to human communication inquiry not only for his analysis of the logic of sovereignty but also and specifically for the parallel he draws between it and the structure and function of language.

Reading Agamben, I argue, extends the space of interpretation opened by the presupposition about the impossibility of noncommunication to the sphere of contemporary continental philosophies of language and law. The present chapter enters into that sphere by way of Agamben's thought, which, I will demonstrate, enables us to radically reframe and assess the sense of the presupposition in the following way: There is a ban that is fundamental to human communication. It is semiotic, which means it is embodied. The ban communicates and is experienced in the form of an injunction, "one cannot not communicate." It is experienced as law.[4]

The sense of law and language that are of concern here is a matter of ontology, not of right and wrong—the latter of which is a matter of morality and/or ethics. Language is a basic ontological condition of being human, of being both defined by as well as empowered and guided in it. As Émile Benveniste puts it, there is no human being that is not always a speaking being.[5] It is from the perspective of language as our basic, defining ontological condition that human being may be understood to be what Nancy calls "abandoned being," banned from any imagined state prior to or outside of language. Ontologically, we are before language, present and presented to it, just as one can be said to be before the law. Drawing on Nancy's philosophy, Agamben argues further that to be in language is therefore to be held in a ban, "both to be 'at the mercy of' and 'at one's own will, freely,' to be 'excluded' and also 'open to all, free.'"[6] If this is so, as I explain here, then new communication questions may be legitimately raised: How, or by what authority, if any, does language hold us in a ban? If language operates like law, carrying principles that bring meaning to life and guide action, calling us in the "sound" of being named, whence does the power of this law derive? How is it in force? Who, or what, declares that noncommunication is impossible—that one (*you, I, him, her,* or *them*) cannot not communicate?[7]

Philosophically innovative responses to this enduring and discipline-defining problematic may be found once we consider the relation of language to the being who speaks as a relation of ban. Using Agamben's pursuit of questions of language and law as a guide, the pages to follow examine human communication in terms of the experience not merely of self-difference, as described in chapter 1 of this volume, but of the ban of language and law of communication.

Outside-Inside: The Relation of Exception

To develop the potential for philosophical inquiry opened by presupposing the impossibility of human noncommunication, we can begin by looking carefully at the distinction between communication and noncommunication that is reflected, and perhaps even taken for granted, in thinking and/or debates about the presupposition itself. The distinction can be approached as that between an interiority and an exteriority of communication, or an inside and an outside of communication. From the perspective of common understanding as well as of modern theory of communication, the "inside" of communication may be defined as that which includes the phenomena of contact, interaction, and affinity; the practices of exchange or transmission of information and knowledge by means of speaking, writing, and so on; and the goals of learning, informing, shared understanding, and the transcendence of personal differences. The "outside" of communication would be its opposite, or other, such as the phenomena and experiences of separation, solitude, silence, noise, misinformation, babble, nonsense, and so on—in short, so-called noncommunication.[8]

By invoking the terms "inside" and "outside" of communication, what I am calling attention to is the ordering of human communication: its *nomos*, the organized exchange of semiotic material in human contexts. Consider the normative order of communicating—that which is seen from the perspective of modern theory of communication, often depicted in sender-message-channel-receiver and feedback models of information transfer,[9] as well as in common thinking about communication, which is itself influenced by transfer models. Here, the inside of communication (again, identified by what it includes: namely, the phenomena, experience, and/or goals of informing, clarity, determinate meaning, identity, transmission, dialogue, understanding, and affinity) is privileged and preferred over what it excludes, which we can call its outside (again, identified as the phenomena and experience of separation, silence, solitude, and difference, as well as so-called failed outcomes such as inaccuracy, indeterminate meaning, misleading information, noise, and misunderstanding). However, the problem with this, or any, rigid inside-outside image of ordered human communication is that its rigidity severely limits what we can think of as "communication." It conceals by working to maintain the very distinction between communication and noncommunication that stabilizes the order and, in so doing, frames debate about the presupposition of the impossibility of noncommunication.

In contrast to a rigid inside-outside picture of this order, we would do well to consider how human communication in fact includes its outside (e.g., noise, silence, misunderstanding, indeterminacy of meaning, difference and separation of agents) so as to rule it out, that is, to exclude it both theoretically and practically, from the ordered inside of human communicating (e.g., understanding, determination of meaning, identity, dialogue, interaction, and affinity). It thereby stabilizes this very order by privileging of one set of phenomena, practices, and experience over another. Note here that "ruling out" does not mean eliminating but rather containing in order to curb and control. For example, consider how "noise," whether it is characterized as excess, confusion, conflict, difference of perspective, or otherwise, is routinely featured in transfer models not merely as disturbance to but as the elemental background of the problem—namely, "communication"—to which such models are designed to represent and address in the first place. If there were no noise—which is a sign of the separation in time and space of subjects, and therefore the possibility for exchange, for difference, disagreement, and misunderstanding—then human communication (defined here as the minimal act of interaction, encoding/sending, receiving/decoding) would be unnecessary for the reason that subjects would be in perfect communication, and as such, there would be no need to engage in, study, and/or model it for improvement. Noise betrays the neutrality and objective appearance of positivist communication theory's transfer model by unveiling the conservative leaning of it toward clarity over distortion and misinformation, accuracy over serendipity, understanding over misunderstanding and conflict—in short, of communication over mis-, non-, or so-called failed communication.[10] The outside of communication must be taken inside, as indicated, in fact, by classic transfer models, for "communication" to be understood as ordered in the first place, for there to be ordered exchange and not babble.

Here we can say that there is communication and the order of its sphere actually includes so-called noncommunication—that category of phenomena and experiences that are seen as such from the modern theoretical perspective of its order. That said, however, locating noncommunication on the inside rather than outside the order of communication does not confirm that one cannot not communicate; it merely offers philosophical direction for reentering the problematic circumscribed by the presupposition of the impossibility of noncommunication. Nevertheless, by underscoring what other scholars identify as the "ideology of communication" sustained by positivist currents of modern communication theory, research, and thought,[11] the perspective I am offering here helps bring into view how the distinction between communication and noncommunication that is established and maintained by both common and theoretical thinking about human communication practices, goals, and outcomes is not clean and clear-cut but is in fact structurally, and not only ideologically, blurred.

If this is so, then has the so-called outside of human communication simply dissolved? That is, if, as I have suggested, the outside of communication is not in fact outside because it is already inside, included within the order of communication as part of its balance and our modern communication-theoretic understanding of it, then what, where, or even *is there* an outside or exteriority to communication? And why does this matter? By "outside" of communication (I want to retain this word), I refer neither to noise nor to the indeterminacy of meaning or indiscernibility of various expressive material. Regarding noise, we know that it is semiotic and announces itself as noise within contexts of exchange, albeit disruptive to (at least according to classic, conservative transfer models) other communication elements, goals, practices, and outcomes.[12] Noise is included in the order of communication, both by way of being assigned a place and a meaning within social-scientific theory about communication and by its own negative self-communication. Regarding expressive phenomena that may appear to lack or exceed discernibility—such as artistic expressions of the sublime in painting, music, and literature, or the words of a language that one is in the process of learning, or even the appearance of other people—all of these are also inside communication, and are not noncommunicative. Communicability and communication, defined as contact, transmission, and understanding, may come with such phenomena, if not at first then perhaps later, as one catches on and "gears into" their expressive content.[13]

Instead, the "outside" of communication that I want to call attention to is an outside or locus from which the distinction itself between human communication and noncommunication is determined. Outside is the place of a ruling or decision, a place where what is communication, what is communicative and what is not, is determined. The place of such a decision must precede any judgment whatsoever about what qualifies for inclusion and what does not in order for the authority of the decision to have both the power and the legitimacy to establish the inside-outside distinction as such. This outside of human communication—that is, the outside of the inside-outside order described previously—must be situated somewhere for any legitimate determination to be made on what is and what is not within its domain, a ruling or determination of what is included (e.g., meaning, information, understanding, and so on) and what is excluded (e.g., noise, disturbance, misunderstanding, and so on) from the normal order and contexts of human communication.

Modern communication theory may refer to the place or locus of this decision as the place of a boundary. Anthony Wilden, for instance, argues that we must speak of a boundary as a signifier of a communication rule for elements/agents to which the rule applies.[14] A boundary is a signifier, not a sign, Wilden says, because it is at the basis of signification. A boundary divides and thereby puts human agents into relation and establishes a codified context for meaningful communication, defined as contact, interaction, exchange, transmission, and/or affinity. A communication boundary—again, a signifier, not a sign—is itself the exception to the rule it founds, the rule regarding whatever is inside or outside a context of communication. The boundary establishes a rule but does not apply to it. Or we can say that it applies by not applying, an exception. It exhibits what Agamben calls a "relation of exception," neither internal nor external to the context for which it functions as a boundary but is related as the exception to it.

The concept of exception is pivotal to Agamben's analysis of sovereignty in what is perhaps his best-known study, *Homo Sacer: Sovereign Power and Bare Life*. Briefly put, an exception establishes a rule by way of its suspension. A rule is suspended, that is, with regard to the exception to it, whose being and function is to ground the rule as such. An exception is not the same as an example, which serves as evidence of something that gives rise to it. Focusing on the nature of the relation between the exception and the rule, Agamben explains, "The exception is a kind of exclusion. What is excluded from the general rule is an individual case. But the most proper characteristic of the exception is that what is excluded in it is not, on account of being excluded, absolutely without relation to the rule. On the contrary, what is excluded in the exception maintains itself in relation to the rule in the form of the rule's suspension. *The rule applies to the exception in no longer applying, in withdrawing from it.*"[15]

Agamben employs this concept to help explain the logic of sovereign power, which according to him, can be understood to operate paradoxically by way of a relation of exception of the sovereign to the political-juridical order established by it, a sovereign whose power to do so is sustained in its exception (L. *ex-capere*) from that very order. The exception explains the distinction between the place or locus, an "outside," from which a political-juridical order is founded, and the function or order of that sphere, an "inside." The distinction between this inside, call it a state, for example, and its outside, call it sovereign power, is not clear-cut but rather blurred and at times indistinguishable, such as in what Agamben calls a "state of exception," that is, the sovereign decision to momentarily suspend the political-juridical order in periods of chaos so as to restore order—even though, Agamben argues, it is in fact the exception that today appears as the norm, a permanent state of exception.[16]

The logic of exception goes a long way to help explain the authority problem mentioned above, namely, of deciding legitimately on what is internal to communication and what is external (inside/outside, included/excluded). The legitimacy problem may be characterized not merely as one of drawing an inside-outside distinction (i.e., what is communication and what is not; can one not communicate; is noncommunication possible). More important than that, the problem is one of making determinations on a set of circumstances while standing apart from or outside of those circumstances and simultaneously maintaining a relation to them—a relation of exception.[17] By what right, or authority, are determinations made in any situation? How is the legitimacy of that authority maintained? With regard to human communication, how is the presupposition of the impossibility of noncommunication grounded as a presupposition?

These questions can be reduced to a master question, so to speak, about how a set of rules, or law in general, applies to the circumstances for which they function as rules or law. The logic of exception, which operates as a relation of inclusive-exclusion, brings into relief the locus or place from which inside-outside determinations are made—that is, that there must *be* such a place for the determination to hold. That place, according to Agamben, is the place of exception, an exclusive-inclusive relation that, like the concept of boundary in modern communication theory, is neither completely inside nor outside the territory or context it marks but is a necessary limit to it. The exception brings into focus how the relation between inside-outside is blurred.[18]

With regard to the presupposition of the impossibility of human noncommunication, Agamben's concept of exception helps by doing the philosophical work of unconcealing, and thereby aids in putting into question, the very distinction between communication and so-called noncommunication. It points to the place outside and beyond the distinction between communication and noncommunication that is required for any decision to be made on what's inside and/or outside communication in the first place (its order or *nomos*) and how the authority occupying that place (who or what makes the decision) maintains itself (its force and authority to decide) in relation—as an exception—to the order itself. As I demonstrate next, the concept of exception offers considerable power to explain the authority, force, and staying power of the presupposition of the impossibility of noncommunication and, in doing so, helps reframe modern communication theory debates about whether or not one cannot not communicate.

To Whom It May Concern: Language as Sovereign

Although the exception provides a critical philosophical clue to questions about the authority of the presupposition of the impossibility of noncommunication posed at the outset of the present discussion, it does not yet offer complete answers. In order to build toward those answers, we must first revisit the topic of language, this time beginning with the principle established by twentieth-century structuralist thinking about language as a contract. That principle goes something like this: the human person, endowed with the cognitive capacity to appropriate language, uses it according to its terms, namely, the grammatical, rhetorical, and logical rules of the combination of signs, which have historically agreed upon meanings necessary for meaningful communication (defined as transmission, dialogue, and/or affinity).[19] In using language for communication, as well as using it to name, there is always sign interpretation, negotiation, cocreation of meaning, and above all, creativity in expression. Humans are not machines. But there are limits to sign use. A sign cannot mean anything anyone wants it to mean: signs are arbitrary but necessary, Saussure says. Meaningful communication is contingent upon context, and although languages evolve, are shaped by, and reflect human agency, language use (according to which meaning is made and intersubjective understanding is possible—i.e., human communicating) is rule-bound and relatively stable.[20]

Regarding the contractual nature of language, we could once again refer to Lacan, as well as to Saussure, and rehearse the explanations that came after them.[21] However, for my purposes of examining the problematic of human communication (its possibility), it is Agamben who offers a decisive and radically innovative perspective on the *sovereignty* of language. He writes,

> Only language as the pure potentiality to signify, *withdrawing itself from every concrete instance of speech*, divides the linguistic from the nonlinguistic and allows for the opening of areas of meaningful speech in which certain terms correspond to certain denotations. *Language is the sovereign who, in a permanent state of exception, declares that there is nothing outside language and that language is always beyond itself.*[22]

According to Agamben, just as a sovereign power can decide, in the establishment of a juridical-political order, that there is nothing outside it except for itself (a sovereign exception), so too can language be understood as a sovereign that, or who, decides there is nothing outside it and that it is beyond itself.[23] Agamben's claim is certainly radical, but its structural linguistic and philosophical basis is well established, both by the distinction made by Saussure between *langue* and *parole* and by the one Benveniste draws between the sign and the sign in context (the existence of language and its manifestation, or actualization, in speech), as well as by Walter Benjamin's writing on language's messianic quality: namely, that there is language.[24]

To explain, two points made in the quotation can be rehearsed. First, language use is governed by language in withdrawal. That idea reflects the structural linguistic principle that speech (*parole*) contains within it an entire language system (*langue*) by way of which instances of speaking are meaningful. Yet with the attention Agamben brings to the relation among language, speech, and speaking beings, this principle receives a distinct inflection: namely, that language may be understood to be included in concrete instances of speech through its exclusion, a relation of exception. Language as such stands outside—it withdraws—as the background to and opening for human communication.[25] Hence the second key point: for Agamben, language exhibits the status and structure of sovereignty insofar as it can be said to be in, or to occupy, a state of exception "both within and lying beyond the set of phenomena it represents."[26]

The phenomena that language "represents" in the political and semiotic sense are its users, subjects of language as sovereign. In its permanent state of exception, language declares that nothing is outside it and that it is beyond itself. There is nothing outside of it that isn't already inside it, namely, subjects of communication. By using language—that is, entering into the language contract that enjoins the community of humans to communicate, a relation that, Agamben will show, actually preexists and thereby undermines the very concept of a linguistic "contract" and point of "entry" into it—a subject grants language the authority of sovereign representation, to communicate as a means for the sign-using subject to communicate for him- or herself.

To explain how this is so, we must first refer to Benveniste, whose writing on the instituting of subjectivity in language directly informs Agamben. The subject—whose basis, Benveniste tells us, is in the exercise of language—cannot, by definition, speak for itself.[27] Meaningful speech requires the appropriation of an entire language, Benveniste says, by which a speaker designates him- or herself as *I*, and interlocutors as *you, he, she, it, them, they* and so on. Agamben pursues this idea throughout his entire philosophical corpus, drawing on Jakobson's and Benveniste's analyses of pronouns as the class of signs that perform the special function of relating a speaker to a language system. Pronouns move a speaker into discourse, from *langue* to *parole* or from the semiotic to the semantic, while retaining their autonomy, Benveniste says, but "do not refer to a concept or to an individual." Regarding *I*, he explains that

> *I* refers to the act of individual discourse in which it is pronounced, and by this it designates the speaker. It is a term that cannot be identified except in what we have called elsewhere an instance of discourse and that has only a momentary reference. The reality to which it refers is the reality of the discourse. It is in the instance of discourse in which *I* designates the speaker that the speaker proclaims himself as the "subject." And so it is literally true that the basis of subjectivity is in the exercise of language.[28]

The above formulation serves, at least in part, as the analytic background of the widely recognized twentieth-century antihumanist principle that language speaks through a subject: language enables human communication as the symbolic structure in and through which expression is formed.[29] But with Agamben, both the political and the ontological significance of this principle is deepened, remarkably so, by his attention to the official, and one could even say austere, function accomplished by indication: pronouns designate (L. *desegnare*, "to mark") and represent a speaker.

In *Language and Death*, a slim volume devoted to the topic of voice, language, and presence in Hegel and Heidegger and whose title intimates the primordial connection of language to human life, Agamben draws on Benveniste to explain that whenever a pronoun such as *I, he, she, it, them, who,* and so on is uttered, the act of uttering does not refer to, or indicate, an individual speaker with whom the sign shares an existential connection but rather an instance of a discourse—the present moment of uttering, as Benveniste describes. More important, according to Agamben, such an act also refers to the agency or taking place of language. After tracing a history of scholarly thinking about deixis, or indication in language,[30] Agamben draws out the legal-political significance of Benveniste's research on uttering (F. *énonciation*) as the act of speech that sets language into motion.[31] For Agamben, Benveniste's "return to the instance of discourse" points to uttering and its sphere—the focus broadens to include all speech acts—as the place and time where language itself takes place. Agamben writes, "The sphere of the utterance thus includes that which, in every speech act, refers exclusively to its taking place, to its instance, independently and prior to what is said and meant in it. Pronouns and the other indicators of the utterance, before they designate real objects, indicate precisely that language takes place. In this way, still prior to the world of meanings, they permit that reference to the very event of language, the only context in which something can be signified."[32] Language exists *and* it takes place; the potentiality of it to signify is actualized in the function of enunciation, within whose sphere (namely, human communicating) language refers to itself, its *thereness, that there is* language. Here, one could certainly refer to this taking place of language not only in speech acts (statements) but also in conversation (dialogue) as well as in quotation (writing), all of which amount to citation, or reference, here and now to text and/or language elsewhere. That point is established by deconstruction.[33] But what the taking place of language in instances of speech and writing calls attention to is not just language itself, its self-reference but, crucially for Agamben, its sovereignty, that which transcends or stands outside of what has been said (language is beyond itself) in a relation of exception to it (nothing is outside language).

To be sure, although Benveniste and Agamben begin with language as an ontological condition of human being (there is no human being without/outside of language), neither argue that language merely imposes itself, dominates, and rules over the person who appropriates it for him- or herself.[34] Rather, the main critical point they share is that subjectivity is "manifest" in language. Language enables meaningful individual expression not only by way of personal and demonstrative pronouns (i.e., *this, that, these, those*) but also by adverbs and adjectives that indicate the spatial and temporal relation (i.e., *then, there, now, here*, and so on) of a subject to a statement.[35] As

Hamacher puts this idea, the subject of language, a being whom we find in the world as a speaking being, "is an effect of speech and writing in such a strict sense that it has no place outside of them."[36] A second critical point shared by Benveniste and Agamben is how the appropriation of language binds a speaker ontologically to the conventions, and thereby the social and judicial consequences, of its use, conventions that are worked out discursively and that apply to an entire communication community. Human being, in sum, both has free, creative, expressive capacity in language and is tied existentially—in uttering *I, you, he, she, this, that, then, there*—to its conventions for which a speaking speaker assumes responsibility.[37]

What interests Agamben most, following Benveniste, Lacan, Foucault, and all that came after in the name of poststructuralism, is how the order of culture, which is constituted in and by discourse, parallels the order of language. Agamben describes how the parallel between language and culture is demonstrated concretely by an act of oath, such as *I swear, I promise, I guarantee*, which, in *The Sacrament of Language*, he labels a "juridical institution,"[38] or what Benveniste calls an act "of social impact . . . a *performative* . . . by which Ego is bound."[39] Without going into detail, by swearing or promising or declaring (a performance rather than description of the very act of swearing, promising, and so on), a speaker admits to the cultural-linguistic network within which such an act is meaningful—that is, socially and judicially consequential—and which binds him or her existentially-ontologically to it and to all of its users.[40] For Agamben, what is at stake in taking an oath (again, a performance of act in speech by which the social-judicial reality of oath is placed upon its taker) is not the verification of truth of fact or event but rather *being before* "the very signifying power of language," a sovereign power.[41]

Why sovereign? Again, because like the sovereign who has the power to decide to temporarily suspend the rule of law if necessary (a state of exception)—a power that founds and justifies an entire judicial-political order—language, in its self-reference to the reality of discourse whenever *I, he, she, them, now, here, I swear, I promise, I declare* and so on are uttered, suspends momentarily the normal signifying function of the language system. To reiterate, for Agamben, in every speech act, language refers not merely to a thing or a speaking speaker but to itself, its taking place, the time-space of its event. It refers to the fact that *there is* language and that language is the pure potential for human communication. Oath-taking in particular, a performative "which pledges me," says Benveniste,[42] discloses the status and logic of sovereignty that Agamben attributes to language as such: namely, a sovereign with the power to interrupt the signifying function of its own system, thereby creating the sphere of its reference and establishing itself as the source of logical coherence of that very system. He explains,

> The performative substitutes for the denotative relationship between speech and fact a self-referential relation that, putting the former out of play, puts itself forward as the decisive fact. The model of truth here is not that of adequation between words and things but the performative one in which speech unfailingly actualizes its meaning. Just as, in the state of exception, the law suspends its own application only to found, in this way, its being in force, so in the performative, language suspends its denotation precisely and solely to found its existential connection with things.[43]

In momentarily suspending its normal signifying function by referring to itself rather than that to which signs stand for in an instance of speech, language establishes its sovereign connection to the world of things. It enables communication; that is its power.[44] In human communicating—which requires positing oneself as *I*, a sign, and another as *you*, thereby designating both as subject to a signifying order—language as sovereign speaks, a self-reference made to its status outside and beyond itself, an exception audible in the communication acts of human speakers.

Crucially, Agamben shows how language functions much less like a contract and more like a ban, a relation to something nonrelational. I explain this in the next section. In structurally the same way that there is no original social contract instituting human community by lifting it from a prior, chaotic state of nature, Agamben insists that we do not simply enter into language, nor can we break with it, as one can enter into and/or break with a contract. Rather, like community, human being is always *in* language, presented to and held existentially by it as sovereign—which is to say banished from any imagined prelinguistic state of being prior to communication.[45]

Abandoned to Language: The Law of Communication

It is in the self-connection of language to world, which goes beyond a power to name and includes the ontological foundation of human expressive being, that we arrive at Agamben's major insight into language and law that is essential to a contemporary continental perspective on the presupposition of the impossibility of noncommunication. That is, in the process of becoming a speaker—appropriating a language, which establishes *I* and *you* as personal/existential symbolic representatives—human being is abandoned to and by language as the sovereign potentiality to signify. For Agamben, language, which "provides the very definition of man,"[46] is not merely parallel to but coextensive with law. The structure of law, he argues, is founded in the structure of language, which, as we have just seen, binds the speaking being to it and to all for whom it represents (a *Lebenswelt*) through language's exceptional relation to regulated instances of its taking place.[47] Hence the relation of humans to language as a relation of ban, which is a relation of law: like law, whose essence is the very life of human *being*, coming prior to and outlasting us all,[48] Agamben says that "language holds man in its ban insofar as man, as a speaking being, has always already entered into language without noticing it."[49]

Drawing from Nancy, Agamben defines ban, in part, as a force—a power "of delivering something over to itself, which is to say, of maintaining itself in relation to something presupposed as non-relational."[50] For Agamben, language is this "something" presupposed as nonrelational. He explains, "Everything that is presupposed for there to be language (in the forms of something nonlinguistic, something ineffable, etc.) is nothing other than a presupposition of language that is maintained as such in relation to language precisely insofar as it is excluded from language."[51] This idea—the presupposition of language maintained in relation to language—can be understood as another way of expressing the logic of sovereignty described previously: namely, that nothing is outside the sovereign, and it is beyond itself, a paradox of relation by way of exception (a relation of nonrelation) to instances of the sovereign's taking place. As Agamben explains, the ban issuing from language, which is simultaneously removed from and delivered over to itself, as can be seen concretely in the reality of discourse, has the function of tying language as sovereign to instances of its taking place, namely, to speaking subjects, a tying by way of exception, a *ban* as the form of relation to something presupposed as nonrelational: "As the pure form of relation, language (like the sovereign ban) always already presupposes itself in the figure of something nonrelational, and it is not possible either to enter into relation or to move out of relation with what belongs to the form of relation itself. This means not that the nonlinguistic is inaccessible to man but simply that man can never reach it in the form of a nonrelational and ineffable presupposition, since the nonlinguistic is only ever to be found in language itself."[52]

As mentioned already, the subject cannot communicate on its own. Language is required. Language as sovereign offers that provision. It defines human being as a speaking being—that is, a subject who, in appropriating language, admits to its logical and cultural order. Abandonment is therefore a form of relation, albeit negative, a relation of ban: Language is nonrelational, which means human being cannot move in and out of relation with it. Language withdraws from instances of speech, abandoning human being to speak, while simultaneously remaining in force, its taking place being audible in acts of speech. With regard to language itself, the nonrelational relation of ban is, as such, a relation of exclusive inclusion: the sovereign stands back but at the same time keeps its constituents in check. Human being is both abandoned to language, subject to its law (we cannot be outside it), and abandoned by language, endowed with the capacity for signs and rules of combination but nevertheless left to its own skill set to communicate freely.[53]

François Raffoul's interpretation of Heidegger's notion of "thrownness" helps clarify the nature of this relation to language as fundamentally ontological and points to its significance in inviting new understanding of the presupposition of the impossibility of noncommunication. In an essay on the concept of abandonment,[54] Raffoul explains that in being thrown into existence, the human *Dasein* (being-there) does not know why it is there. The origin of its being remains an enigma, hence the meaning of being is raised as a question for it. Being thrown into existence, and not knowing why, *Dasein* as such is not merely a being-there (*Da-sein*) but is, more profoundly, a *having-to-be*. It does not just exist—it has to. Its condition is precisely what Nancy calls "abandoned being." Human being is—and it *has* to be—abandoned.

Having-to-be is, as such, and essentially, an obligation. "In one stroke," Raffoul explains, "the throw of thrownness is also the throw of an obligation, a having-to-be. . . . Abandonment is delivered over to an obligation."[55] In other words, because we don't just exist, we have to, our being consists in/as an ontological obligation *to be*. Now, if what has been said thus far about language as a fundamental ontological condition of human being is true, then we must add that human being is not merely in language but, because it is defined by language ontologically, it has to be. Because we are thrown into existence (having-to-be and not knowing why) and, by virtue of one's humanness, are given over to language (there is no human community outside it), human being is obligated to language, which means we are obliged to appropriate and exercise our subjectivity in it—to live meaningfully. We are obligated to speak, to *communicate*. Humans cannot not communicate because, ontologically-existentially speaking, we have to.

Drawing again from Nancy's Heideggerian-inspired philosophy, Raffoul calls attention to the root of the term "abandonment," *bandon*, which he says "designates an order or a prescription, a decree, a power. To abandon would thus mean: to remit to a law, a sovereign power."[56] To abandon—to give over to a ban—means not only to be held before it (a relation) but also to live (to exist) by its rule: abandonment is "delivered over" to obligation. To be sure, abandonment to and by language does not simply mean choosing to yield to its command or law, its injunction to communicate. Rather, it means not having that choice. The law of communication is ontological. To be human is to think, and thinking takes place in language. As a semiotic being, human being is held to (defined by) language and ontologically obligated to use it, to communicate in/as its *having-to-be*. Abandoned to language by its withdrawal—that is, being held in a relation of nonrelation (a ban) to that which presupposes itself as nonrelational, namely, language as sovereign—not only is it impossible not to communicate, but also one must communicate.

It is worth stressing here that obligation is ontological, and only later does it take on moral or ethical features (ethics is not first philosophy). Obligation is what being gives itself over to in abandonment, as Raffoul says, an "abandonment of existence *to an obligation, and the assignation of the injunction of this obligation to the having-to-exist.*"[57] To be human, which means to coexist, is having-to-be in language and being responsible for (obliged to exercise) one's expressive capacity in it. The obligation of language, of being in language as a condition of having-to-be human, is thus an obligation of communication, a being held in obligation to the freedom of expression given in and by language. As I address in the concluding chapter of this volume, what is at stake in human being's having-to-be, its primordial obligation, is not merely communication as transmission but communication as affinity, the having-to-be-*with* others in human communities. Read from this perspective, "one cannot not communicate" may be now understood as the injunction or command of sheer being, of having to be with one another in our shared abandonment to and by language. It is a command, a ban, to which one gives oneself over in obligation by way of making sense of (thinking about) how to be.[58]

From this perspective—on the condition of being in language (Benveniste), and having no choice but to be (Heidegger), which means being held in a ban

(Agamben)—we recognize not only that language enjoins users to communicate. We see also that its law, that "one cannot not communicate," is self-imposed. The force of authority to decide on what is inside and outside language, a sovereign decision, is sustained in language *use*, the appropriation of it by speakers whose subjectivity (*I, you, he, she, them*) it founds and whose subjectivity is manifest in language's taking place (*now, here, then, there*). In using language and being defined by it—*a-ban-doned* to and by language, which means being given to it and left to one's expressive capacity—the law of communication is embodied, and consciously experienced, because it is actualized in speech, and heard, as if it were a voice speaking through the speaker.[59]

For Agamben, speech, or what he specifies in *Language and Death* as "voice," indicates the place of language, the sovereign who issues its ban.[60] If, as discussed previously, the taking place of language is indicated by the utterance, then what the utterance also indicates is the very place of this taking, the place or location of language. Where is language? It lives in speech.[61] To refine a point made already, language is not outside or external to moments of its taking place but in fact resides within them and can be heard there and then (in speaking, in voice in general) where it *takes place*.[62] Language the sovereign constitutes the possibility for a language system to signify by its withdrawal from (as an exception to) particular speech acts, by which it remains immanent to those instances as a relation of exception, instances that, universally, indicate its place: speech. Speech is the place of language's ban that holds a speaker (abandoned to and by it) there in its taking place, issuing from the voice of a speaking being who has-to-be.

If all of this is so, then we understand in a new way why one cannot not communicate. Noncommunication is ruled out, ontologically, by language. Its authority to institute a ban (a *bandon* of noncommunication, of anything outside language other than itself) is founded by a relation of exception, its standing outside instances of communication (language is beyond itself), which in themselves—this point is crucial—uphold that authority and refer to, before anything else, its movement, order, and place (nothing is outside of language). Ours is a condition wherein we are not merely enjoined by the human community's language "contract," but we appropriate and entrust it, embody it, and in our existential obligation to pursue it, we do so freely and sometimes with abandon. Human being benefits from language's provisions as a being who, in having-to-be—the experience of being named *I, you, he, she* and called into culture by language as law, which is to say, its permission—cannot but be communicative.

Scholarship on language and communication affirms Agamben's philosophical findings. I will mention three traditions. First, as we saw in the previous chapter, psychoanalytic theory offers perspective on how a person is subject to language rules. According to this tradition, language acquisition for the purposes of communicating requires the person to assume the place of *I*, a universal plural signifier. However, in order to assume the place of this signifier, a separation must first be introduced: the child develops a unified image of itself apart from, and in contrast to, the lived, disorienting experience of its body. It is a body image that is separated from (external to) but recognizable by the child as him- or herself and to which the child will eventually refer or "misidentify" as *I*.[63] Assuming the place of a signifier such as *I*, *you*, *he*, and *she*, as well as proper names, depends on the child's cognitive capacity to imagine and thereby take up (to internalize) him- or herself as an object-self in language's signifying system. Words may represent the speaking subject, but they do so poorly because not all can be expressed in language. Language rules therefore must pull the subject along, represent it for another signifier, as Lacan says, in the promise and potential of more words and perhaps more effective communication.[64] There is an emotional impact that may arise from self-separation in the developmental stage of learning to speak a language and being spoken about in and by it. Notwithstanding that, the significance of a person's capacity to perceive his or her body image as distinct from others, and hear him- or herself being named in the call of language, is that the person recognizes him- or herself as bound to the expressive and perceptive conventions of his or her lived—that is, embodied—communication community.[65]

Second, research in symbolic interaction, especially in its classical sociological phase, teaches that in order for the person to imagine him- or herself as *he*, *she*, or *I*—that is, for the person to appropriate language and inhabit the semiotic domain of the human life world—the person must be able to picture him- or herself not only as distinct from but also alongside others. G. H. Mead famously calls this the capacity of "taking the attitude of the other," a conscious process whereby a self perceives others, and their expressions, not as objects or merely as others but as other selves.[66] In this learning process, the person takes what Alfred Schutz calls mental "snapshots"—to which the person refers at a spatial and temporal distance, there and then—in the sense-making process of interacting with others here and now. In human communication, a person appears meaningfully to him- or herself as one among others, as if in a "phantasied filmstrip," Schutz says, which precipitates consciousness of a self that is subject to, or impacted by, the viewpoints (attitudes or snapshots) taken by others.[67]

Third, social semiotics confirms how the person is guided in communicating with others via processes in which human consciousness develops by way of attending to the experience of oneself as a sign. Even if a person were able to choose "not to" communicate—which a naïve theoretical perspective assumes may be accomplished simply by refusing to speak, write, or by leaving the presence of another—that person nevertheless remains impacted by language and other sign systems because he or she is implied by the discourses and circulation of meanings enabled by it. We are named in language, constituted by "sign material, linguistic material which are always signs of the other and words of the other."[68] We freely speak words that come from others (F. *langage*—community norm), and our statements (F. *parole*), spoken freely, will in turn inhabit other people by entering into their conscious experience.[69] "The signs in which the human being's conscious and unconscious are engendered arise in the community, the public sphere," says Susan Petrilli, which explains the essential human feature of our relation and projection toward one another.[70] As Jacqueline Martinez summarizes, "Existence is fundamentally intersubjective and semiotic. As human beings, we are simply and profoundly connected through our mutual location and participation within sign systems."[71]

Taken together, the psychoanalytic, phenomenological, and social semiotic perspectives on human communication add rigor to the basis of the present chapter's interpretation of the presupposition of the impossibility of noncommunication. They show how noncommunication is impossible for the reason that language is an ontological condition of being human—a being that as such has-to-be in communication, in language's pure potentiality to signify, a being that lives intersubjectively, "which alone makes linguistic communication possible"[72] and that embodies, shapes, and is enfolded into "a complex of expressive media"[73] of which language is the most crucial. Noncommunication is not simply ruled out theoretically but is from this perspective impossible ontologically: because of its relation to language—neither prior to nor after language but present *to* as coextensive *with* it—the being who speaks (*I, you, he, she, them*), and who speaks with abandon (*now, here, there, then*), cannot not communicate. Human being exhibits "the ontological peculiarity of *being within* a structure we institute and sustain and yet that transcends us."[74] We are beings of language, semiotic materiality through which meaning circulates and its order passes—is actualized, communicatively, case by case. Language, and expressing oneself in it, is (in short) what separates being human from the sphere of what Agamben calls "bare life." As he writes in the final pages of *The Sacrament of Language*,

> When language appeared in man, the problem it created cannot have been solely . . . the cognitive aspect of the inadequation of signifier and signified that constitutes the limit of human knowledge. For the living human being who found himself speaking, what must have been just as—perhaps more—decisive is the problem of the efficacy and truthfulness of his word, that is, of what can guarantee the original connection between names and things, and between the subject who has become a speaker—and, thus capable of asserting and promising—and his actions.[75]

Human communication, whether it is defined as transmission (expression, perception) or as interaction and affinity (dialogue, understanding), or both, is made possible and occurs by way of the embodiment and actualization—the "taking up and recreating in experience"[76]—of sign material that includes the sign-using being as its exterior.[77] This is the being to whom language as sovereign applies existentially, with which language's taking place coincides, and therefore into which, as Agamben insists, the very stake of its potential as *human* being is placed.[78]

Ban, Law, and Philosophy of Communication

Points of clarification are necessary before developing and extending these ideas further in this book. First, I am certainly not suggesting that the person is merely passively subject to and burdened by the ban of language and law of communication. Language is both restrictive and productive. People creatively use, are shaped by, and are invested in linguistic, visual, acoustic, and nonverbal semiotic resources that structure perception and one's capacity for expression: "We cannot escape these semiotic structures, and they are always at work, both enabling and constraining what is possible for us to think, feel, or experience."[79] Being in language without room for escape does not mean, however, that the values, attitudes, beliefs, and styles held by a group over time are, or will be, taken up and acted upon by everyone in exactly the same way. Far from it. Nor will the network configuration of ideas within which meaning circulates remain permanent, for the reason that "each expression deforms and reforms the fields of meaning to which it responds and yet that it paradoxically sustains."[80] There is room for interpretation, as we say, as well as discord and disagreement.

What I am arguing is that as an expressive being, what the person is more or less aware of in human communication—what one feels and is concerned with—is not only one's own ability to perceive (to sense) and make meaning of (to take up, activate, and move forward with) the expressions of others but also the consequences to perceptions of oneself and world of the ability of others to take up and make meaning of (to perceive) one's own expressions. Simply put, this is a matter of just being aware. But not only that. Human "communication" need not be reduced to messages, information, or understanding, where an occurrence of one (an exchange of signs in a given context) presupposes a mutual and thereby successful sharing of other. Although language enables speech and writing as vehicles for idea transmission, *communication* must also be understood ontologically, as fundamental to being human—that is, as having-to-be a linguistic-semiotic being obligated to the expressive and perceptive (communicative) freedom enabled by language. Existence outside of language—a medium offering access to the discourse systems or communication communities of which one is a part—amounts to no human existence at all.[81] In later chapters, I address the ontology of human communication in terms of our embodied relation, if not direct contact, with other beings as *being-with* one another.

Second, I do not wish to imply that solitude, for instance, is impossible. It is possible. However, because consciousness is by phenomenological definition consciousness *of* self, other, and world, and because human being is fundamentally a social-linguistic being among and with others, solitude is neither the absence nor the opposite of communication. Thought, feeling, and experience are shaped by language, whether we are alone with those thoughts and feelings or actively sharing them with others. As discussed previously, there is never a "pure" self that is independent of language; there is always a subject of language that shapes it, and that it (a subject) in turn reproduces in speech. When asked what makes a person "truly" him- or herself, for example, recourse is routinely taken to a description of values, beliefs, traditions, and memories—discourses of a community or culture (an outside, as it were) that are not invented by oneself but are disbursed and absorbed over time, the time of abandonment, informing a person's sense (an inside, as it were) of who she or he "really" is. As I have shown, the distinction between inside and outside communication is blurred by the fact of language, whether one chooses to interact with others or not.

Third, questions may be raised about using the terms ban and law rather than *axiom*. Law, like language (the one has its foundation in the other, Agamben says), shapes consciousness; the language of law (its code) gives form to thinking, which is worked out in expression (speaking, writing, being named)—is worked out in life, outside of which law has no existence for itself, just as language is only pure potentiality outside of its use. To be sure, although human being is abandoned by and to language, it is obviously impossible to rigidly follow its law. The difference between recognizing a law, rule, or convention of a culture and comporting oneself according to it in strict fashion is a significant one. We may share a language, and in it we may try to overcome our differences, but we don't always say, mean, or understand the same thing, at least not in the same way in the same context. Language structures speech and enables communication. We are caught in its cipher, but our expressions are free. We are all, in a way, *banditos*. Axiom, defined as a self-evident truth, is rigid by contrast. It does not afford the philosophical flexibility that a term like "law" does, which refers to a structure gathering us together as semiotic beings geared into, grounding, and exhibiting its code. In its application—that is, in life, as is discussed in the next chapter—law requires interpretation. Unlike an axiom, it isn't followed exactly to the letter.

The above reframing of the presupposition of the impossibility of human noncommunication could be dismissed, perhaps relatively quickly, if one were to restrict understanding the presupposition to its historical connection to the Palo Alto group and all the communication theory that came after, including its critique. There, one could say that the authority to determine what counts as communication and what doesn't is located in a specific institutional discourse, psychotherapy, and the contexts of its application to embodied beings, whose "behavior," when seen from the perspective of agents of a Western medical gaze, is determined as information and therefore, as "communication." The outside stands apart, but with the power to determine what is inside, what is "communication." End of story. But to reiterate, *one cannot not communicate* is not merely a mid-twentieth-century research outcome. As an axiom of modern thinking about human communication, it weighs on human awareness, on consciousness of self, world, and existence with others, our coexistence.

Agamben's thinking about abandonment and law broadens our vocabulary and therefore our philosophical perspective on communication. His terms help underscore the absence of any outside to human communication other than language itself. Language transcends instances of speaking, but that does not make it a transcendental. It speaks, and commands, but nevertheless requires a mouth (a body) from which to issue.[82] Neither is the law of communication imposed from beyond. We inhabit it, as communicative subjects, and it inhabits us (it is immanent) to the extent that we use language to communicate, are conscious of being with one another (we coexist), and are conscious of other people, too, as expressive and perceptive (i.e., communicative) beings. Language holds us together *and* offers terms to maintain our distinction. It frees and restricts; it empowers and it can immobilize. As Irving Goh writes, "the fact of existence of each being is the expression of that law and the freedom that accompanies it."[83]

Perhaps one might suggest that noncommunication is possible, for instance in monologue, when interlocutor expressions are ignored, or in reflective thinking about one's perceptions as interpretations, or even under the mask of solitude. However, this would require one either to believe in a reality that exists outside of language but is nevertheless accessible by way of it, which would amount to being language the sovereign,[84] or to presume that communication is a domain of absolute conscious control, where its possibility may be turned on and off by personal whim. Belief in the possibility of noncommunication can be undermined, on one hand, by reflecting on communicating within oneself, such as in the uttering of *I* and *you* or, radically, in premeditating the act of uttering a forged document, where even in the appearance of noncommunication *there is* communication. On the other hand, reducing communication to interpretation, to a skill set in encoding and decoding, eliminates far too much from critical observation. Particularly, as I discuss later in this book, it ignores the existential-ontological fact of relation and contact, where being in communication is understood as primary to human life—the embodied experience of sense and meaning.

In that regard, Agamben helps us understand why the consequences to life of being banned by and to language are what he calls "biopolitical," where being and language—or to put it another way, life and law—are entwined by way of the management and regulation of one through the power and/or force of the other. If language defines human being (an ontological condition proving the point that one *cannot* not communicate) and abandonment to it obliges human being to take responsibility for our shared condition, then the consequence of having-to-be in language is exposure to communication. Exposure calls for at least some degree of protection. With regard to human communication, we may even go so far, as I do in the next chapter, to say that communication calls for, and in fact is a form of, immunization.

CHAPTER 3

Of Communication and-as Immunization

The previous chapter demonstrates how Giorgio Agamben's perspective on language, law, and the logic of exception broadens thinking about human communication—in particular, the presupposition that "one cannot not communicate"—as a contemporary continental philosophical concern. The present chapter extends that perspective to thinking about communication as both threat and protection, as contagion and immunization. If, as previously argued, there is nothing outside of language except language itself, which institutes and regulates an order of communication, then being ontologically defined by it—that is, abandoned by and left to language's mercy—is coextensive with being exposed. Human being is exposed within this order, I argue, both to the threat of communication and to its protective or immunizing function. This threat is defined here as the figuration as well as disfiguration by the linguistic-semiotic codes, conventions, and values of a community and also the possibility of disruption, confusion, misunderstanding, disagreement, and conflict offered by the actions of employing them. The protective or immunizing function of communication is defined as the use of semiotic-linguistic materiality to bring meaning to sense and structure to experience—to build knowledge, learn, develop mutual understanding, and also affirm and expand or potentially challenge the prevailing community order by active subjective expression within it. Communication protects human being in the long meaning-making process of having-to-be at the same time that it threatens the linguistic-semiotic identity boundaries of its material existence.

To develop this thesis, the present chapter turns to the work of Roberto Esposito, whose best-known volumes—*Communitas*, *Immunitas*, and *Bíos*—critically explore the relation of bodies and social formations by way of a rigorous examination of the origins of ideas about life, law, and community advanced in the major works of modern political and twentieth-century continental philosophy.[1] The chapter focuses mostly on *Immunitas*, the centerpiece of the above trilogy, for its powerful and provocative analysis of immunity as a conceptual device that Esposito shows has become decisive today in how both human and nonhuman life is perceived—and thereby how it is experienced, valued, and regulated within what he and other continental philosophers and theorists call a modern biopolitical paradigm. Esposito defines immunity as "a protective response in the face of a risk," and what constitutes such a risk (threat) provoking an immunizing response, he argues, is "the trespassing or violating of borders."[2] Crucially, whether it is the threat of contamination from a common flu virus, the potential risk of unauthorized computer access, or perhaps for some, the threatening appearance of strangers, "what remains constant," Esposito says, "is the place where the threat is located, always on the border between the inside and the outside, between the self and other, the individual and the common."[3]

The topic of identity borders—their existence, maintenance, protection, and threat of violation—is a fundamental communication topic. Modern information theory, for example, posits an organism interacting with its environment and defines "communication" as an interactive response to the environment. The main goal of inquiry from the perspective of that modern tradition—that is, the cybernetic study of communication command and control—is to understand how organisms relate to and learn from environmental stimuli in order to reduce doubt and anticipate, predict, and better manage future communications.[4] For the human organism, the environment consists of other organisms, humans being the most obvious, and interaction within it is always symbolic: human communication occurs within a context, a bounded environment of social contact and interaction within which responses to environmental stimuli, including social agents, gain meaning through sign systems. The logic that organizes a context of human interaction, whether micro, such as dyadic interpersonal and group, or more macro, such as community, state, and nation, can be read from its symbolic content (for instance, differentially valued linguistic couplets such as self/other, man/woman, us/them, human/nonhuman, inside/outside). *Semiotics* is the name for the study of this logic, and *phenomenology* is the name for the study of its conscious, embodied experience. Esposito's perspective on the concept and function of immunity adds insight into both the semiotics (sign logic) and phenomenology (lived experience) of communication's identity-making borders. It helps us understand communication as the name of the threshold between self and other, us and them, inside and outside, at which identity border threats and protection occur. For my purposes, Esposito offers an intellectual pivot point for the continental philosophical perspective advanced in this book on the intersection of human language and subjectivity, human communication and the impossibility of noncommunication, and community and embodiment.[5]

To establish the direct relevancy of Esposito's work to contemporary continental philosophy of communication, I begin with a sketch of his study of the origins of the idea of "community" represented in modern thought. Through his command of the canon of modern political philosophy, which is nothing short of dazzling, Esposito links the origin of the thinking of community to modern discourses of "immunity"—that is, the protection of identity boundaries by way of the very threats against them. But rather than approach immunity and community as strictly opposed, Esposito instead offers an account of how these ideas coincide and overlap. It is in the etymological core of both terms, *munus*, that he finds not only the conditions of this overlap but also an opening for an affirmative philosophy of both. In so doing, Esposito offers perspective on the practical political, ethical, and existential benefits of thinking about human communication as both threat and protection—that is, of communication and-as immunization.

Community and Immunity: *Nothing* in Common

Esposito's philosophical oeuvre, which is thoroughly deconstructive in orientation, may be summarized by its address to what he calls the "antinomy of community": namely, that there *is* community and that it cannot be realized.[6] On the one hand, to say that there *is* community means that it is "constantly present,"[7] for the reason that being is primordially co-being, or that existence is coexistence. There is no being that exists outside of, and that cannot be identified other than in terms of, its relation to other beings. Insofar as the being of human being is defined in and by being-together with other beings—including other humans, who, as previously discussed, have-to-be—there *is* community. For Esposito, community not only "constitutes our originary condition" but also precedes it ontologically by "the fact that we have always existed in common."[8]

On the other hand, and paradoxically, community cannot be realized. This is because, as Esposito argues, community "is" neither a substance nor an attribute. Like language, it is less like a concrete and rigid totality and more like a threshold, an articulated social unity that we share. Because it separates each human person from the limits of his or her identity by exposing each one to another, community is not a thing, Esposito says, but rather a no-thing, a nonentity—that which, while not being a "that," cannot be filled or raised to the category of a something.[9] A summary quotation from *Communitas* captures this critical point:

> Community isn't an entity, nor is it a collective subject, nor a totality of subjects, but rather is the relation that makes them no longer individual subjects because it closes them off from their identity with a line, which traversing them, alters them: it is the "with," the "between," and the threshold where they meet in a point of contact that brings them into relation with others to the degree to which it separates them from themselves.[10]

To suggest that community is not a thing, that it "is" a nonentity and therefore impossible to realize because we are already in common, is not to deny the importance and necessity of what typically comes to mind whenever the term *community* is invoked. There are communities, and communities can be imagined and built.[11] What is at stake here, philosophically, is the idea rather than the phenomenality of community, the latter of which, when raised to the level of discourse, can quickly dissolve—a dissolution in nomination that in fact justifies raising "community" as a philosophical question, in this case, of relation.[12]

That said, although relation itself is an abstract concept, Esposito's intent in identifying the no-thing of community by raising it to the level of philosophical discourse is not to defer its thinking to another, potentially more abstract, term. Nor is it, again, to undermine the necessity of community and the importance to individual life of sharing it with one another. To the contrary, emphasizing the ontological fact of relation, that to be human means to be with one another—relation as the essence of any identity, including community[13]—helps explain its rise in modern thinking and the failed attempts to realize it, particularly since the idea of community bears with it two major consequences.

The first consequence of community, according to Esposito's reading of it as a foundation problem of modern political philosophy, is that community fails to protect individuals.[14] As an original relation (a nonentity) shared by all its members, community does not itself secure the ability of individuals to exercise personal freedom while at the same time limiting others from exercising too much of their own. In an undifferentiated mass of individuals existing together, there is the possibility of conflict, the threat or fear of potential violence, and for those reasons, a need for protection. But because of its nonbeing, community has been thought of as "utterly incapable of producing effects of commonality."[15] It neither warms nor protects us, Esposito says, but on the contrary "exposes us to the most extreme of risks: that of losing, along with our individuality, the borders that guarantee its inviolability with respect to the other."[16]

The second consequence of community, inseparable from the first, is that attempts to realize community by overcoming its lack of protection in a state of undifferentiated mass (to realize what there is already, which makes realizing it logically impossible) may in fact threaten its members. In the creation of identity boundaries throughout the world—the act of cutting into the globe to secure sovereign territory and establish group independence, the political-juridical process of so-called nation or community building—individual as well as collective freedoms may be imposed upon, narrowed, and curtailed. In that process, as the modern record of pursuing statehood makes evident, life itself can become threatened, especially when identity myths about blood, sweat, and bone (in the recourse they take to biology's vocabulary of contaminants like *bacteria, viruses, parasites, cancer, infection*, and so on that may "weaken" community) are employed as a means to identify, justify, and govern the rights to and protection of one's own.

It is in response to the threat of an undifferentiated and thereby unprotected community, and the impossibility of realizing it, that modern political theory, as Esposito carefully reads it, develops what he calls an "immunitary paradigm."[17] Philosophically, this paradigm is guided by the immunization theory and practice of harnessing potential threats to a body-system in order to protect against them. A basic example is the vaccine practice of injecting a small amount of a disease-causing virus in order to stimulate a human body's natural production of protective antibodies or, in the example of a nonhuman system, the installation of virus-protection software into computer code so as to anticipate, detect, and better control threats of system compromise. Crucially, immunization means not that system threats are absorbed, later expelled, and thereby eradicated. Rather, it means that the threat is stored and contained in the body-system, becoming part of it, internal and vital to the system's healthy function. By definition, immunization entails the persistence of a threat or contamination in the form of its containment or cure. As Esposito explains this important point, "The immunitary mechanism presupposes the existence of the ills that it is meant to encounter, not only in the sense that disease makes it necessary (it is the risk of infection that justifies the prophylactic measure) but also, in even stricter terms, that the immune mechanism functions precisely through the use of what it opposes. It reproduces in a controlled form exactly what it is meant to protect us from."[18]

An example of immunitary thinking in modern political philosophy, as Esposito reads it, is social contract theory.[19] Cursorily put, this theory posits that a human being recognizes within him- or herself the power of violence—to hurt and be hurt by other people who are similarly capable. Therefore, in order to preserve one's life and prevent community from dissolving into a threatened state of conflict, an agreement, or contract, must be established whereby the power to institute and maintain order is granted by community members to a power who, or that, imposes measures to protect individual freedom and thereby sustains community life. This power, a sovereign power, represents the potential for violence that arises from group life. It carries and wields that potential as the defining feature of its power *as* sovereign and, in doing so, maintains the obligation of individuals to one another—only this time as having-to-be for community. The social contract immunizes the "inside" of the individual (secures its personal freedom to live by containing its violent capacity to destroy), protecting it from the compromising contagion of what appears to be its "outside" (namely, the wider human community and its potential for violence, to which all members are exposed) and thereby strengthening the armor or identity boundary of individuals.[20]

With regard to modern social formations, the interrogation of which is Esposito's primary concern, law (or the modern legal system) may be identified as "the immune apparatus of the entire social formation."[21] Esposito argues that being in common under the modern social order means being free to make claims upon and take possession of available property—to own, to keep, and to make a living more so than to merely exist as separate entities "whose very separateness functions as the invitation to the common."[22] The problem, however, is that if such freedom is available to all, then the ability to make and uphold claims to what is one's own (the proper) must be secured: everyone cannot lay claim to the same property because whatever belongs to all (the common) belongs to no one.[23] Lest it devolve into a state in which what is one's own is defined solely by one's power to rip it away from somebody else, where uncertainty about what belongs to whom threatens social order, community must be bound together—that is, protected—by measures that keep individuals apart. Law performs this vital immunizing function:

> The legal form safeguards the community from the risk of conflict through the fundamental rule that things are completely available to be used, consumed, or destroyed by whoever can legitimately claim to possess them, without anyone else being able to interfere. But in this way, it reverses the affirmative bond of common obligation into the purely negative right of each individual to exclude all others from using what is proper to him or her. This means that society is legally governed and unified by the principle of common separation: the only thing in common is the claim to whatever is individual, just as the object of public law is precisely the safeguarding of that which is private.[24]

In the modern order, law compensates for the community's lack of resources to protect individuals. It stands as an immunizing mechanism to preserve group life by providing consistent and predictable answers to common questions about property, freedom, and their limits. Whenever conflicting claims arise within this order, those that prevail do so not by way of personal force but by the effective employment of law, a codified system for governance that applies to the community because it is authorized to do so by members whose well-being it serves and, in theory, is designed to protect.

This brief sketch appears to indicate two opposing problems: the idea of an undifferentiated community that compromises the difference and independence of individuals by fundamentally exposing each one to the potential for conflict with another on the one hand, which, on the other hand, gives rise to the idea of immunity in order to fortify the individual with protective mechanisms that help close it back into itself, thereby hardening both the community and the individual against whatever threatens to compromise them. However, Esposito shows the contrary: that the ideas of immunity and community indicate circumstances that overlap and even coincide. To explain, he calls attention to the etymological core of both terms, *munus*.

Munus: A Double Lack

Munus may be defined as both "gift" and "debt." It refers at once to the gift of human existence—that is, life and the freedom that comes with such a gift.

We are born free; we live. However, because life's freedom is a gift given to all and not only to some, it must be shared. We live together; we coexist (*co-munus*). *Munus* therefore, and also, refers to a debt in two senses: debt in the sense of obligation and, crucially, the sense of lack. First, as obligation, *munus* refers to a basic expectation to give back in return for the gift of life. Individuals ought to give up some of their freedom (a donation) so that others may enjoy theirs, an "ought" that Esposito calls community's unwritten "law of reciprocal gift-giving."[25] Humans ought to be for community, "the expenditure of self for the other,"[26] so that life's gift may be shared harmoniously (*cum-munus*).

In addition to the reciprocal obligation to give back for the gift of life, the second sense of *munus*, as lack, refers to the debt structure of human community in an original, undifferentiated state. *Munus* refers to the absence—the lack—of any real mechanism binding human community other than the personal obligation of having-to-be, the experience of which has been represented in modern philosophy as "guilt."[27] To reiterate, community isn't a thing we have in common, such as land or a job; rather, it "is" what there is—namely, life, a coexistence.[28] It is in precisely this sense that Esposito says we hold nothing in common—*nothing*, that is, other than the *with* or *co-* of being, an ontological relation.[29] Hence we have an obligation to give back by being for what there is, the nonentity of community, which is as such defective because although life is its essence, community lacks the means to protect and regulate that gift—of being, which means to live.[30]

With Esposito's analysis of the *munus*, which I have only glossed, we recognize how the ideas of community and immunity converge more than diverge. It shows that community is not exactly external and thereby opposed to individual members, who, if it were, would clearly need immunizing protection from its threat to compromise their individuality—its threat of eliminating difference in communal life. Instead, the analysis of *munus* shows that community is already internal to individuals: life, or the gift of the *munus*, "exposes each person to a contact with, and also to a contagion by, another."[31] In short, being is by definition co-being: human community is what there is because no human being exists outside of, or other than within, relations to others. Not exactly an alien threat to the individual's domestic constitution or what can be called "subjectivity," community is more so "the exteriorization of what is within,"[32] moving from what is inside and proper (one's own) to what is outside and shared (the common).

Next, in exposing each being to contact with and thereby contagion by another, *munus* (the gift of life, of co-being) bears within it (is cause for) community—a protective, shared identity. Once established, however, the more the individual needs to protect from others what is his or her own, the more he or she ends up relying on the community, which may thereby infringe upon and appropriate the individual. As Esposito says of law, for instance, it is "*of* the community and *from* the community."[33] Nonetheless, community cannot be realized, as was just explained, not only because it lacks more than the relation that it "is" already (it is a no-thing) but also because of the internal tension and unsociability of its members to which being in relation (which means being human) may give rise.[34] This tension limits community structurally and leaves it exposed, which makes it not dysfunctional but "inoperable."[35]

Finally, and crucial to Esposito's critique of community and interest in the positive potential of immunity, he calls attention to how the immunitary paradigm may begin to offer too much protection, such as in response to the circulating mixture of people, products, and ideas in a thoroughly globalized world. We may see the potential for too much immunizing protection in an era of heightened security consciousness, wherein both individual and group identity boundaries may become rigid and inflexible more than open and yielding to other individuals and different groups. In extreme circumstances, such as with the rise of nationalist movements guided by essentialist, racist desires for purifying protection, the immunitary paradigm can mutate into a threat, a political-juridical mechanism that "determines and orders the destruction of life."[36] Under extreme circumstances of protective, immunizing closure, boundaries that were once established to limit the sovereign territory of states and secure individual life within them may be looked upon as "thresholds within human life itself that allow the division of one part that is said to be superior from another that is said to be inferior"—a division, Esposito suggests, that can reach a point at which decisions are made about which "life is no longer worth being lived."[37]

Such circumstances call for *autoimmunization*—the protection from an excess of immune system protection. Autoimmunization is "a protective attack against protection itself,"[38] a process by which an organism attacks not a foreign element but its own capacity to fight it off in an effort to protect rather than reject that element.[39] For Esposito, the concept of autoimmunization is crucial. It helps turn thinking back toward the *munus* of community and specifically the affirmative qualities of being in mutual contact with and exposed to identity contamination by one another. The goal of retaining the immunitary paradigm for its constructive potential, which Esposito sees in it, would be to posit the globality of human life and operate immunizing mechanisms as its custodian—that is, to gear the immunity paradigm toward strengthening borders not as thresholds of separation but rather as invitations to community. Such thinking, Esposito says, "is to commit to a full reversal, back to the *munus* understood as gift/donation, expropriation, and alteration."[40]

What Esposito's analysis of *munus* shows us, in sum, is that neither the individual nor any group, state, or nation can be returned to a fully unified, contained, originally undifferentiated, and pure state because such a state was never there to begin with.[41] Defined as protection against exposure, immunity is not simply an external and independent response to the fact of community, a relation of exposure. Nor is community—defined as gift, debt, and alteration—the mirror opposite and moral high ground of immunity, the absence of obligation, and the elimination of debt. Rather, each is the internal horizon of the other.

To clarify, a focus on the *munus* (as gift, debt, alteration) blurs the very distinction between inside (proper, individual) and outside (common, community). Every identity is limited in its completion—no identity is complete—because identity is relational, constituted in difference from other identities. Existence is coexistence—*munus* is shared, *co-munus*. A human being is first and foremost a social being: it lives intersubjectively, lacks complete independence from other beings, and is thereby exposed in mutual interpersonal contact. Next, not only is lack of completion an ontological condition of human being, which is defined by its thrownness (*Dasein*) together (*Mitdasein*) in having-to-be, not as a fall from fullness but out of emptiness (being is the opening of being[42]), but there is also the lack or defect of community, which Esposito shows is doubled: community is not a thing or identity but is "itself" a relation, a nonentity—it lacks being and is absent or lacks an origin because it is already between us and is for that reason as impossible to realize as to return to. The lack that is *munus* is simultaneously inside (institutive of community) and outside (constitutive of individuality). It invites identity protection (boundary limits) and threatens it by making identity closure structurally impossible.

For its part, immunization does not just overlap with the inside-outside structure of community but in fact coincides with it, moving the outside to the inside in a way that makes the one nearly indistinguishable from the other. In its "progressive interiorization of exteriority"—that is, the appropriation and preservation of the extrinsic and foreign by the intrinsic and domestic[43]—the point to reiterate is that immunization is not the elimination of whatever external/foreign element threatens the internal/domestic function and so-called health of a system. Rather, immunization is the containment and curbing of that contaminating threat. Akin to the biological insertion of antigens into the human body so as to control for them by stimulating the internal production of protective antibodies, law in the modern order, for example, functions to immunize the social body from the threat of conflict and potential violence (that which is outside the law). It does so not by erasing the threat of violence but instead by presupposing, containing, and curbing, as well as employing its potential by internalizing it within the legal system to preserve individual freedom and group life for a relatively stable state of interaction.[44] The outside becomes inside through immunization, is excluded as threat by way of inclusion as protection against it. Immunization does not protect by purging and purifying but by containing and contaminating. In so doing—and here is the explanatory power of the concept—immunization helps call into question the stability of, and our ability to maintain, any distinction between whatever is perceived, and therefore valued, as different, foreign, and/or external as well as self-same, domestic, and/or internal.

Although I cannot do justice to the intellectual dexterity of Esposito's thinking, which is stunning, I can insist that in unconcealing the coincidence rather than emphasizing the divergence of community (unifying/exposing/defective) and immunity (separating/closing/protective), not only does Esposito substantially broaden the intellectual space for a "new thinking of community,"[45] of which his work is emblematic. He also opens space, as I demonstrate next, for a new thinking of *communication*, a contemporary continental philosophical perspective in which the concept of *munus* and the function of immunity can be harnessed for their power to explain the coexposure and interdependence (the *com-muni-cation*) of human being that invites community in both its constructive and its restrictive qualities.

For example, consider how law, the immune system of modern social formations, need not be reduced to its negative form, that which transforms "the bond of common obligation" into the individual right to private property. Its function may be understood more widely, and practically, as having an affirmative impact on co-being, as that which "augments its members' capacity to interact with their environment, so that community can actually be fortified."[46] Here, we must recognize how the appropriation of the *munus* by law in the modern social order is not merely a subtraction but precisely an act of inclusive exclusion.[47] The gift-giving *munus* that institutes a logic of obligation is excluded from the community by way of its containment and integration—that is, its inclusion—into the system of law. The inclusive exclusion of the *munus* (its removal from the community and its appropriation by law) does not mean that community members are thereby immune from it—free, that is, of the gift/debt/obligation inherent to being in common. Far from it, because community, a relation of co-being, an inside that moves to the outside, "is" what there is: there is no place from which to stand apart and be immune. Law's inclusive exclusion of the *munus* immunizes community from its members who internally constitute it. Law secures the obligation of being in common and in so doing becomes a legal *order* by and to which individuals are held, not merely morally obliged, in protecting community from the potential threat of descending into eternal conflict, violence, and chaos.[48]

For the purposes of communication philosophy, it is crucial to note how the code of modern common law—which, in essence, operates like a language in being expressed in statutes, opinions, and sentences—assists in avoiding chaos and the threat of potential violence by reducing doubt and increasing predictability about decisions regarding the rights and freedom of both individuals and the community. In that way, law performs a basic communication function. In fact, by developing from past environmental stimuli and responses, such as with case law, in order to anticipate, predict, and better manage conflict in the future ("substituting uncertain expectations with problematic but secure expectations"),[49] the legal system performs an immunizing communication function, one that, although flawed, is nonetheless vital to life and a potentially harmonious coexistence.[50]

Co-*munus*: The Antinomy of Com-*muni*-cation

As mentioned at the outset of the present volume, the *OED* identifies two primary senses of *communication*: (1) affinity/association and (2) imparting/transfer.[51] Although these two primary senses are entwined and difficult to distinguish from one another, both make sense, and can be seen to do so, from the point of view of what we know about not only the etymological root of communication (*communis*) but also, and most importantly, its core: *munus*.

As we just saw, *munus* is both gift/alteration and debt. It refers to the gift of human existence and the obligation to give in return, the presence of a debt that cannot be repaid because of a lack that cannot be filled. This existence, one's life, is a coexistence, a mutual interdependence and therefore lack of a completely closed identity. *Munus* exposes each one of us to contact with and contagion by another, *contagion*, Esposito says, because no identity is pure but rather constituted ontologically by the contaminating presence of another, which does not complete it, or itself, but instead taints the purity of both and limits their full closure. Human being is ontologically lacking, coexposed in its coappearance with other beings in the world. Based on this line of reasoning, we can define *communication* (co-*muni*-cation) as the putting into contact, and thereby the exposing to contagion, of one to another, a relation of mutual exposure, one *with* another. Communication is a name for the threshold between oneself and another, the relation separating one from oneself, thereby altering it, and opening it to another and others, maintaining itself as the opening of one to others that calls for as well as provides the means, media, and channels for its overcoming—as transfer/imparting and affinity/making-common. Communication is a "basic constituent of our intersubjective existence."[52]

Now if communication is a basic constituent of intersubjective existence, then it is loaded with consequences. For instance, note how *communication* is defined in the *OED* by way of a deferral of its meaning to other terms, such as "interpersonal contact," "social interaction," "association," and "intercourse."[53] These terms are offered in response to a prior problem, or condition, which is presupposed by the senses of communication as affinity and as transfer. That prior problem is the separation of individuals, one that invites communication. Modern communication theory, exemplified by mechanical sender-message-channel-receiver-feedback models of information transfer, typically characterizes the problem of "communication" (a noun of action) as a problem of overcoming separation, of crossing the distance between individuals by way of the activity of encoding and decoding of messages, for instance. This gives rise to the challenge of increasing redundancy for channel noise reduction, which, if successful, can help promote exchange and interpersonal and/or group association. In this modern model, the goal of communication, particularly the traversal and conquest of space-time separation by way of transport, contact, and interaction, is characterized as clarity of transmission (quantity and quality of information passed through lines, or channels, of communication; choice selection to ensure redundancy and reduce entropy), determination of meaning (effective message encoding to promote and control for accurate decoding), and mutual understanding (overcoming difference, managing dialogue, avoiding conflict, resolving disagreement by way of deliberation in decision-making, and so on).[54] From the modern theoretical perspective, communication is typically approached not only as a problem (of interpersonal separation, want of commonality) and a possible outcome (the success or failure of sending-receiving) but also as a goal (of overcoming) and a solution (the activity of transfer, contact, and interaction).

The concept of *munus* significantly expands the sense of communication as affinity and transfer by drawing our attention to not only the problem to which communication (noun of action) responds but also, and most importantly, the one to which it in fact gives rise. *Munus* shows us that identities are not exactly separated in the first place because they are already linked by a common lack. To reiterate one more time, all identity is partial because of the presence of other identities, a common presence that is constitutive of each and any identity by way of being a "not part" internal to them. With regard to human identities, this is not to say that everyone is the same and that there are no interpersonal differences. Rather, it is to say that no individual identity is complete, pure, and fully closed in on itself. Every identity is lacking and partial due to its constitutive relation to other identities. The lack that humans share makes us common: "it" places us into community; human being is ontologically lacking and therefore already in relation.

The fact of co-being gives rise to the problem, or what I will call the *antinomy of human communication*—namely, that there *is* communication and that it cannot be fully realized. In light of Esposito's analysis of the *munus*, it is reasonable to assert, on the one hand, that communication (co-*muni*-cation) is what there is—it is already there—because being is co-being, interdependent, in contact with the world of beings. There is no human being that is not first and foremost a social being. On the other hand, communication cannot be realized because it is not a substance but a relation, a *no-thing*, a threshold between oneself and another that separates individuals from themselves and alters them by putting each into contact with, and thereby exposing each to contagion by, another. To assert that communication cannot be realized, however, is not to say that it is impossible. It is not to deny the experience of human interaction or, for example, that the words on this page are imparting information and sensible ideas. There *is* communication, and as previously discussed, one cannot not communicate: we are always in relation. However, with regard to the goal and process of overcoming (co-muni-*cation*), we can reasonably assert that it cannot be realized, or at least not fully realized, because of the permanent lack in identity that communication institutes and by which it is called to action. The problem created by com-*muni*-cation—namely, lack in identity, relation of contact and mutual contamination—is responded to by the actions, practices, and means of com-muni-*cation* (transfer, affinity). There *is* communication and it cannot be fully realized because if it were, then there would be no evidence of previous attempts at transfer, discourse, intercourse, or affinity, and certainly no reason for ongoing contact and/or future communications.

Communication carries with it, in fact it *is*, the problem to which it is itself pressed into service as the solution. The problem or challenge of communication—the antinomy that there is communication and that it is not fully realizable—is not only the possibility of transmission of information or the possibility of affinity and shared understanding, which are themselves modern theoretic responses to the presupposed problem of overcoming a distance or gulf that separates and differentiates individuals. It is also the problem and practical challenge of the indetermination and slippage of meaning, the potential for confusion, disagreement, and conflict that are introduced by and as outcomes of the ontological-existential fact of always being-in-communication. Communication exposes (it "is" the exposure of) individuals to the challenge of being-in-common, of being-in-communication, and it functions simultaneously as the actions and the means (self-expression and other-perception) as well as the mode of that being (having no choice but to communicate). It is not as if there are self-contained, preformed human individuals existing in monadic separation and *then* there is communication, which gives rise to the problem and challenge of communicating. Rather, there *is* communication (an ontological condition of co-being, of human coexistence) and for that reason, simultaneously, the problem and challenge of communication: namely, the fact that complete, guaranteed agreement, understanding, clarity, and fixity of meaning cannot be fully realized. In short, being human is not to be in isolation and complete independence, like the image of preconstituted senders and receivers in transmission models of communication would have it, but rather to coexist, to be already in communication, which raises transfer, intercourse, affinity, shared understanding, and so on as challenges and problems of and for human communication.[55]

Three Senses: Communication and-as Immunization

If the previous is true, then it is reasonable to assert that communication calls for or, more precisely, bears within it the cause for identity protection. Communication inaugurates the need for protection from the identity-contaminating relation of being-in-common (com-*muni*-cation), a relation that alters individuals (institutes a lack in identity) by separating them from themselves in placing them into a contact with, and thereby exposing them to an identity contagion by, one another. As the name of the threshold relation between self and other, individual and community, not only does "communication" call for the practices, and patience, of interaction, dialogue, transfer, and sharing (com-muni-*cation*) aimed at the intended goals of clarity, understanding, agreement, and affinity. It also, in so doing, poses a threat of communication, the threat of potential uncertainty of meaning, misinformation and deception, confusion and misunderstanding, interpersonal and intergroup disagreement, and conflict.

What is at stake here is not only the two senses of human communication summarized in the previous section but in fact three more: human communication as a fundamental contaminating relation of contact (*first sense*), which gives rise to communication (affinity and/or transfer) as protection (*second sense*) from communication (affinity and/or transfer) as potential threat (*third sense*). We have a grasp of sense one. Let us now consider sense three, and then return to sense two.

Communication as threat may be understood broadly as a consequence of the opening of human beings to one another, as well as their abandonment to language and the impossibility of noncommunication, as discussed in the previous chapter. It can also be understood specifically as the figuration and disfiguration of subjects (their manifestation in language) by discourses that address them, the sharing of ideas, as well as the possibility of uncritically accepting those ideas, what at one time was called "propaganda" and has been more recently referred to as "semantic contagion."[56] Human communication threat may also be characterized in basic communication theory terms as not only goals but also outcomes, such as noise and nonsense rather than clarity, confusion rather than understanding, slippage of meaning as opposed to its fixing, and disagreement and even deadlock rather than openness and harmony—all of which fall outside of, and in so doing may be perceived as disruptive and destabilizing threats to, the so-called normal order of communication.[57]

With regard to the second sense of communication, as protection, we immediately find a paradox: what does communication protect against? The answer is that it protects against itself. Communication protects from the threat of communication (sense three) by way of communication. As protection, communication may be understood as the employment of linguistic-semiotic resources that bring structure to sense and meaning to existence, employed to figure against the threat of disfiguration by way of active individual, interpersonal, and/or group expression, whether in speech, writing, or other expressive forms. Communication as protection may also be understood conversely, as the action and means for upholding and maintaining a prevailing order (fix the slide of meaning, promote understanding, resolve conflict, and so on) and simultaneously, as we shall see, the potential to unsettle and even tear it down by way of challenges to prevailing discourses, attitudes, values, and beliefs.

If it is indeed necessary for communication to protect against communication—to struggle against itself—then why is this so? The reason is that in giving life, *munus*, the shared etymological core of *communication* (sense one), as the inaugural "togetherness" of beings, is the "there is" of community and communication, and as such is the source of the limit of realizing both. *Munus*, we also recall, refers not only to the gift of life and the freedom to live but also to the debt and obligation that simultaneously accompanies it. *Munus* gives life and threatens it as a weak relational mechanism lacking the capacity to ensure balance of resources necessary for all individuals, leaving the onus on the latter to give back (or take less) as the only means to address the defect of the former. In order to protect life and make it worth living rather than devolve into a threatened state of conflict, the "poisonous fruits" of the *munus* (debt/obligation) must be removed from community, thereby immunizing its members from it.

Why would the *munus* need to be negated and somehow appropriated in communication? The answer is because *munus* is what institutes the problem and challenge, or the antinomy, of communication. It raises the problem that *there is* communication (com-*muni*-cation, commonality, the gift of co-being) and that communication (com-muni-*cation*) cannot be realized, at least not fully realized, if "communication" is understood as, or desired as, the guaranteed success of transmission, the full fixing or determination of meaning, and the overcoming of confusion and disagreement as well as the eradication of interpersonal and intergroup conflict by way of securing each of their opposites. Not only that, but also, and most important, the *munus* that throws us together obliges the individual to communicate. Communication ontologically precedes individuality, opens self to other and the sharing of differences, and for that reason enjoins one to negotiate his or her coexposure (negotiate identity boundaries) as members of a community "whose traditions are sedimented in one's natural being."[58] Being in common/communication on account of the *munus* leaves the individual with no choice: one cannot not communicate.

The immunization paradigm is community's immune system, protecting individuals and the community from the ontological condition of being-in-common. In the modern social order, as we saw, the legal system functions as a kind of debt collector that assumes the obligation to protect life by threatening individuals with the community's power to take it back. With regard to communication, it is communication that, paradoxically, provides the immunizing function. Communication protects the individual from the obligation of being-in-common/communication by offering the possibility and means to communicate, whether in speech, writing, gesture, or other forms and channels of expression. At the same time, although one cannot not communicate, communication, at least in the West, cannot be legally coerced, such as with forced confession or testimony, nor can it be legally surveilled: there are constitutionally binding provisions that communicate this personal privacy protection, as well as provisions that protect open speech, discourse competition, the flow of ideas across channels of mass communication, and so on. Community is also immunized from the onus to communicate by way of communication provisions that restrict speech, writing, and other communicative actions that are publicly disruptive, infringe upon others, and/or violate community standards of decency.[59]

The point to reiterate now is that immunization operates not by way of excluding and eliminating threatening contagions but by including and appropriating them, integrating threats in the struggle against them. With regard to communication, it protects against the threat it faces—communication faces itself—not by eradicating and dispelling communication, which would mean self-destruction, but by internalizing and using the threat against the threat itself. It is in this very sense that we may characterize communication *as* immunization: the means and actions of communication contain rather than eradicate the threatening potential of our being-in-common in it, such as the potential for difference, disagreement, miscommunication, misunderstanding, and so on, of which communication is itself the cause. For that reason, although the *nomos* of communication privileges clarity, understanding, agreement, and affinity, it always runs the high risk of causing further confusion, misunderstanding, disagreement, and potential conflict. Communication cannot eradicate the potentially disturbing fact of difference, nor eliminate the unsettling risk of disagreement and conflict, for the reason that both are already part of it, internal to and integrated into its function, sense, and order.

As a threshold between self and other, us and them, interiority and exteriority, communication exposes one to the other, a contaminating exposure that alters the identity borders of individuals and thereby calls for protection from the identity-breaking effects thus given rise. As an immunizing exposure, however, communication simultaneously secures the individual by way of enabling the practices of contact, association, and interaction as well as the actions of encoding/expression, transfer, reception, and decoding/perception. This is so because communication and immunization do not indicate separate and divergent conditions. Rather, like the circumstances characterizing community and immunity, each is the horizon of the other. It is not that there is communication (affinity/association, imparting/transfer) that is then followed by immunization from it. Communication is not an antidote administered after contaminating exposure. Rather, as with community and immunity, communication and immunization coincide. As Esposito puts it, "Communication is *already of itself* immunization. Or, in complementary fashion, immunization is the very form of communication: its *non*-communication of anything other than communication, that is, once again, immunization."[60] It is by way of the coincidence of one with the other that communication *and-as* immunization protects against its own threat as contaminating exposure. The solution to the problem of communication, which is not merely the problem of overcoming of interpersonal separation but of always being in communication, is offered in the form of the cause of the problem itself: namely, that *there is* communication and that it cannot be fully realized. There is no perfect communication.

Communication is the immunizing antibody to the effects of exposure that it essentially is.[61] Realizing complete or perfect communication is impossible because it is fundamentally and permanently threatened by the practices, potential outcomes, and sheer fact of communication itself. This is true whether those outcomes are constructive, such as the opening of the mind, as we say, by way of the wonders of reading, writing, and speech, or the more detrimental kind, such as exposure to antagonizing differences of opinion or unwanted remarks, whether these are direct and intrusive or offhanded and unintentional—all of which can create the potential for misunderstanding, uncertainty, disagreement, conflict, and even the turning away of individuals in an attempt at separation and self-closure. Immunizing protection from the potentially threatening problems of communication is, from this perspective at least, required for ongoing and productive communication. That is, it is necessary for the potential for clearer expression and better perception, for openness and welcoming interaction and so on, the objective of which may be to learn, cultivate mutual recognition and agreement, increase certainty of intended meaning, and perhaps accomplish shared goals—in short, to secure commonality and promote well-ordered exchange. The goal of immunizing communication, or of communication *and-as* immunization, is, in sum, "improved" and "effective" communication to protect against its own identity-breaking power and threat of its disorderly and disruptive potential.

Consistent in impulse with what we saw of Agamben and the ban of language and law of communication, Esposito adds new perspective to the philosophy of communication principle that what communication communicates most of all is communicability.[62] With Esposito, this principle obtains a distinct inflection. The immunizing function of communication demonstrates how, at a metalevel, beyond any content or meaning, communication communicates not only the fact of being-with (an identity-altering relation) and the possibility for transport or making known but also, and thereby, the threat of possible contagion—the fact that communication spreads. Henceforth, the principle can be reformulated as follows: *there is* communication and, although not always fully realizable, it cannot not take place except by immunizing, as immunization. The dual function of communication, both contaminating and immunizing exposure, illustrates how the immune system itself "is not only the protective shield for something that precedes it, but the object itself of protection: self-protection."[63] This is the crucial point we must grasp next.

Autoimmunization: Communication and-as Community

In the overlapping circumstances just described, what can arise with human communication's power to protect is the potential for overprotection, a reversal of the immunizing function whereby community life and individual health is not only compromised but also threatened. Too much immunizing protection from communication may occur unintentionally—for instance, by routine dismissive reference to "common sense" or in the absence of time for dialogue and debate within group decision-making processes. The threat of too much protection may also occur intentionally—for instance, with mass communication efforts to fortify and amplify and even to saturate prevailing perspectives when faced with the opposition of different, or subordinated, discourses, especially those that are publicly communicated. The threat of too much immunizing protection of communication can take its most explicit, and potentially destructive, form in instances when open dialogue, debate, and the sharing of ideas are curbed and contained in an effort not only to delegitimize different viewpoints but also to eliminate them, to permanently silence any "noise" considered disruptive and thereby threatening to the normal order of communication. This is accomplished by way of, for instance, blocking access to media of public expression, restricting channels of transmission and open association, censoring, ex-communicating, or even imprisoning visibly or vocally prominent sources of dissent.

The implications of an immunizing overprotection against communication's boundary-altering potential should seem obvious. They range from unawareness, due to the inaccessibility of knowledge about different perspectives, whether in speech, writing, or other mass mediated means; to a lack of confidence in speaking out or posing questions, leading to deference to dominant perspectives; to more threatening overprotection situations where communicative agreement and certainty preclude the communication of alternative procedures, innovations, and imagination of how the world could be different. The most dangerous outcome of communication's potential over immunization, which all the previous examples indicate, is the enclosure of the individual and/or the community back onto him-, her-, or itself, a narrowing of the irrevocable lack that opens one to contagion by another and thereby enriches both the individual and the community, making life worth living.[64] Too much protection of communication is especially undesirable if we understand the exposure to difference, and/or to contrasting perspectives, whether in dialogue or disagreement, as a fortifying exposure—not to build up resistance but rather to shift self-perspective and encourage interactive communication and not only one-way or reversible transmissions. Overprotecting human communication by way of an immunizing restriction on what is communicated, how, when, and by whom stifles the benefits of its opening and thereby poses a protective threat to community health and vitality.

Consider, for example, how the discourse of citizenship today places a heavy emphasis on the secured person. Just as humanities scholarship has been persuasive in analyzing the implications of consumer discourses in shaping the meanings we make of our experiences of race, class, gender, and sexuality as historically articulated to persons,[65] thinking about communication and-as immunization adds critical perspective on the stability and endurance of discourses that address and shape us. On the one hand, it helps us recognize the role communication plays in discourses that place "them," by way of exclusion, into the category of threat (outside community but included within the order of its political-juridical power), which is then responded to and justified with publicly financed security measures that encroach upon "us." *We* are included in the effects of *their* exclusion by a potentially overprotective communication immunitary practice (discourse about who's in and who's out) that risks closing perspective on commonality and new social relations, placing the freedoms of both them and us at risk. On the other hand, thinking about communication and-as immunization shows how communication offers itself at the same time as a resource to stimulate discourses that may aid in refiguring the expressions and perception of individuals, groups, and even institutions that may be infringed upon, ridiculed, silenced, and/or excluded by prevailing legal/regulative and biomedical/technological discourses, an affirmative practice of communication autoimmunization.

Protection from an excess of immunizing protection, or autoimmunization, was defined previously as an attack on the very immune system that is vital to the health of an organism, whether human person or community. It is, in other words, a self-fighting for self-protection. Based on this line of reasoning, an autoimmunizing communication response to circumstances of excessive communication/immunizing protection can be defined as an attack on communication's own immune system, a self-fighting of communication's order, or *nomos*, done in an effort to protect and vitalize precisely what that system functions to discourage and depress: namely, com-*muni*-cation (contact and contagion) as well as risks inherent to attempts at com-muni-*cation*, such as, but not limited to, the plurality of meaning, differences of perspective, uncertainty, misunderstanding, disagreement, and conflict.

What would human communication's autoimmunizing response to, by way of an attack on, its own immune function look like? To be sure, it would not be merely the rejection or refusal of communication, a protective hiding from the discourses that shape how we perceive and make sense of our experiences of world, self, and others.[66] Refusal of human communication is not only rationally but also ontologically impossible. Instead, an autoimmunizing communication response would be the conscious and overt attempt to engage in communication. Critically engaging that which gives the individual and/or the community too much protection, that which may sometimes shield us under the blinding glare of a heavily polished armor of identity, can in fact help expose any identity to what it might be all too protected from: namely, different perspectives, new ideas, knowledge, and even itself—differences that one may never encounter, or perhaps is prohibited from encountering, within the horizon of his or her protective communication community.[67]

The possibility of a protective attack on a communication's system of self-protection can be made sense of, at least in part, by reference to the

Anglo-American academic tradition of the study and teaching of human communication in its historical connection to the project of modern democracy.[68] The primary goal, there, has been to develop a communication skill set in speech, writing, and argument (rhetoric) to enable men and women to contribute to, by making claims upon, the shape of the common. In this sense, learning to "communicate effectively" in a field of competing discourses can be understood, on the one hand, as protective of the community values according to which individuals live, such as, in the West, the freedom to gather and be expressive. On the other hand, the teaching and learning of communication skills can also be understood as a tactic to protect from too much protection, a tactic for speaking up and out rather than to remain seen but not heard. Refusing to engage in communication by turning away, or inward, or not speaking out implies a risk of being spoken for by others and therefore a risk to all.[69] Communication study "immunizes against an excess of immunization" thanks to the resources of communication.[70]

Communication's immunizing self-protection from communication and-as immunization, or the autoimmunization of communication and-as immunization, is not a contradiction in terms. Human being is exposed in communication by communication and-as immunization from human communication. Immunization from the threat itself, of communication's immune system—in this case, a threat of too much immunizing protection of communicating—does not eliminate but rather appropriates the threat and uses it against its own self-protection. And therein lies its most potent potential: an autoimmunization attack on the threat of too much immunization of communication returns communication, in this reversal, to the initial, threatening potential of the *possibility* of communication. Protection against too much protection of communication may be obtained, that is, from precisely what has been strengthened and fortified by its immune system—namely, communication, the original threat, currently stored, curbed, and contained. Communication's threatening potential (the indeterminacy of meaning, lack of understanding, differing perspective, discord, disagreement, and so on) always remains and may be protected in an autoimmunizing attack on its protective function, an attack against the threat of self-overprotection: in short, communication as immunization of too much immunization as communication.

Here we arrive at immunity's affirmative dimension, which emerges against the backdrop of its most potentially destructive form. As with too much immunizing protection of community, the destructive features of communication and-as immunization—namely, too much protection from communication that threatens to destroy potential attempts at communication by overprotecting its threshold between one and another—calls back to the thinking of *munus*, defined favorably as gift, alteration, and expropriation. That is, thinking is called back to the gift-giving of community, of life. The goal of turning thinking toward community is neither to stabilize its majority nor to recast immunity in opposition to community as a singular function unburdening individuals from the obligation of being-in-common. Instead, the goal is to regard immunity "as a way for the individual *to open up to* what is threatening to him or her in order to alleviate the grip that one's own self-protection has over the individual." With respect to human communication, thinking about immunity "as a way of protecting oneself from too much protection"[71] invites reopening com-muni-*cation* to difference, disagreement, uncertainty, plurality, and other potentially disruptive threats—opening to that from which its order may be overprotected but that may in fact add flexibility in complement to its strength and stability.

More important than that, however, perspective on the affirmative aspect of immunity turns thought to the role of com-*muni*-cation in/as com-*muni*-ty, the threshold relation of one being to another. It is perspective that helps identify the task, and perhaps challenge, of regarding self-separation, contact, and mutual exposure as potentially agreeable qualities. In French, to regard (F. *regarder*) means to observe, which works as relation, an opening to look with respect.[72] The fortifying potential of human communication's identity-altering power may be seen (regarded, respected) with perspective on the *munus* as the condition that establishes the possibility for human communicating in the first place. Even if communication is never fully realizable or always successful, *munus* invites the sense or, better, the thinking of affinity, contact, transfer, and access—a thinking, which is not a glorification, of one's own sense of being-in-common. In other words, communication may be regarded from Esposito's perspective as the basic invitation to community. Communication is a shared possibility, a resource, and a means for individuals and communities to engage differences productively and perhaps even to resolve disputes. As Christopher Watkin confirms, "Community is not threatened by, but relies on, the conflict engendered by claims of unjust distribution that would seem on one level to threaten it with disintegration. It is precisely because the community has mechanisms for dealing with different narratives and challenges to accepted narratives that it can persist as a community at all."[73]

"Opening" to what may be threatening in human communication does not mean, however, a simple acknowledgement of interpersonal and intergroup differences, their divergent values and beliefs, and whatever disagreeable tensions may result, only to then curb and control them in an effort to overcome them, as may be the goal of communication theories of, say, deliberative democracy. Instead, the challenge is to protect from too much immunizing communication protection by using the power of immunity against itself by turning toward rather than turning down or away from contact, transfer, and association, or at least their possibility, with regard (as respect) to being-in-common as the ontological fundament of one's own being-in-communication. As Jean-Luc Nancy puts it, "We have to expose ourselves to the sense of the world and to the complex intermedialities that seem to regulate and deregulate it. Only from there can we return to the *problem* of our communities and the identities they claim."[74]

To be sure, I am not advocating for a community that is functionally disabled by a communication order of constant confusion, lack of agreement or disagreement, misinformation, conflict, and so-called noise. Rather, disagreement, discord, difference, plurality of meaning and perspective, and the possibility for conflict brought by communication (being in com-*muni*-cation) must be understood as elements of healthy communication (of being in com-muni-*cation*) that support and do not always weaken a vibrant community. Exposure to elements that are part of and included within community is beneficial not as a means to build resistance or tolerance by containing and curbing them but rather to retain and sustain the opening of community—as politically, philosophically, or psychologically daunting as that may appear to be.

Community, Immunity, and Philosophy of Communication

Critical questions must now be raised. First, regarding the assertion that communication identifies or is a name for a threshold of contact that alters the individual (institutes a lack of pure identity) by separating everyone from him- or herself in being put into relation with others, was this not the function, to say nothing of the problem or antinomy, of *community*? The answer is, yes. Is it therefore reasonable to substitute community with communication and attribute to the latter what Esposito teaches us about the former? The answer is, once again, yes, with the supporting evidence of each term's etymological core, *munus*. But this line of reasoning does not lead to an immediate conclusion. Communication is not equivalent to community. A distinction must be made, although not in terms of the divergence but rather in the coincidence of one with the other.

Community is what there is. Human being is a being of coexistence. And yet, community cannot be realized. For its part, communication may be understood as the action, the doing, the "of" of this coexistence. It is the place of occurrence of the *munus*, the shared gift of life, of being-in-common. *There is* community, as *there is* communication, and it takes place, even if unrealizable, in and by way of communication, which itself cannot be fully realized. To take place does not mean "to realize." The latter is a kind of finality, a closure. Rather, to "take place" means to occur, to happen, to actively pass and then disappear, as was described previously with the taking place or event of language and its withdrawal in the act of speech. Community, like language, is not a *fait accompli*. It occurs, takes place, is given shape in communication and by way of communication as immunization. Pragmatist John Dewey identified this existential condition in one of his most oft-quoted assertions: "Society not only continues to exist *by* transmission, *by* communication, but it may fairly be said to exist *in* transmission, *in* communication."[75] Put another way, communication is the taking place of community, which explains why neither can ever be fully realized.

Second, is all communication equivalent in force and effect—that is, in power? In one important respect, the contemporary continental philosophy of communication perspective on offer here complements the critical theory perspective that discourses compete in a social formation, or community. Discourses can be forged, can be promoted, and can spread (they are possible) within social formations, out of which political identities emerge, articulate, change, gain momentum, and may alter public perception or falter and fade. If, by appropriating a language, one appropriates the values and beliefs of a community, which does not mean that one follows them to the letter or agrees with them completely, and if discourses are the instituting means through which sense is made of human experience, then "communication" may be understood as the action, channel, and practices of language appropriation as discourse competition, and as Raymond Williams defines it, as the objects (e.g., letters, reports, opinions, and so on) "thus made common."[76] By "communication," therefore, I do not mean to imply that all of it is equivalent and that power of access, control, and knowledge is not essential to the action, channels, practices, and production of objects made common. Not all communication is equivalent because power in its manifold form is essential to instances of its taking place. Communication has the power to both threaten (to compromise identity, to persuade through propaganda and misinformation, or to shut down the free flow of competing ideas) and protect (from threatening communication as well as from too much protection), and thereby reopen, broaden, and invigorate ongoing and future communications.[77] For its part, the concept of immunity guides us in this regard to think affirmatively about communication exposure, threat, and protection that derive not from a foreign outside—for instance, other people, or "them," as if "they" operate according to an alterity sign system that is radically different from "ours." Rather, communication exposure, threat, and protection come from inside an order of exchange of signs (a culture, a community), a field of competing discourses shared, inhabited, and embodied by human communicative beings.

Third, is communication as immunization implicitly an effects model of communication, such as modern communication theory's functionalist "hypodermic needle" model, captured best by Harold Lasswell's classic definition of communication as *who says what to whom with what effect*?[78] Despite the biomedical imagery shared by both, communication as immunization confronts several assumptions hidden within such transfer models of communication. First, communication as immunization does not assume preconstituted subjects within a transmission chain, subjects who are willingly, uncritically, and equally affected by exposure to communication. It emphasizes instead communication as a relational process that shapes subjects by way of both constraining and enabling expressive freedom. Next, communication as immunization sheds light on the general effect of communication, namely, communicability and the impossibility of noncommunication, rather than focusing narrowly on isolated message effects in a transfer chain and specific context. I have argued that communication performs a general immunizing function, exposing subjects to its effects—such as the possibility for learning, understanding, and agreement, as well as misunderstanding, disagreement, and conflict—while at the same time equipping subjects with empowering expressive capacities, such as creativity and the ability to disagree, to differ, as well as to conform. Third, the model of communication as immunization does not assume a separation of channel and content, as a transfer model of communication does, where "channel" is theorized in terms of its capacity to accommodate, or distort (noise), message content. Communication as immunization is more holistic than that. Human expressive content does not precede its transfer and sharing but is in fact shaped by and through that process of being made common.[79]

Finally, does invoking the value of "free speech" and its instituting political-juridical mechanisms take the discussion too far afield from the philosophical focus on communication as a fundamental, ontological condition of human being? I do not think so. Any suspicion in this regard must be rejected for the reason that the connection between ontology and politics is a primary finding of scholarship produced by contemporary continental philosophies and critical theories of biopolitics, as well as by semiotic phenomenologies of human communication. The ontological is, or at least has become, in the modern immunitary paradigm, thoroughly political. To reiterate the point made by Esposito, in the context of too much security—the encroachment of too much protective immunization—bodies and life itself become threatened. A body is regarded as not only being on the front line but also *being* the front line of life and death, he says, a threshold that has become territorialized by the state, whose power in the struggle to define life, and end it, is nearly absolute.[80] With regard to human communication, which on its face seems weak regarding life and death questions, it would be naïve to dismiss the power of its spoken, written, and rhetorical forms as elemental to the modern biopolitical paradigm. Communication takes place, even if not fully realizable; it has already taken place, ontologically. It is not outside but inside, inside-outside, embodied in and as words, discourse, gesture, style, and so on. A lived body (a linguistic-material phenomenality) is opened in, and to, valued, and shaped by way of communicating in communication (being-with, contact, exposure, and association) through its and our communication (interaction, transmission, expression, and perception).

Communication is by definition exposure of the same to what is held in common with the different: namely, the experience of relation—of communication, by way of communication, sustained in communication.[81] The challenge for thinking now, monumental as it may be, is to affirm those forms of relation and their expression, whose "contagious exposure to others gives way to constitutive openness."[82] For it is by way of exposure to human communication's identity-altering potential, in the movement of the individual and/or the collective toward that which does not belong properly to either, that anything like subjectivity and/or community may be constituted, challenged, and/or lived out as real to begin with. Perspective on the function of immunization, the objective of which is protection from and by way of exposure of a body, whether that body is individual or collective, highlights the importance of communication to the discourses spoken and lived regarding what we want both our bodies and our communities to be.

CHAPTER 4

Body as Index

Human communicating threatens and protects identity-making borders. It threatens with the potential for affiliation, expression, transmission, and the possibility of exposure to contagions of misunderstanding, disagreement, and conflict—a threat to the closure of identity that accompanies communication's gift of interaction, affiliation, expression, transmission, and the possibility of agreement, understanding, and the deepening of self-awareness in the process of learning from difference. Communication thereby also protects identity borders, defending the possibility for difference and for community, and the latter's potentially restrictive consequences, it was argued in the previous chapter, communication immunizes against by way of its power to contain and curb the boundary-threats (both affirmative, closed/opening, and destructive, opened/closing) for which it is itself the cause. In extreme cases, the risk of too much immunization by communication may be counteracted by an attack on the system of protection itself (autoimmunization). This is done as an invitation to reopen the threat to identity brought by communication in an effort to maintain identity exposure rather than close it in on itself in its protective indifference to community.

The critical point to reiterate at the outset of the present chapter is that the boundary-threatening potential of communication is in fact its most constructive characteristic. It is through communication that self-identity is constituted in and opened onto difference, and thereby community; it is also through communication that community-identity is constituted in and opened onto individuality, and thereby to difference. Identity, whether individual or collective, is not pregiven, preformed, and prior to communication but instituted originally in it, an ontological relation (being-with one another) whose lived, practical consequences may not only compromise but in so doing also expand the exposure of being.

The present chapter explores conditions of exposure as possibilities for maintaining the openness of the human communicative subject. Building on what we know about the subject and its relation of communication within and to community, the focus of this chapter is the identity borders of the communicative body. Strands of the ideas about language, self and other, subjectivity, community, communication, and immunity developed over previous sections of this book, are deepened in connection to the philosophy of Jean-Luc Nancy. Although Nancy is best known for his writings on community, developed over the course of his entire career, he has also written extensively on the topics of painting, literature, the media arts, and most passionately, human embodiment.[1] The discussion to follow focuses mainly on Nancy's volume *Corpus*, which, as may be glimpsed in the lively passage here, announces the problematic of embodied being and its exposure in a compelling and inviting philosophical style:

> More than five billion human bodies. Soon to be eight billion. . . . What is the space opened between eight billion bodies, and, within each one? In what space do they touch each other and stray from each other, with *none* of them, or their totality, being absorbed into a pure and empty sign of the self, into a body-of-sense? Sixteen billion eyes, eighty billion fingers: seeing what? Touching what? And if it's only to exist and be *these bodies*, and to see, touch and sense the bodies of *this world*, what might we invent to celebrate their number?[2]

Published in 2006 and translated into English in 2008, *Corpus* offers on one level an erudite critique of Western reason, taking as its analytic point of departure the Latin phrase *hoc est enim corpus meum*, "this is my body."[3] Addressed throughout *Corpus* are the continental philosophical topics of being and nonbeing, presence and absence, identity, difference, and alterity evoked by "this is" in that ritual phrase. Crucially, what occupies Nancy's attention is not only what he calls our "obsession" in the West with asserting that the *this* that cannot be seen or touched is indeed *here*, and takes the form of a body, "thanks to which," he says, "those who form a *body* with God can commune," but also the doubt cast by this phrase, especially in its repetition, on the certitude of the body.[4] On the one hand, Nancy says "*hoc est enim* displays the body *proper*, makes it present to the touch, serves it up as a meal"; however, on the other hand, "the body on display is foreign, a monster that cannot be swallowed."[5] And so begins Western thinking, secular as well as religious, about the body *tout court*: a paradox of the most foreign (*this is*) that also appears to be most proper (this is *my* body), a two-thousand-year insistence on a present absence.[6] "That's why," Nancy claims at the outset of that exquisite text, "the body, bodily, *never happens, least of all when it's named and convoked*."[7]

To assert that the body "never happens" is not to rule it out as *some thing* beyond the reach of conscious awareness, discourse, or philosophy. Rather, in Nancy's unique phenomenological-deconstructive style, "never happens" helps call into question presuppositions about the presence and unity of the body, both its *what* (parts, functions, modalities, weight, and sum) and its *where* (its location among bodies) that are essential to its being—its disunity and disintegration and not merely unity and integrated totality. Drawing attention to the *some where* of the body unsettles humanist thinking about corporeal integrity (body as closed, proper) and the permanence assumed about it and its correspondence to self-identity. *Corpus* matters for contemporary philosophy of communication, I argue, because in calling into question discourses about bodily order, totality, and integrity, Nancy challenges us to confront, but not necessarily resolve, the limits of identity in our exposure to difference. In support of that thesis, the present chapter engages two themes: first, body as index, defined as measure and as list, and second, the spacing-timing of embodied being, its openness, or what Nancy calls *exposure*, its *some where*.

Although *Corpus* can be read as continental philosophy of Spirit,[8] it can also be read as contemporary continental philosophy of communication. It offers a critical resource for thinking about human communication as the experience of relation, with others and oneself, which is fundamental to the sense and meaning of being human. To be sure, relation itself is a complex philosophical concept. As discussed in previous chapters of the present volume, relation is not a substance, not a thing that can be pinned down or formalized. Although it is itself incorporeal,[9] relation can be approached indirectly, as it consists in actions that occur among and within bodies, especially between oneself and one's body. I turn to *Corpus* for the perspective it offers on the relational dynamic of bodies, what Nancy calls "the *distinguishing oneself* in which the distinct comes into its own, and it does so only in relation to others, which are also distinct."[10]

The objective of this chapter is to specify Nancy's perspective as central to a contemporary continental philosophy of communication, embodiment, and community. It is perspective that blunts the sharper edge of modernist thinking about our separateness, both individual and collective, in its effort to narrow, or seal off and defend, points of access for new social and communicative relations. Nancy shifts our thinking from a body as pregiven, unified, and one's own (as proper) to thinking about embodiment as a dis-integrating integration, an exposure of being in the active-passive withdrawal of human life, what I will here call an "index of existence." The discussion concludes with critical remarks on the limits of a philosophy of the dis-unified body and its relational exposure.

Corpus, Index, Dis-integration

Rather than think of the body as unified, integrated, and under more or less rational control of the self, the model Nancy offers for thinking about the body is *corpus*, a catalog or inventory of organs, functions, sensations, and so on that compose a body—a compilation that is, as such, "always extendable."[11] For the purpose of discussion, and to offer a flavor of Nancy's style, I quote two of the fifty-eight indices on the body located at the end of *Corpus*:

> 36. Corpus: a body is a collection of pieces, bits, members, zones, states, functions. Heads, hands and cartilage, burnings, smoothnesses, spurts, sleep, digestion, goose-bumps, excitation, breathing, digesting, reproducing, mending, saliva, synovial, twists, cramps, and beauty spots. It's a collection of collections, a *corpus corporum*, whose unity remains a question for itself. Even when taken as a body without organs, it still has a hundred organs, each of which pulls and disorganizes the whole, which can no longer manage to be totalized.[12]

> 39. "Body" is distinguished from "head" as well as "members," or at least "extremities." In this respect, the body is the trunk, the bearer, the column, the pillar, the built of the building. The head's reduced to a point: it doesn't really have a surface; it's made of holes, orifices, and openings, through which various kinds of messages come and go. The extremities, likewise, are informed by an ambient milieu, where they accomplish certain operations (walking, waiting, seizing). The body remains alien to all this. It perches on itself, in itself: not decapitated, but with its shriveled head stuck onto it like a pin.[13]

As indicated by the quotations, the term "corpus" may be understood in the interplay of two senses: first, a compilation of written texts, such as a body of research, diagnostic manuals, case law, and so on; and second, the anatomical core of a structure, such as a torso, the trunk of a tree, the body of an essay. What connects both senses is the inscription—the shaping and incorporation—of a body by signs and codes of communication, by discourses, such as those of institutions and public policy, through which meaning is made of its function and experience.

Although a body has the structure and capacity for freedom—the power, that is, to do as much as to have done to it—a body is not merely organized but ordered, not simply shaped but governed. It is, Nancy says, a body that "obeys a law that passes from case to case."[14] A body is not given, but brought together by the semiotic logic (discourse, ordered speech) of a culture; however, rather than define it in terms of an essence, or merely as an object of discourse, Nancy instead insists on the importance of thinking of a body *as* corpus: parts, sensations, and operations whose terms "may be repeated from one list to the next, but always with new additions and in different combinations."[15] In short, a body is a collection whose unity is a question for itself.[16]

Why is this important? Why corpus and not merely a discursively ordered organism? Answer: because if there *is* a body ("this is my body," *hoc est enim corpus meum*), then it is to be located (situated, positioned) and made, not simply found. Its sensation remains prior to and after what has been written about it, its capacities abstracted and developed outside of the unity of the lived body. For Nancy, a body comes in parts, is perceived and interpreted by way of the index it offers of its presence, and in its presence, its presencing—*this is*. Hence his rationale: "46. Why indices? Because there's no totality to the body, no synthetic unity. There are pieces, zones, fragments. There's one bit after another, a stomach, an eyelash, a thumb-nail, a shoulder, a breast, a nose, an upper intestine, a choledoch, a pancreas: anatomy is endless, until eventually running into an exhaustive enumeration of cells. But this doesn't yield a totality. The pieces, the cells, change as the calculation enumerates in vain."[17] Because there is no rigid totality to the body, which is a humanist notion of bodily unity that is no longer tenable in the context of world-integrated communications, we must read it (*this is*; *hoc est enim*), in part, as a *some*, as parts, taken together. This *some*—not only a quality (a description offered, for instance, by Western medicine, or philosophy, of bodily parts, functions, and zones) but also a quantity (a sum but nevertheless not a finite totality)—means that the body (its *this is*, *hoc est enim*) is not only extended and integrated but also distributed, *dis*-integrated, and multiple in its relations.[18] A body is not simply here (*this is*) but is taken here, drawn together, collected. I address the political significance of this perspective later.

But first, to explain Nancy's viewpoint further, we can also read him as playing on, by moving between, two main senses of the term "index." One sense is Peircean-semiotic: namely, a sign associated with its referent by contiguity (sequential occurrence) or connection (contact, proximity). An index in this sense is typically defined as a natural and causal sign, such as paw prints or a bullet hole, which, for a meaningful association to be made by a perceiver, requires an "existential or physical connection between it and its object,"[19] such as the past presence of a cat or a round of ammunition. The other sense of index operating in Nancy's usage is the more common sense of index as a list of items, such as a product inventory, or a list of subjects, such as those enumerated in the final pages of a book, which functions as a reference to the existence of those items (in stock) and the location where they appear (their position).

Among the questions raised by thinking of a body as parts, operations, sensations, and so on—"a collection of collections"[20] classified and indexed, a thinking that challenges the essence and certainty of a body presupposed by a phrase like *hoc est enim corpus meum*—the most important question, indicated by Nancy's fifty-eight indices, is, *Where* is the body? And where (or what) is *the* body? Nancy's interest in *hoc est enim*, provoked by the *this is* (or *here*) of being, puts into question the presence, unity, and meaning of *human* bodies, not just the absent body of Christ.

Inquiry into human being, which is the root task of continental philosophy, is inquiry into how and where it appears—its presence, or its meaningful expression. For Nancy, this question is a matter of not merely how a body is expressed (written about, represented) in language but also how it expresses itself, "*how the body declares.*"[21] We saw this kind of problem in chapter 2 of the present volume: namely, the problem of demonstrating in language, in personal pronouns specifically, the spatial and temporal relation of a subject to a statement, wherein, as Giorgio Agamben argues, what *takes place* is language. Nancy takes the problem of showing or indicating what has no body (Christ) as the *this is* (a demonstrative pronoun) in the direction not of language but of what is at its limit—bodies. I have argued that the subject is language's "outside"—it is that through which language takes place and without which, strictly speaking, it cannot speak, which is another way to say that there is nothing outside of language that is not already inside it: namely, human being, the speaking subject. If this is the case, then a body is that which remains (*hoc est, this is*), showing itself all the while that language shows itself. A body declares, takes place in its being-there (*da-sein*), and thereby demonstrates the indeterminable: namely, life. Body is a sign, an index of existence.[22]

From this perspective, the relevance to human communication inquiry of Nancy's perspective on the some and where of a body (its positions) becomes clear: a body is composed (organized by the logic of a culture), assembled (drawn by thought through which it is sensed and understood), shows itself (is expressive of life, existence), and is counted (some and a sum—a meaningful existence). The primary importance of understanding a body as index, for contemporary continental philosophy of communication, is its correspondence to, or declaration of, the *spacing-timing* of existence. I turn now to this topic.

Now Here, Then There: The Exposure of Bodies

The Latin *hoc est* (*this is*) implies that *some thing* is here, now. Or, it is now, here—two words that when combined spell *nowhere*. For its part, a body *is some where*. Where, exactly? Now, here. "Here, in the where of nowhere," Nancy says—nowhere other than its presentation, its showing or presenting, which means its exposure.[23] This "now here" is in fact nowhere because a body is not simply here but rather always en route, withdrawing into the past while projected into future moments.[24] In *Speaking and Semiology*, the classic study of Maurice Merleau-Ponty's philosophy of communication, Richard Lanigan summarizes the some-where/now-here condition of a body: "A body has neither a here or now (space or time) except indirectly as not being there or then."[25] The here-and-now-only-because-not-there-and-then (the spacing-timing) condition of a body makes it semiotic, an index of *some thing* there, manifest here.

Later, I discuss how a body's material presence shapes perception of it as one's own and why Nancy rejects that perception. For now, let me continue with this explanatory thread of thinking about how a body as index helps draw our attention to it—to a body in its gathering together, its presencing rather than its totally unified *this is*. This is key to Nancy's critique of modern philosophy and his unique phenomenological perspective on the spacing-timing of being. A quote from *Corpus*, regarding the *there* of a body, summarizes his perspective:

> Bodies aren't some kind of fullness or filled space (space is filled everywhere): they are *open* space, implying, in some sense, a space more properly *spacious* than spatial, what could also be called a *place*. Bodies are places of existence, and nothing exists without a place, a *there*, a "here," a "here is," for a *this*. The body-place isn't full or empty, since it doesn't have an outside of an inside, any more than it has parts, a totality, functions, or finality.... It is a skin, variously folded, refolded, unfolded, multiplied, invaginated, exogastrulated, orificed, evasive, invaded, stretched, relaxed, excited, distressed, tied, untied. In these and thousands of other ways, the body *makes room* for existence.[26]

The body "makes room" for existence—room, a place, a location, an opening "for the fact that the essence of existence is to be without any essence.... The body *is* the being of existence."[27] For its part, the human body offers a site, or ground, of human existence, is finite in terms of its relations, but open to (in communication with) others, in the open.[28] It is a being whose essence is exposure, to be exposed, abandoned. Body as index is a showing or appearance of existence.

Exposure from this perspective does not imply that something was previously hidden, revealed only because of a defect in its obstruction that results in broadening its visibility. Rather, exposure of the body is for Nancy the fact of its being.[29] Typically, we think of a body as closed, sealed, on its own and unto itself, the basis of self-identity: body as interiority, wrapped in skin, covered in cloth. However, for Nancy, such a thing would not be a body but a mass, a substance without extension, blocked and impermeable. By contrast, and to reiterate, for Nancy a body is "a thing of extension ... a thing of exposition. It's not just that the body is exposed but that the body *consists* in being exposed."[30] Consisting in being exposed, *exposition* is not a matter of coming out on stage or putting into view or on show that which is concealed or shut in under ordinary circumstances. Rather, exposition is equivalent to the expression of being, its coming-to-be (how the body declares) by way of its presencing and withdrawal, its unfolding, "where the being, as a substance, has for its essence self-positing; self-positing here is exposition itself, in and of itself, in essence and structure. . . . The body is the being-exposed of being."[31]

The idea that a body is the being-exposed of being—which is another way to say it is an index, that exposure is fundamental to being a body—offers a foundation, if not the foundation, for a contemporary continental philosophy of communication. A natural sign of human life—an index of existence (now/here only indirectly because not there/then)—the human body appears (declares, shows itself) as a being blessed with and burdened by the existential capacity for expression, perception, and reflection. A fascinated phenomenon. In turn, it is in, or because of, the exposure of being—the body as it consists as an exposure of being—that the signs of a culture find *their* vitality and reason for being: namely, to code the exposure of human being in its manifold contexts and, in so doing, to offer resources for self-expression and other-perception in our fundamental ontological condition of being-with one another.[32]

Nancy continues, "If the body isn't mass, if it isn't closed in on itself and penetrated by itself, it's outside itself. It is being outside itself."[33] According to this perspective, a body is by definition outside, *ex-posed*, literally standing out in front of (before) others. And it is at the same time in withdrawal: its apparent presence dissolves. For example, consider that whenever I deliver a speech, I am here, "presenting," just as my body is "here," present before others (S. *de cuerpo presente*). The before of *this* body—me, a singular and particular embodiment—is both spatial (*here* it is; here *I* am) and temporal: I am here *first*, as one to another, an embodied consciousness that constitutes the presence of *you* and *others*, just as the appearance of you and others before me (*ex-posed* by the being there, the presentation, of bodies present to me—your or their *first*) renders me, correspondingly, constituted.[34] My place, *now*, *here*, as first in the order of noemata (or "world"), fades and becomes second in the noematic presentation of you and/or another, a first appearance, a *now*, *here*, that from my objective perspective, seems already to have been *there* and *then*. But, in fact, it is not, not until, that is, it (your presence, the presence of others) is presented with another presence, another *here and now* (intuitively constituted as a noematic correlate)—in this case, *me* or, in another case, another embodied consciousness.[35] Your first appearance (given objectively before me) turns out to be third. It is a first presentation whose firstness in the order of presentations requires a second appearance (a *me*, *her*, *him*, and/or *others*) that perceptively constitutes that present place (as first) in time, despite seemingly having been there already. Because it requires a second time (a perception of it) to be constituted as first, that first presentation dissolves and becomes third.[36] The same applies to me from you, or others, but without reducing one to another: in the interpersonal nexus, my present appearance as first (now, here) is demoted, not to second but to third.[37] In other words, a body (*me, you, others*) is in a reversible relation of communication. It is (we are) co-exposed, co-present, and co-appearing. *Hoc est enim*: here and now only indirectly because not there and then.

At this point, a comment on the overlap in thinking between Nancy's perspective on the space-time of bodily exposure and the existential phenomenology of Merleau-Ponty is warranted. Merleau-Ponty characterizes the body as an enclosure, but by *enclosure* he does not mean an exclusive interiority. Rather, from his perspective, the body is intertwined, spatially and temporally, with its lived-world environment. As Lanigan explains, the body "*inhabits* space and time but is not *in* either one."[38] Body, in the spacing-timing of its existence, both is shaped by and acts upon its environment. We may call it an interior exteriority, both inside and outside itself. The phenomenon that exemplifies Merleau-Ponty's thinking of bodily enclosure is well known: flesh, "a synergetic, co-present immanence and transcendence."[39] It is by way of flesh—skin (F. *peau*), the body's largest organ, a boundary between inside and outside that is neither fully one nor the other—that the person obtains an acute sense of her, his, and our *ex-peausure*.

That said, the crucial point raised by phenomenologies of the flesh, that material medium of human communication par excellence, is that flesh communicates the fact that one has a body (human being is an embodied being) and that a body has it. The issue raised here, not just by Nancy but by other continental thinkers as well,[40] is not the separation of mind and body but possession—a double possession. In index 34, Nancy explains,

> 34. In truth, "my body" indicates a possession, not a property. In other words, an appropriation without legitimation. I possess my body, I treat it as I wish, I exercise a *jus uti et abutendi* [L. the right to use and misuse] over it. It, however, in its own turn, possesses me: it pulls or holds me back, offends me, stops me, pushes me, pushes me away. We're both possessed, a pair of demonic dancers.[41]

Consider how we sense the "me" of "my" body—*me* by way of *a* body—in cold and warm temperatures, especially while in contact with other bodies.

We also sense the "me" of, or as, "my" body by way of awareness of the fact that we can make it do things, such as come out of the cold or heat. In its turn, however, a body limits us from what can be done to it, to "my" or other bodies. It can't fly, but it can sit, stand, walk, and run. But it tires and weakens. A body requires care, limiting the extent to which it may be tasked. With regard to the bodies of others, one may touch but never possess them. If I make contact with another, I do so in *its* presentation, a relation of exposure as the mutual unfolding of being. For Nancy, bodies not only present but also *are* limits, limits that are material (spatial-temporal) and psychical (cultural-historical), therefore meaningful. A body is singular, a "line of separation that allows beings to appear as distinct" and always in relation, a "point of their connection and contiguous existence."[42]

The upshot is this: "We sense ourselves as an outside."[43] It is from then and there (a body *as* and *in* exposure *of* and *as* world) that the person, about which we can speculate, gains access to, or awareness of, him- or herself here and now, an outside that enters into his or her conscious experience. "I am addressed *to* my body *from my body*," Nancy says.[44] We are in relation to one another and ourselves as a primordial outside. "The body," Nancy argues, "is the stranger 'out there' (the place of all strange things) *because it is here.* Here, in the 'there' of the here, the body opens, cuts, displaces the *out-* 'there.'"[45] Hence body as index—lists, entries and exits, a corpus of access points to a whole that never adds up.[46] The attention Nancy calls to the double possession communicated by and with a body—such as in our experience of flesh, or in our experience of speaking *of* a body (*a corps*) *from* a body (*de corps*)—helps justify raising the body as a topic of philosophical discourse in the first place: *hoc est enim corpus meum*—this is "my" body, distributed, extended, and exposed *some where*.[47]

Not Mine: Body Between Inside and Outside

The summary philosophy of communication concern of *Corpus* is body consciousness, which does not merely mean body image but also awareness of oneself distributed (*some where*) in one's being. Of chief importance for contemporary continental philosophy of communication, from a Nancean perspective, is to understand the human body as a location/exposure not only of existence but also of psyche. Cursorily put, human being is a thinking being. The body of the human is inhabited by consciousness—a psyche or *ego* in phenomenological terms—and is perceived as such. It is from a body that one becomes aware of oneself. This does not imply a separation of body and consciousness but a relation of distinction. Lanigan explains this relation: "It is the awareness of this 'body' that allows the individual to come to know or be aware of his psyche or consciousness *as his body*." He adds: "The lived-body experience is fundamentally the recognition by the person that his body is the agency of his psyche so that one is a body-subject in the phenomena of living."[48] *Body not as separate from, but agency of, the psyche.* A body is the ground or home not only of existence (life) but also of consciousness of one's existence and for perception and expression (that is, communication) of the lived/living experience of being in a world of and with other bodies.

Nancy's description of indices of the body defined as a corpus, or corpus of *corpora*, affirms in a lively fashion what phenomenologies of the body-psyche relation explain: that neither the ground offered by the body for consciousness nor the relation between it and psyche is as stable or as unified as they may appear.[49] As Diane Perpich explains, "rather than defining a self, a corpus records the fault lines of the self's identity, lines that both separate and join the self with itself and with the world."[50] Thinking of the body as corpus destabilizes perceptions of it as being one's own, as coterminous with self-identity. A body is *me*, but is it *mine?*[51]

In order to explain how this is so, and why it matters, we can refer not just to phenomenology but also to structuralist-continental philosophy of language. As discussed in previous chapters of this volume, the signifier *I* requires a person to posit and think of itself apart from itself in order to say "I"—that is, to speak as a subject. According to Émile Benveniste, subjectivity is defined "not by the feeling which everyone experiences of being himself . . . but as the psychic unity that transcends the totality of the actual experiences it assembles and that makes the permanence of consciousness." That subjectivity, he adds, "is only the emergence in the being of a fundamental property of language."[52] However, by thinking of the body as exposure and as possession (*corpus meum*), Nancy seeks to address precisely those feelings and experiences of material being that are inaccessible in language and unavailable in strict phenomenologies of perception. Writing after poststructuralism, yet within the paradigm of phenomenology, Nancy attends to what *ex-sists* alongside language: namely, a body right at language, *exscribed*, the corporeal points of entry and exit between which the *I* finds and is capable of learning to speak of *me* or of *myself* at all.

Exscription is a term in Nancy's vocabulary that Donald Landes calls a "deconstructive invention"[53] employed in an effort to question the relation between writing (inscription, signification) and writing's "outside"—the relation between word and thing. As Nancy explains,

> "Exscription" means that the thing's name, by inscribing itself, inscribes its property as name *outside* itself, in an outside that it alone displays but where, displaying it, it displays the characteristic self-exteriority that constitutes its property as name. There is no thing without a name, but there is no name that, by naming and through naming, does not exscribe itself "in" the thing, or "as" it, while remaining this *other* of the thing that displays it only from afar.[54]

The concept of *exscription* should not be mistaken as a denial of Agamben's position, discussed in chapter 2 of this book, that there is nothing outside language, that language as a system (F. *langage*, community use) withdraws from instances of speech and writing (F. *parole*, individual use) and in so doing frees up (enables) the possibility for language use within the limits of its rules. *Exscription* for Nancy is a term employed to inquire into those limits.[55]

With regard to bodies, *exscription* for Nancy indicates resistance to complete symbolization, a body's material pushing back or declaration. The body "speaks"; it is speech in action. Exscription in this sense may be understood to refer to the body in its nakedness or pure *ex-position* after or prior to inscription, which does not imply an unsymbolizeable Real (Lacan) but an expressive body lived materially as sensed and sensing. Landes confirms this reading in a passage worth quoting at length:

> Bodies, as they come to be formed by their material parts and their technical relations are individuated in an irreducible process of expression, for they never admit to being re-absorbed by a sense or discourse pre-existing their being. . . . As such, there is no *the* body, and no single discourse that might gain access to the essence or principle of bodies. There are only bodies, sharing meaning in their material being and technical relations. Bodies are the collections of their exscriptions, their expositions, and their *ecotechnical* milieu, bodies are *corpus*, and the world of sense is the failure of encompassing the many *corpora*, and *corpora of corpora*.[56]

Returning to the main thread of the discussion, although one typically thinks of one's body as one's own, particularly in its distinction from foreign bodies, Nancy maintains that just like the languages we speak and through which thought and perception are shaped, one's body is not, phenomenologically speaking, properly one's own. A body is neither an attribute of one's substance nor a possession by right, he argues: "It is proper insofar as it is me rather than insofar as it is mine. If it was mine like an attribute or possession, I could abuse it to the point of destroying it. Me destroying myself only shows that it is me and not mine."[57] The emphasis on *me* rather than *mine* is crucial for understanding Nancy's way of thinking about the body both as movement/exposure/spacing-timing and as being not one's own (F. *propre*). For Nancy, a body ("one's" body) is carried along with language, *exscribed*, while simultaneously being enmeshed within it. A body remains: it continues to be *there* while being expressed *here*, *here*, and *here*. We can say that it serves as a constituting reference point (a spatiotemporal location) for an *I* (a signifier), a *me* to *myself*. It is me, myself (body as psychic agency), but me myself "on the outside, myself outside as outside me, myself as the *division* between an inside and an outside."[58]

Evidence proving Nancy's point about the blurred inside-outside relation between a body and a self (body and consciousness) is offered by the mundane but nevertheless alienating feeling of seeing oneself, whether externally—given by an image in a mirror, a photograph, or the expression on another's face—or internally, as may be exposed by CT or X-ray scans, say, of one's bones, brains, or teeth. More complexly, proof that a body is not mine but me outside is offered by the biological-material fact and experience that a body—a corpus of cells, organs, systems, and precisely choreographed involuntary operations to which both body and psyche remain alien—alters over time.[59] As it grows and stretches, and then eventually slows, weakens, and disintegrates, the body may disrupt the familiar sense of intimacy one has with oneself. By way of its points of entry and exit, it can intrude upon, inconvenience, and even abandon the self, especially in the experience of malfunction and illness, betraying "the self's *proper* immersion or submersion in itself" and, in so doing, forcing it "to identify itself materially and thus in ways it never had before with this body."[60] What we call *health* Nancy calls "life in the silence of the organs, when I don't sense my stomach, my heart, or my viscera."[61]

How could *it* do this to *me*? Because *it*, "my body," is outside, *exscribed*. The body is me, myself, but only by way of being not *mine*, a meaningful relation (sense) rather than attribute (thing) that I have and am with *a* body, "my body," which I do not entirely possess.[62] Body (*me*) is *some thing* that I experience *some where*—namely, "me-outside." Nancy confirms,

> Yes, me-outside. Not "outside me" because in truth the only inside is not "me" but the gaping in which a whole body gathers together and pulls itself together in order to find a voice and announce itself as "self," reclaim itself and call itself, desire itself in desiring the echo that will perhaps come back from the other bodies around it. Stranger to itself in its call from itself: otherwise, it would not be called at all, it would not express with all its extension the demand to meet this stranger.[63]

A stranger to oneself, *corpus meum*—one's body, if we can still use this phrase—would be, in a way, uncanny, although not because repressed. Rather, like a shadow, it is there with and alongside *me*. It is well known that *uncanny* (*das unheimliche*) is the word Freud assigns to the rare and unsettling experience of an encounter with what appears to be strange, not because foreign and unknown but because familiar, albeit forgotten. Freud's best example of the uncanny is drawn from his own experience of an encounter with what he thought was an intruder while traveling by rail to Vienna. Awoken late at night by a violent jolt in the passenger cars, Freud got up, moved toward the exit of his cabin to investigate, and was startled by the appearance of an elderly man in a dressing gown coming toward him, a man whom Freud recalled "thoroughly disliking."[64] As it turned out, what Freud believed to be an intruder—by definition, they break in by force from outside—was in fact a reflection: the door to Freud's cabin restroom had swung open in the movement of the train, and he had come face-to-face with an image in its mirror that, for a brief moment, Freud had failed to recognize as his own.

Even though there are other examples that demonstrate how the fragmenting tendencies of media such as mirrors, televisions, phones, and so on radically undermine the humanist notion of a unified body,[65] the Freudian uncanny's significance here can be connected to the early period of Heidegger's phenomenology, a connection that David Farrell Krell has done brilliantly in his interpretations of the works.[66] According to Krell, *das unheimliche* is a fundamental structure of human being, which Heidegger identifies by a different term: *concern* regarding one's existence. Without rehearsing the details, although Freud's theory informs Heidegger's analysis of concern, for Heidegger, the source of the uncanny is not the unconscious.

Rather, what fills the human *Dasein* with uncanny feelings of anxiety and even dread is *consciousness*, the person's awareness of his or her presence (time), which raises as a question its meaning and unity (being).

Concern (existential consciousness) is not merely felt for others. Uncanny is the unsettling experience in the presence of not what is different, foreign, or alien but what has been there all along, what is familiar albeit unreflected upon, uncared for, forgotten, and/or perhaps repressed. What may be forgotten in being with others, but returns exposed in their absence, is *oneself*.[67] Freud's experience on the passenger train to Vienna illustrates nicely the unstable and *dis*-integrated relation of self to body (body as agency of psyche) underscored by Nancy's perspective on the body in its withdrawal from the self: the exuberance of the child who rejoices, *That's me!* in the mirror phase of identification becomes the disbelief of the elder who, late in life, is shaken by the misrecognition of his or her reflection: *That's me?* The same expression, separated in space and time and marked by a different point: the exclamation point of childhood droops and bends into the question mark of old age, punctuating the weightiness of time and the dread of being that may accompany memories of where one no longer is, and awareness of where one will end up.[68]

Corpus Meum: Grave Site

We are talking about a body as index, an index of places of existence—what can also be called *plots*. Technically, a plot is a terminus toward which one moves (*terminus quo*) and from which one proceeds (*terminus quem*). It is singular, a "horizon" in the sense that Husserl employs the term, both an ending and a beginning.[69] We recognize the body as the index of a crossing of two axes, space and time. Each body is singular and unique. Each begins at some point or plot (*now, here*) and proceeds from it (*then, there*), moving through the world, occupying space and distributed in time, sharing or "dividing," as Nancy often says, the space-time of existence in what we call our, or the, world. Nancy explains this unfolding of being:

> When a baby is born, there's a new "there." Space, extension in general, is extended and opened. The baby is nowhere else but *there*. It isn't in a sky, out of which it has descended to be incarnated. It's spacing; this body is the spacing of a "there." Thereafter, things do indeed become more

complex: the "there" is not simply there; it isn't there as a geometrical point, an intersection or a marker on a geometric map. The "there" is made only of opening and exposition.[70]

Every existent (*some*) has a there (*where*). But to repeat, this "there" is not simply there; every existent is *ex-posed* (standing out), *this is*, opened/opening onto the world of bodies. To make the point explicit, "existence" is another word for *life*, where each life—every existence—corresponds to a body for which it is an index. The horizon of a life takes on meaning from the space-time intersection marking "the coming to presence of things,"[71] including me and a body, the front line that we (*me, you, him, her*) are, and it (a body) is, between life and death.

In the study of human communication, there is a lot of talk about the lived body, the expressive and perceptive human body (both actively and passively) as a sensing, sensuous, meaning-making, and meaning-filled body. But in its lifetime, in its coming to presence and withdrawal, a body lived is also a body dead. It is "the body of a dead person, this dead person that I am when alive."[72] What of it? Of what is the "dead person that I am when alive" an index?

One possible answer is that a lived body-subject (*me, you, others*) is an index of the dead person it *will have* become. It is a living sign here and now (presencing, being) of the not yet there or then (absence, nonbeing). On the general cultural significance of cemeteries in the modern era, for example, and the particular significance of bodily remains, Michel Foucault remarked in passing that the dead body "is ultimately the only trace of our existence in the world and in language."[73] Not only there (out of sight) but also in visual images (Barthes's famous phenomenology of the photographic *punctum* comes to mind[74]), as well as the tradition of lying in state (the public monstration of a revered ruler's lifeless body, embalmed and wrapped in glass) exemplify this basic semiotic principle: body is an index of the location (space-time) of an existent, the *some where* (presencing) of an opening or plot, a site of existence, out in the open, lived from terminus to terminal along life's tranquil ground. Unto its end.[75] For Nancy, "Corpus would be the topo-graphy of the cemetery *whence we come*, which isn't filled with the petrifying medusa-phantasmagoria of Rot. A topography, a photography, of graveyard tranquility, not derisive, simply potent, making room for the community of our bodies, opening the space that is *ours*."[76]

Such imagery of a "topo-graphy of the cemetery *whence we come*"—or in other words, life's termini presented by a body, meaning "a presentation of the difference between life and death"[77] and not some kind of zombie resurrection—reflects the influence of *Dasein*, in its Heideggerian usage, on Nancy's philosophy. The crucial meaning of *Dasein*, its gravity, as it were, is not only *life* but also the *time* of human being, an existence.[78] *Dasein* is not here, now (*this is*); rather, it is there and then, always ahead of itself (*Da-sein*). As such, it is less a thing than an action, "never 'localized,' but localizing; it must be thought of with movement, in the accusative."[79] Moreover, the human *Dasein*, a body in action, is there *with*—not only with others, coexisting and coappearing, but also with and, in fact, as the *there* or space-time opening of being disclosed to it by way of its whole lived-body experience.[80] The "there" of being is an opening at which human *Dasein* is exposed to world, others, and itself, and from which it is propelled, a crossing of the axes of space and of time that ground it *here*, en route *there*, in this world. Until its end. *This is* my body: here lies my body—life returned to the silent ground of coexistence.

I will stop short of rehearsing Nancy's examination of the soul in *Corpus* because doing so would require an independent study beyond the scope of the present research. But I will say that what is at stake regarding the soul, from Nancy's point of view, is understanding the condition of a body as being open and outside, a me-outside, *partes extra partes*. It is an open space, a room for existence structured by relation points of entry and exit rather than a closed, contained, and sealed interiority into which Spirit breathes and out from which the soul departs.[81]

Corpus and Philosophy of Communication

Why body, today? Why *this is*, after all? In human communication studies, there is a lot of talk about race, class, gender, sexuality, and nation as each of these and their associated meanings are read off of bodies, for better or, usually, worse. Within such discourse, *body* is a term that is mentioned but then typically denied, or at least presupposed, in order to establish emancipatory discourses of race, class, gender, and so on. The critical strategy of "mention and deny" is central to both contemporary rhetorical criticism and discourse analysis.[82] The problem, however, is that the element named and denied, in this case, *body*, remains. It does not go away once the rhetorical/linguistic critique of its plurality of meanings is set in motion. In order to transform assumptions about race, class, gender, sexuality, and so on, and thereby improve lived conditions, one must also transform discourses about bodies in order to see and live with bodies differently. It is to this task that Nancy's philosophy is relevant.

The primary importance of *Corpus* for contemporary continental philosophy is the ontological scope it offers for human communication inquiry. The focus it brings to the exposure of being broadens our perspective on the lack of wholeness constitutive of what we call *identity*, a lack or defect in the shell of subjectivity that makes us common. This is the point at which we are enjoined in language and invited to community, what *there is* but that nevertheless remains unrealizable. In discussing how the essence of existence is to be without essence (what I have called our *some where*), and how the "self" in relation to its body as well as to others may be integrated but neither pregiven nor entirely closed (*non corpus meum*), Nancy provides a vocabulary with which to talk about human embodied being as a being-exposed in configurations that are both singular, in this case, and plural, in multiple contexts.[83] Although our horizons will differ, and sometimes greatly so, what makes us common is being a body—singular, particular, enfolded, and also plural, universal, and exposed in multiple relations, a body whose outside, Nancy says, is "precisely the *inside* of the world."[84] Body is an index of the exposure or spacing-timing of being in communication and community with other beings.

Bodies, Nancy shows us, are indexes of life and of people and not merely of matter—they are indexes of people that matter. "People," says François Raffoul, "are not the anonymous They, but distinct singularities, 'bizarre' because singular, not dissolved in a genre."[85] The people we encounter matter, which means they are meaningful, because we encounter them as they encounter us—we coappear as family, colleagues, and neighbors, as well as strangers, foreigners, and others, differing singular pluralities whose human existence, in which we share, is made meaningful by conscious, creative engagement with the world.[86] "Humanity or humanness is not an essence on this view," Perpich explains, "but the product of difference, and it is a difference not just of linguistic signifiers but of heterogeneous bodies."[87] To see bodies as people, as indexes of embodied beings that are meaningful in their unique exposure, requires perspective—that is, ontological and not merely moral scope. The greater the distance between people, the more we can see, and the nearer in proximity, the greater the detail. But being too close results in a loss of perspective, or even blindness, that can lead to indifference.

For its part, *Corpus* helps us to regard a body as integrated and dis-integrating, an index of a quantity equal to others not in mass but in exposure, distribution, and coming-to-be.[88] Perspective on the exposure of existence indicated by bodies (the *some where* of a *these are*) dignifies bodies on the basis of equality among them, as "absolute and irreducible singulars that are not individuals or social groups but sudden appearances, arrivals and departures, voices, tones—here and now, every instant."[89] To assert that bodies are equal in exposure is not, however, to imply that they are merely equivalent. This would be to regard bodies from the perspective of a system of general equivalences (i.e., currency), wherein bodies and their capacities are regarded (valued) as bodies of labor, which may lead to inequality and even to exploitation.[90] Bodies are nonequivalent. With regard to "community," thinking the body as index is neither to reduce bodies to life alone nor to overlook the consubstantiality of life and community and thereby skirt the urgent political fact that some lives are often less advantaged than others because of the privileges, rights, and wrongs brought upon them by modern history, as well as philosophy, which have been justified on the basis merely of the perception of bodies.[91]

That said, critical questions must still be raised. If, as Nancy argues, a body isn't one's own (*non corpus meum*), then whose body is it? Is a body *there* merely to be picked up, claimed, kept, and/or employed, not just for work but to use? The answer obviously is that it is not. Nancy's main philosophical point is that there is no body *proper*. A body is not closed and completely integrated. On the contrary, it is dis-integrated, *ex-sisting*, presenting itself as a collection of parts, points of contact and openings, both to intrusion as well as to new, and different, relations.[92] There is no Body; there are bodies (*corpi*), "discrete, multiple, and swarming."[93] There is no *one*; there is *we*: a community of bodies, singular pluralities, none belonging properly to any other. If, as Derrida argues, "the proper escapes from contact, from contagion," then a human body is disqualified as proper because it is by definition exposed to contact, open to contagion in relation, in com-*muni*-cation.[94] Human bodies are always in communication, with other bodies and other selves, the latter of which may call the former its own but remains nonetheless exposed to contact and thereby compromised in the presumption that identity is contained by and coterminous with "one's" body.

What we can say is that being a body is common. Common is juxtaposed to "one's own," to property, which is not common.[95] We are common (subject), *im-proper* (as individuals). By that logic, although what is common may be shared, it belongs to *no-one*. Human existence, our embodied existence, is common—what *there is*—a gift shared, divided.[96] This simple point is worth emphasizing to the extent that it sharpens focus on how we are more the same than different. Sameness, however, and to be sure, is not equivalent to commonality. These terms are also juxtaposed. One is self-same (the definition of "identity") but our bodies belong to us and we to our bodies, as to community, by a relation of nonbelonging—a keeping of freedom and order by maintaining the openness for diversity and distinction.[97] It is in this regard that Nancy's term "singular plurality" makes sense, not to erase differences but to refer to what makes us common: namely, the sharing of relation in which bodies coexist as not property, predefined, or pregiven.[98]

But what is at stake, ultimately, in Nancy's undermining of the metaphysics of the unified body as origin of creative, human communicative capacities? Perpich raises critical questions about the limits of such a philosophy of dis-integrated bodies. She reminds us of the accomplishments made by critical scholarship that call attention to the violence done to bodies both by systems of thinking and of representation that reduce it to parts and functions and by the encroachment further into the interior of bodies—women's bodies in particular—by legal, governmental—that is, biopolitical—discourses in an effort to gain greater control over decisions regarding *one's own* body. And yet, although Perpich admits reason to move cautiously in adopting the entirety of Nancy's philosophy, she nevertheless identifies "significant resources" in his effort to undermine thinking the body in terms of rigid inside-outside and subject-object dualisms posited by modern philosophies of consciousness. Specifically, she identifies Nancy's innovative philosophy of singular plurality, "that emphasizes the possibility of new modes of connection and community even as it records the fault lines with current historical configurations,"[99] as perspective that strengthens current critiques of gender conventions by inviting careful consideration of the political inadequacy and danger of therapeutic discourses about bodily integrity, as well as market-driven myths about becoming whole, which, as the discussions of Nancy and others in this book make clear, we never were to begin with.[100]

Thinking corporeality as a task of acknowledging the distinct, nonequivalent, integrated-disintegrative unfolding of human embodied being not only expands but also invites critical inquiry from a contemporary continental philosophy of communication perspective. The topography required for human communication to come (the spacing-timing of human being that makes it semiotic, an index of existents equal to but nonequivalent with one another) and the loci of its experience (the discourses that ground and flesh out perceptions of self-expression and expressions of other-perception) are both corpus matters. For its part, a body (a *me, you, him, her*) is the "materiality of what is coming,"[101] an index of the perceptive and expressive, sensing and sense-making phenomenological agency of the humanly communicative life world. There is no shared sense, no community of sense, and no common sense other than sense of and from a body, each singular and plural, free but composed, shaped in its expressive capacities, and open in its coexistential relations. For its part, *Corpus* does not burden a body with the weight of added philosophical discourse. Rather, it extends what we know about being human by focusing on our relational exposure and the communication experience of coming meaningfully into contact in the breaking-through onto reality of every life—*this is*. It illuminates how we are joined by sense (of our differences as well as our similarities) and not merely by cause.

CHAPTER 5

What Remains to Be Thought
Community, or *Being-With*

"Naturally," writes Michel Henry, "the essence of community is not something that is; instead, it is that which (*cela*)—not being a that (*ça*)—occurs as the relentless arrival of life into oneself and thus the arrival of each one into itself."[1] Consubstantial with the life of its members, community will occur, or arrive, in multiple ways. However, if the concept and phenomenology of community (*its* life) coheres in shared understanding of one's being within it (life, an abstract concept, must be given a form of representation, and the body, as we saw, is that form), then to speak of community is, at least in part, to put the stability of it at risk—risk that expressions of community may not only confirm and shore up but also possibly lead to its unraveling. This is to say that if community is taken to be (it arrives, so it must be received, or taken) that which, in not being a "that," inheres in a kind of intuitive and therefore unspoken acceptance of its nature, contours, and limits (the *connaissance* of a community's *savoir*, so to say), then speaking of community in discourse, as in philosophy must, in its turn, be taken or regarded as part of the uncertainty inherent to *communication*—the life-giving openness of oneself that, in the company of others, may itself be accompanied by the desire or fantasy of its closure. Instability of the identity of community shares in the uncertainty of the subjects who speak of it—that is, the experience of not being outside of language and therefore always traversed by the common. From that perspective, we appreciate more deeply how the idea of community is bound irrevocably to the possibility of human communication, both its protection and threat, its freedoms and constraints. The question of community is a question of its communication, a sharing, which means its and our dividing.

The concept and phenomenon of community are long-standing as thematic guides for human communication inquiry. Yet within mainstream social science and humanities scholarship, "community," or what Zygmunt Bauman calls the "dream sign of a paradise lost,"[2] is routinely presupposed as a certainty, a *that which* can and should be built or maintained, usually through so-called improved communication.[3] *Dream sign*, however, does not imply that community is not real or is simply imaginary. Rather, the sign of and discourse about community bring structure to sense and shape the meanings made of our experience of the world, and for that reason it is as much real (embodied) as it is symbolic. However, although community features prominently in academic scholarship as well as in routine talk about who we are, what is meant when speaking about it is often vague and dreamlike. It is in that sense that the task of thinking, rather than presupposing community, not only remains but also persists.

Thought of community is, to be sure, a thinking of our time. As Jean-Luc Nancy argues, it is a task of "thinking through what will become of our common existence (which is to say our existence itself)."[4] From the shadows of what he calls "the work of death" carried out in the "frightening appeals to community" of modern history (e.g., ethnic cleansing),[5] the task brought to light by contemporary continental philosophies of community is to broaden the horizon for reflection on the meaning of being-with-one-another. This is a thinking of *relation*, or of what Nancy calls "being-in-common beyond the being thought of as identity, as state, and as subject; the being-in-common affecting the being itself in the depths of its ontological texture."[6]

The goal of the research presented in the present volume, summarily put, is a philosophical description of human communication in its law-like, immunizing function within a social formation, a mode of enabling and limiting individual expression that also contains and curbs the potential for collective conflict. The objective of the description thus far has been to draw attention to the constituting role played by language and communication at the intersection of subjectivity (consciousness), human embodiment (life), and human community (the semiotic crossing of identity boundaries). Building on that discussion, this final chapter focuses on the task of philosophical thinking about "community." From a contemporary philosophy of communication perspective, such a task deepens the discussion thus far of relation, existence, difference, communication, noncommunication, community, and immunity by way of an examination of coexistence, or *with*, that is elemental to thought and experience of self, other, me, you, us, them, and how *we* are together. If the problem of community is semiotic and phenomenological, then its thinking, I argue, helps identify the task and demand of human communication philosophy in a contemporary continental key.[7]

To support that argument, this concluding chapter engages what I call Nancy's semiotic phenomenology of community. As mentioned at the outset of this monograph, "semiotic phenomenology" is recognized under the communication-disciplinary name *communicology*, an established paradigm of philosophical inquiry into the union of consciousness and embodiment, perception and expression, rhetoric and ethics, person, world, and media that shape human communication.[8] Although to some it may appear odd to link Nancy to semiotics or phenomenology (for instance, Ian James and Ignaas Devisch have persuasively characterized his philosophical program as post-phenomenological),[9] I argue that semiotic phenomenology is an appropriate descriptor of Nancy's philosophical approach. This is because his goal is to interrogate the discourses of Western philosophy and develop new terminology aimed at broadening the horizon for thinking about what it means to be human. He emphasizes terms such as exposure, relation, exposition, exscription, and touch over presence, appearance, and contact, because, as James explains, Nancy finds the language of existential phenomenology insufficient "to account for the nature of world-disclosure."[10] In that sense, Nancy's philosophy exemplifies the semiotic-phenomenology couplet as "a continuous, mind-opening, and nontotalizing *discourse* where the problems and shortfalls of both classical philosophy and contemporary theory meet with insights into existential, psychological, and aesthetic issues that were consciously bracketed and excluded after the structuralist turn."[11] As I will demonstrate here, Nancy's intellectual project, which is both literary and philosophical, is precisely "a phenomenology of the lived world, and a philosophy of signs."[12] It is a meditation on the experience of our shared world, or what I will here call a semiotic phenomenology of touch, communication, and community.

What follows is a description, reduction, and interpretation of *being-with*, a key albeit underdeveloped sign in the vocabulary of contemporary philosophical discourse of what it means to coexist or be in community. It is against efforts to realize community, which in the modern era have sometimes ended in catastrophes to life, that Nancy has throughout his writing called attention to the critical significance of what is indicated by the preposition *with*—"a category," François Raffoul explains, that Nancy "considers to be still without usage and status, nonetheless harbor[ing] all that is to be thought for us today."[13] As a sign, *with* signals for Nancy the demand of thinking about being-in-common, community, and communication—a thinking of relation (*with*) as our having-to-be. Such a task is a task not only of our time but also of our being, and not merely of philosophy. In his efforts to extract the significance of this wee term, Nancy adds critical insight into why the concept of community is not simply stable and guaranteed, nor is being in it avoidable, just as communication is not reducible to self-expression and other-perception, nor is it avoidable.[14] The objective of this chapter is to deepen the connection between philosophy of communication and the contemporary continental perspectives already engaged in this book, which cohere as an implicit project of philosophical justice "to confront and explode the denial of existence"[15] inherent in late-modern, globalizing forms of human indignities. That said, what follows is not a roadmap for so-called community building through communication. It is instead groundwork in semiotic phenomenology offered as evidence of, and perhaps even a modest guide for, a contemporary continental philosophical approach to human communication—a practical thinking of the idea of community to come.

Semiotic Phenomenology and *Being-With*

Allow me to begin with a few words on semiotic phenomenology as a three-step method for critical philosophical inquiry. Doing so brings a philosophy of communication framework to understanding Nancy's conviction that the preposition *with* is originary to, but underthought, regarding what it means to be human. The first step in a semiotic phenomenological analysis of the human life world is to describe the prereflective state of consciousness.[16] According to Richard Lanigan, preconscious moments are those when "we are 'not thinking' or 'day-dreaming' or otherwise not cognizing our lived-moment."[17] These moments occur as we live through everyday practices without necessarily actively attending to the meaning they have for us, now or in the future.[18] Examples of prereflective experience is habit, or something as mundane as walking or driving to work, routine practices that are part of one's style or system of living but that remain unapparent until that system malfunctions (e.g., break a leg, blow a tire, lose your job, and so on), thereby exposing how parts and system interact. Crucial for semiotic phenomenology is the human prereflective state as a starting point from which to work backward in the descriptive phase of analysis. Conscious awareness invites philosophical introspection prior to whatever meanings we later make of our basic sense experience "not yet articulated in propositional form."[19] The question that guides a semiotic phenomenological description is this: What is our basic condition of being aware and having a world? Lanigan's answer is straightforward: "Our everyday condition is one of *encountering other people* and the world."[20] Human consciousness is consciousness of a world of others (*Mitsein*).

Turning to Nancy, the first step in what I call his semiotic phenomenology is a description of this basic human relation. Throughout his work, and particularly in his three best-known volumes, *The Inoperative Community*, *Sense of the World*, and *Being Singular Plural*, Nancy describes the normal condition of being and having a world as "being-with." Prior to reflection on the sense we make of our experiences within the world, there is the everyday fact of existence. And that existence is coexistence. Being-with is a priori and predetermined, essential to the experience of being human and what that means.[21] In Nancy's vocabulary, *being-with* is a privileged sign, a conceptual sign. That is, it selects a context and thereby thematizes thinking about the human world as shared. It is the linguistic sign of a fundamental relation constitutive of and ground for human awareness.[22] Nancy's description of the experience of being human specifies *being-with* as thematic of the basic relation that shapes human consciousness.

To be sure, Nancy's relational ontology shares not only in the spirit of Husserl's perspective on the pregiven sense-world—its visual, tactile, and acoustic presentation, and its lived-through togetherness—but also, as I discuss below, in Heidegger's philosophy of *Dasein*. Not only that, Nancy's emphasis on coexistence as a basic ontological condition of being human also aligns him squarely with Lanigan's existential phenomenological philosophy of human communication. Just as Lanigan's phenomenology emphasizes that humans are "able to *understand* the *other person* whom we recognize as *having* this existential condition which is the *very condition of our own being* in a shared Lived-World,"[23] so too does Nancy insist on co-being as the absolute condition of human conscious awareness. *Being-with* as primary to being aware of one's existence precedes self-reflection and offers the ground for both the possibility of communication (the impossibility of noncommunication) and for thinking about community.

Although semiotic phenomenology, as a method, begins with a description of the constituents of conscious awareness, the procedure moves forward by drawing its focus back (refining the description) to consider the active *experiencing* of awareness. The goal here is to narrow focus on the dynamic experience of living in a world of perception. The second step of the analysis therefore moves from being aware of existing to the awareness of one's own awareness—that is, from a description of consciousness of the world to a reduction of the description.[24] The aim of the phenomenological reduction is, Lanigan explains, "to determine which parts of the description are essential [to conscious experience] and which parts are merely assumed."[25] With regard to Nancy, if *being-with* is at first a sign of the basic human condition of being in a world (a thematization of the problematic of human community), then the description must be further refined: How is being-with experienced?

By "experience," I mean experience as a journey (G. *Erfahren*), the activity of living-through, over time, that accumulates into shared knowledge or so-called common sense.[26] In the second step of Nancy's semiotic phenomenology, a step focused on awareness of awareness—that is, conscious experiencing of the shared world—*being-with* may be understood as an empirical signifier. It is an expression in Nancy's vocabulary used to call attention to what is essential to (that is, what are the primordial ontological conditions of) human conscious awareness of coexistence, our being-in-common, the most important of which is embodiment.

Semiotic Phenomenology and Embodiment

Human embodiment is a central thematic to research employing the method of semiotic phenomenology.[27] Lanigan defines human embodiment as "having and *being* a body," not merely occupying space and persisting in time.[28] Embodiment is to have and be a material form of the sign systems that bring structure to sense and meaning to human experience of the world.[29] Isaac E. Catt and Deborah Eicher-Catt tell us that "embodiment is the *essential point of mediation* between us and the cultural signs and codes of discourse under which we inescapably live."[30] Frank J. Macke draws our attention to the body as the medium of conscious awareness: not only are we conscious of our bodies but "by way of my body and its thinking and reflective properties, I am also conscious of being conscious."[31] With regard to the importance of embodiment in continental philosophies of human experience, Anne O'Byrne argues that although "knowing may be the province of the mind and sensation may be the province of the body on Descartes' account, *experience* is derived from the union of the two."[32] In sum, embodiment is a basic, semiotic, and phenomenological condition of being human, of being an expressive and perceptive (i.e., communicative) being. As I will discuss, reduction of the description of *being-with* to the experience of embodiment refines Nancy's perspective on community and thereby puts new light on why the phenomenology and semiotics of human communication are privileged philosophical domains for its inquiry.

To set up that discussion, I want to rehearse Lanigan's inventory of verbal and nonverbal codes of communication, or semiotic systems, that relate directly to Nancy's philosophy.[33] Lanigan identifies ten code systems, beginning with linguistics, mathematics, and logics, which he classifies into the typology of "eidetic" or conceptual codes: verbal systems of concepts arranged by logical function, linguistic signs being the most complex, followed by mathematical signs, and logical signs. The other seven code systems are classified into the typology of empirical codes: nonverbal sign systems experienced in zones of space (proxemics) and time (chronemics), as sight (ocularics), motion (kinesics), touch (haptics), sound (vocalics), and smell and taste (olfactorics). Three of these systems are especially relevant to the present discussion.

The first is kinesics, a semiotic system concerned with movement of the human body as visually perceived—awareness of awareness based on seeing bodies. Examples include head and facial movement in private and intimate contexts of interaction, bodily gestures that may be codified in behavior profiling code systems, and the significance of bodily movement in contexts of work as well as in contexts of aesthetic performance. The second major semiotic system relevant to my purposes is haptics, which concerns communication by way of bodily contact—awareness of embodied awareness based on the expression and perception of touching bodies. Examples include contact and noncontact in public contexts, the intensity of contact, and its duration and location, all of which are invested with meaning and heavily regulated by rules of moral appropriateness. A third semiotic system is vocalics, which concerns voice sound production and reception as a communication system—awareness of awareness based on hearing bodies. Expressive features of this semiotic system include loudness and silence, duration and quality of voice, and qualities such as pitch, timbre, and resonance.

Several points can be made about each of these semiotic systems as they relate to conscious awareness of one's particular intentional project or style of being in the world. I will mention only two. First, and most obviously, these semiotic systems draw attention to the sense experiencing of our world. That is, they codify the experience of our capacity to see, touch, and hear the bodies with which we coexist. The content of these semiotic systems—namely, "human *sensations as perceptions/expressions* arranged by human *embodied modalities*"[34]—relates directly to Nancy's interest in broadening Western philosophical understanding of the sense of *being-with*. Sensing is, Nancy says, "always a perception, that is, a feeling-oneself-feel."[35] Awareness of being aware, such as feeling-oneself-feel, is acquired by way of reflective attending to the phenomena of life world situations—public, communal, and/or intimate—made meaningful by and through the sign systems that shape sense and regulate the expressive (signifying) and perceptive (signified) practices of human interaction. However, what is crucial for the purposes of my discussion is the focus *being-with* brings, as a signifier in philosophical discourse, to expression and perception as experiences of contact in human communication. For example, in vivid fashion, Nancy writes that language "cuts me / from you / from myself / from the same / and from the other. It is in cutting that it attaches me, adjoins me to something, to some*one* whom neither you nor I know."[36] In language, the dynamic and continuous human experience of the lived world is cut or chopped into discrete bits (as called attention to by the slash marks in the quotation) that attach us in shared semiotic systems, in discourse (F. *discours*). I discuss Nancy's perspective on contact, or touch, in more detail later.

The second important point to emphasize about kinesic, haptic, and vocalic code systems is the analytic focus they bring to the reversibility of human communication. This is crucial. We typically take for granted that one's consciousness of world is acquired in the company of others. However, semiotic phenomenology emphasizes the relationship between body and psyche, or ego, as that which stabilizes the person's reflective attending to what it means to be a person, for other people as well as for oneself. As Lanigan explains, human embodiment is "the necessary condition of observing in oneself just that same *self consciousness* that is perceptible in the *other's consciousness.*"[37] It is worth quoting Henry's technical summary of the relation between ego/self and other in Husserl's phenomenology; all that developed after it has shaped sociological, anthropological, and communication inquiry into human symbolic interaction. Particularly important is Henry's account of the assimilating apperception of a body inhabited by an ego:

> The other enters into my experience as a body appearing in the sphere of ownness pertaining to my primordial nature. The other is perceived within my ownness with the meaning of being an organism, which is to say a body inhabited by a constituted ego. Given that in this primordial nature only my body can, according to Husserl, be constituted as an organism in an original way, this other body is only capable of being given as an organism as well, inhabited likewise by an ego, as the result of an apperceptive transfer. This transfer starts from my own body, which transports this sense of being an organism from my body to the other's body, which is henceforth perceived in the same way. This resemblance reconnects this other body to mine in the primordial sphere and allows my body to be conceived by analogy as another organism, as the body of an other.[38]

Apperceptive transfer among embodied egos explains the principle of the reversibility of human communication: self-expression is bound to other-perception just as other-expressions become the objects of self-perceptions. Understanding subjectivity as intersubjectivity—and from that perspective, human communication as a reversible relation—refines our thinking about the general problematic of "community" to which Nancy responds with the term "being-with."[39]

Returning to semiotic phenomenology, the third step in the analysis is hermeneutic—that is, an interpretation of the reduction. If step one is a description of awareness, and step two aims at the essential features of the awareness of being aware, then step three is a representation—that is, a new interpretation of the awareness of being aware. As Lanigan explains, interpretation is crucial to the method of semiotic phenomenology for the reason that it "allows the researcher to specify the [essential] *signified* or *perceived* elements in the reduced signs of the description."[40] The interpretation itself is another description—namely, a description of a perception of the meaning of what the reduction reveals. As such, the interpretation must be acknowledged as a value—a judgment. It is, Lanigan explains, "a hermeneutic judgment or specification of existential meaning—that is, the meaning of the phenomenon as the person lived it in the *flesh*."[41] Nancy advises that the judgment to be arrived at vis-à-vis our coexistential experience (i.e., meanings made of lived experience) is as a task.

Demonstration of the crucial third step of Nancy's semiotic phenomenology of community is offered in the English translation of one of his most straightforward essays, "Conloquium."[42] It was originally published as a preface to the French edition of Roberto Esposito's *Communitas: The Origin and Destiny of Community*, a synthesis of modern philosophical thought about the idea of community in the works of Hobbes, Rousseau, Kant, Heidegger, and Freud. "Conloquium" can be read as an expression of a perception of the problematic thematized by Esposito as well as an interpretation (third step) of what remains to be thought—an interpretation of the reduction of a description not only of Esposito's argument but also, and most importantly, of the modern philosophical problematic of community sketched in Esposito's volume. To the extent that Nancy's philosophy can be read as a major effort to develop new terminology for thinking about what it means to be human, we see in what I have identified as a third step in his analysis that *being-with* becomes a signified: an object of consciousness representing new meaning of our shared human condition.

Let me turn the discussion to the main implications of this crucial third step. My goal, specifically, is to draw attention to how Nancy adds to what we know about, and therefore how we perceive, the semiotic and embodied conditions of being-in (or, as I discussed in previous chapters, abandoned to) language—our having-to-be in communication and community.

Communication/Community

If *community* is a sign of a philosophical and practical problematic, then its point of entry for thinking is both semiotic and phenomenological. In "Conloquium," Nancy reduces the problem of community to a question: namely, "how to say 'we' otherwise than as a 'one' (= everyone and no one) and otherwise than as an 'I' (= a single person, which is still no one)?" He adds, "There is for us a deep semantic and pragmatic hesitation in the pronouncement of a 'we,' instantaneously vaporized or on the contrary cemented."[43] Nancy's reduction of the problem of community is underscored by Émile Benveniste's explanation of the personal pronoun that is at the root of Nancy's question. He writes, "In 'we' it is always 'I' which predominates since there cannot be 'we' except by starting with 'I,' and this 'I' dominates the 'non-I' element by means of its transcendent quality. The presence of 'I' is constitutive of 'we.'"[44] In Indo-European languages, Benveniste says, *we* is "an 'I' expanded beyond the strict limits of the person," which, he explains, results in two opposed uses of the ordinary sense of this plural: "On the one hand, the 'I' is amplified by 'we' into a person that is more massive, more solemn, and less defined; the royal 'we.' On the other hand, the use of 'we' blurs the too sharp assertion of 'I' into a broader and more diffuse expression; it is the 'we' of the author or orator."[45]

What this tells us is that perhaps the challenge for thinking community in ways that unhinge it from a politics of identity (i.e., to think being "beyond the being thought of as identity, as state or as subject"[46]) is to locate and attend to the communication conditions of awareness (i.e., expression and perception) and thereby develop new ways in which awareness of awareness may be represented (i.e., address ontology where it becomes epistemology). If this is the case, one solution, which is Nancy's, is to subordinate the constituting "I" described by Benveniste and focus instead on the experience of the signifier *we* in its expression. As Nancy argues, "We are *together* and it is only there or thus that I can say 'I.' I would not say 'I' if I were alone . . . since if I were alone I would have nothing from which to differentiate myself."[47] His approach exemplifies a core tenet of the semiotic phenomenology of communication: that perception is grounded in and shapes language. When seeing, hearing, or touching others, what do we *think*?[48]

To be sure, Lanigan has made virtually the same point as Nancy regarding the importance, for contemporary philosophy of communication, of attending to the experience of the intersubjective nexus at which the signifier "I" appears. *I* constitutes the meaning of *me* as other and *you* as different—different, that is, not only from others (the plural "you") but also from oneself (the lived versus image/perception of one's body).[49] The key word in that last sentence is "from." Difference *from* others and also *from* oneself indicates a context characterized by both distance and proximity, separation as well as primary contact, a lived-world context within which human as well as nonhuman bodies are thrown together while remaining distinct. It is this basic ontological feature of being human (being-with in and as relation) upon which Nancy focuses his interpretation. *From* (a sign) presupposes *with* (F. *avec*, a signifier), the meaning of which (a signified) is "co-occurring" or "being-with." Like Esposito, Nancy prefers to emphasize the preposition *with* rather than the pronoun *we* (or *I*) for its power to indicate the spacing-timing, or separating, of beings, their coming and going, inside to and from outside, that characterize the fluidity of life-world experiences.[50] A summary quotation from Nancy explains,

> If there is indeed something which constitutes this "being" or this "existence" in which, or according to which, we are—or this existence which

we are, if you prefer—it is that we are with one another. We are *with* (someone, others and the rest of the world) just as much and exactly as we are *tout court*. Even "to be alone" is also a way of *being-with*; to be with the lack or in the absence. Without *being-with* I would not be alone. I would be, purely and simply, absolutely. I would be all (or nothing!), but neither alone nor *with*. . . . *With* is what gathers us together, in so far as we are all origins; and separates us, in so far as the origins are inevitably incommensurable with each other.[51]

Nancy's emphasis on *with* moves thinking away from a metaphysics of presence (brute being) to an ontology of relation (being-*with*)—relation as communication. Consider how we often say, "To speak with, to enter into marriage with, to break up with, to become angry with, to compare with, to identify with, to play with, to dine with," and so on.[52] Nancy's interest in the phenomenology of these basic situations calls attention both to context (the lived world as shared) as well as to "contact, or at least a proximity or *virtuality* of contact."[53] As Lanigan, Wilden, Bateson, and others have established,[54] context and contact are determinant factors of human communication. Jakobson's classic model of communication, for instance, demonstrates how contact is a "phatic" function of communication, where simple learned greetings and salutations establish a physical and therefore psychological connection between addresser and addressee—and in so doing affirm basic commonality.[55] Nancy's attention to the *with* of human being-with brings focus to how, even if addresser and addressee don't yet make contact in actuality, they are nevertheless already in contact virtually (i.e., existentially) by way of inhabiting space and time in the same world. The two categories (space and time) frame human coexistence, are modalities of human embodiment experienced by way of code systems (proxemics and chronemics). Within the space-time contexts of a shared world, human embodied contact is both already and not yet. Emphasizing the *with* of our *being-with* one another calls attention to why there is human communication (virtually), or, why there is community, and why its outcome is not always guaranteed (in actuality)—why "community," as discussed previously, is unrealizable.[56]

Consider the title of Nancy's essay: "Conloquium." The term "conloquium" typically means to hold a conversation, conference, discussion, or interview.[57] But Nancy employs it to emphasize sharing, or "exchange (a *communicatio*, a *commericum*, a *commentarium*)" as a dividing with another person, especially one who is absent.[58] Although the essay was written to preface the work of another, it is done so *in conloquium*, a contribution to, by way of sharing in, a conversation of which both philosophers are already a part, and apart. To have a conversation or to hold a meeting (i.e., to talk *with*) is to give (a piece of) oneself to another, to offer perspective (one's expression, a judgment). However, at the same time, it is to hold oneself together, to keep one's ground, maintaining perspective for the reason that everybody has one—to give, that is, but not simply to give up or give in. Why else would we converse? Like the preposition *with*, the genitive noun *conloquium* indicates how, in conversation (discourse) everyone gives and maintains him- or herself in his or her being, *being-with* any other.[59]

Touch, Contact, Communication

The nature of self-maintenance while *in conloquium* is crucial to Nancy's semiotic phenomenology of community. Among the insights, what Nancy adds to the study of community is perspective on the phenomenon of touch. Touch indicates concretely a fundamental aspect of coexistence (*being-with*) and its lived, embodied experience. However, Nancy's emphasis on the experience (sense) of touch is offered in critique of metaphysical philosophies of presence and immediacy. For Nancy, touch does not indicate merely an overcoming of distance (immediacy) through a grasping of objects or confirmation of identity (presence). Rather, for Nancy touch is "a figure of withdrawal, discontinuity, and separation."[60] It marks a point of contact and separation, a spacing-in-contact as ontologically fundamental to human coexistence. Touch calls attention to how bodies in interaction (all bodies with mass and weight) not only interact but also maintain their distinction. "It is by touching the other," Nancy writes, "that the body is a body, absolutely separated and shared."[61] Bodies do not simply fuse or dissolve into one another when touching; instead, they maintain their separation. As Graham Harman puts it: "To touch something is to make contact with it even while remaining separate from it . . . to caress a surface that belongs to something else, but never to master or consume it."[62] Bodies interact and maintain separation for the reason that they have no individual character outside of the relation of their mutual touching: "The community of bodies resists."[63]

Regarding human bodies, touch is heavily invested with the semiotic systems / moral conventions of a culture that regulates the spacing-timing of bodies and the contexts within which they come into contact. Touch is an embodied measure of self-preservation, of keeping oneself at a distance and therefore distinct, albeit within the necessarily originary condition of being exposed to and interdependent *with* one another. O'Byrne finesses the consequences to one's self-understanding (identity and difference) of the interplay of touch and distance: "If I can keep my distance, I can preserve my self-understanding as an autonomous individual; but this becomes increasingly difficult the more I come in touch with the world, whether through the touch of a lover, or of a mugger, or of the mass of people on a crowded street. In each case, touch has the capacity to challenge and compromise my identity as it impinges on me, encroaches upon me, intrudes upon me, presses against my boundaries."[64]

Nancy's philosophy of touch complements communication theory of boundaries, which function according to the logics of both/and and either/or (neither/nor). To reiterate a point made earlier in this book, a boundary is both part of and distinct from (a part of and apart from) the context it marks, neither completely inside nor completely outside. It operates as a rule, "neither real nor imaginary, but symbolic."[65] Boundaries establish a relation of choice, hence possible communication in a given context. In the case of human communication, boundaries institute the space of, and are regulated by, semiotic codes, appearing most readily at times whenever they are breached. This is because human being is an embodied, semiotic being, and the body—*a* body—is, according to Nancy, "a thing of *exposition*. It's not just that the body is exposed but that the body consists in being exposed. A body is being exposed."[66] Thinking of the body as exposure is, as we have seen, to understand it semiotic-phenomenologically as a corpus, with multiple boundary limits and openness for multiple configurations.[67]

Boundaries, especially those of a body, immediately stand out, and we are instantly aware of them, in the experience of touch. In touching, we experience both the sensation of another body and our sense of touch, although the two sensations are different and require shifting the focus of attention in order to isolate and perceive one and then the other. In the nexus of touch, bodies don't fuse. They share a relation—of being touched and touching, as well as self-touching, the sensing of embodiment in the act of touch. This haptic relation of human communication is well documented in contemporary continental, especially French, philosophy.[68] For his part, Nancy argues that "I have to be in exteriority in order to touch myself. And what I touch remains on the outside. I am exposed to myself touching myself."[69] Touching another is also to touch oneself, the outcome of which (being in exteriority) is an embodied sense of oneself outside of oneself, a "me-outside."[70] Rather than merely ground and confirm self-identity, a body has the power to undermine it, withdrawing or keeping its distance from a self that may unreflectively call it "its own." It is for this reason that we experience touch as another. In the phenomenon (experience) and semiotics (historical-cultural meaning) of touch, corporeality is intercorporeality, just as subjectivity is understood, and lived, as intersubjectivity. Touch is a boundary experience of being both self/same and other/different that brings human communication into light as a reversible relation.

The coexposure of embodied beings is confirmed by codes that regulate contact.[71] The vocalic, haptic, and kinesic communication codes summarized previously take on new meaning when considered not only as communication but also as evidence of embodied exposure. In bringing awareness to one's awareness of being with others (being-*with* or *in* relation), codes call attention to the contingency of the coherence of both self and other. On the one hand, being a self means being dependent (for expression, sociality) on things other than and separate from it, including a body. Cultural codes expose the self in its lack of completion by drawing attention to the lived body as edges, parts, and zones (*corpora*) to be comported, governed, and protected for the good of others and oneself. The points of human bodily contact, the contexts of contact, its location and duration, are all codified—they mean something. On the other hand, it is through the experience not only of contact but also of understanding the codes (their absorption and sedimentation) regulating the former's meanings that other bodies also appear as matter, zones, and limits, exposed and lacking in their way. The upshot of the semiotic and phenomenological experience of touch (awareness of being aware) is that touch bears with it not only desire, or repulsion, but also knowledge (consciousness) of coexposure and lack of integrated wholeness as a basic fact of being a body in a world with other bodies. "*We are exposed together*," Nancy declares, "body to body, edge to edge, touched and spaced, *near in no longer having a common assumption, but having only the between-us of our tracings* partes extra partes."[72]

Touch, for Nancy, is not an act of possession but rather of "non-appropriative touch."[73] Crucial to this perspective is the emphasis placed on the separation, or spacing-timing, of bodies, what Nancy calls exposure, or *ex-position*.[74] Within that coexistential framework, touch is both a sign of separation and exposure and an experience of the boundary that holds beings in relation. Awareness of being aware of oneself among others—say, of being in community—is an *experience* of that relation. To be sure, awareness of oneself as another among others can lead to recoiling rather than "reaching out" to touch or connect with someone, as we say. If I touch, I do so knowing that I am exposed to that touch and to being touched, exposed to "me-outside." Touch is a reversible relation. In Nancy's philosophy, it is understood to take place in hesitation, as interruption and withdrawal rather than certainty, possession, or confirmation of anything like identity or community. Awareness of being self/same and other/different (*le meme et l'autre*) in human communication thereby calls for protection of the space of exposure rather than its overcoming, or worse, its occupation—the modern objective of community building.[75]

Giving Oneself

I now want to address what thinking of being-with, and touch, adds to understanding the sending or sharing of oneself in communication as *giving over*. In the experience of touch, the mutual relation of contact and separation between bodies radically undermines the gift status of expression—that is, of communication as donation with regard to, say, giving oneself for the common good. Because being-with is fundamental to being human, the act of giving over of oneself or reaching out to make contact with someone or something, such as with active participation in public discourse, must be understood as fundamental to being in language, which, as was explained in previous chapters of this volume, amounts to taking responsibility, ontologically, not morally, for one's having-to-be and having-to-be *in language* that precedes any self-sending or "ethics" of communication.[76] Human beings are already with one another (community is what there is), even if not always in accord (community is unrealizable) or in perfect communication (although noncommunication is impossible, communication when defined as "understanding" is not always guaranteed). In our shared contexts experienced through language that regulates the boundaries that shape us, perspective on touch sheds light on how communication (affinity, self-expression, other-perception) not only brings nourishment but also, potentially, *dis-ease*.

This is to say that touch is a figure of exposure. It indicates disturbance of an individual person's experience of the shared world, an experience of the spacing-timing of being that Nancy, Esposito, and Giorgio Agamben call "freedom."[77] If, as Nancy suggests, language cuts the self from itself and from others, which is a straightforward way to say that language *exscribes*, and if this cutting or separation in language is also part of our attachment (the linguistic-semiotic boundary work holding us together), then although human beings do not fuse in being-with one another, we nevertheless remain exposed, being together (coexisting) in language and speech, in our distance and proximity. Hence the challenge, necessity, and danger of community: because being human is being-*with* others, exposed to and in touch with one another—which means, ontologically, we communicate, we are communicating, and we are always in com-*muni*-cation—then whatever is shared has the potential to spread.[78]

It is with the notion in mind of being exposed together in our mutual existence—that is, of being not entirely oneself because of others, communication as primary contact and potential contagion—that step three of Nancy's semiotic phenomenology may be understood with its fully radical explanatory force. *Being-with* as a sign helps us think about the human life world as shared, and as a signifier it appears as an expression of the already and not yet of contact and communication (we are in touch but not necessarily in communion). If that is the case, then as a signified (a judgment, the third step in the analysis) *being-with* puts more clearly into view the unthought sense of human life: namely, awareness of existence as *co*-existence. In reading Nancy, *being-with* must be read as a conceptual judgment about what it means to be together, the material (embodied) significance of coexistence, touch, and/or being *in conloquium*.

To be sure, judgments are not neutral. And this is reflected in the final passages of "Conloquium," where Nancy insists that being-with is "defined and constituted" by a call, or what he calls a "charge."[79] Although Heidegger says that we are thrown into existence—the consequence of which, among other dispositions, is concern for existence—Nancy argues that we are charged or tasked with our existence. Human being is obliged to exist: it *is*, and it *has to be*. The perspective deepens our phenomenological focus on human existential fate (Heidegger's *concern*, to say nothing of the experience of dread) by adding to it an ontological-political challenge: not simply the grace of giving oneself for the good of all but the labor of being. We are tasked with our *with*, a sign of the *co*-existential situation in which *we* (each one of us) are already in contact linguistically-ontologically, neither completely different nor completely the same together, both self/same and different/other in communication. The fact of human being as being-*with*, indicated by this preposition, is loaded with a demand for thinking. Nancy writes, "Being-together is a *condition* [a sign of conscious awareness] before becoming a *value* (or a countervalue) [a representation of awareness of awareness, a perception], and if it must be a value it can only be one in the sense of that which cannot be *evaluated* [a necessary condition]. . . . This instead raises the question of how to think the condition of being-together other than as derived from a subject, individual or collective, and on the contrary to think no 'subject' without starting from and in this condition."[80]

In short, the question that must motivate living, if not merely thinking (the "driving question" of continental philosophy[81]), is how to safeguard our shared human condition, our mutual relation or *being-with* that we are in its stripped-down, essential feature: namely, to be without essence, our abandoned being. The task is urgent in order to predict and prepare for efforts in this task that may harden into abstract, restrictive appeals to community, or over protection from it (communication as immunization), rather than the more difficult albeit no less individually threatening work of maintaining openness and coexposure to one another.

Being-With and Philosophy of Communication

Nancy's most compelling insight into this task is offered by way of his discussion of *Mitdasein*. For him, *Dasein* in its Heideggerian usage must be understood not merely as a term designating the being-there of human being but being-open, or more precisely, being *the open* itself, an original, singular standing out (*ek-stasis*) of being. Claire Colebrook defines the concept of "open" with reference to Agamben:

> The primary mode of relating is towards the "opening"—not what is simply given as present, but what is offered in terms of potential action, creation, and world production. Humans, after all, do not simply have an environment but are altered or defined according to the degree to which their world is open. (There is, in modernity, an increasing contraction of such an opening, for the world is less and less presented as a domain of potentiality and creation, and more and more as so much fully actualized life that is simply to be managed).[82]

What is at stake for Nancy is to make explicit Heidegger's initial positing of coextensiveness—that is, the mode of being-with indicated in the latter's concept of *Mitsein* (being-together). For Nancy, however, being-with or coextensiveness should not be taken as a dimension added on to an otherwise insulated self (the human *Dasein*), one that can return to itself after being with others. Rather, the crucial point is that *with* defines being, the being of all beings, including human being, the so-called self. As Raffoul explains, coextensiveness for Nancy means, "above all, that the self, as such, is exhausted in the relation-to-another, in the 'with' of Being-with."[83] After all is taken away, or reduced, there is nothing more to being than to be-*with*—an ontologically primary relation of com-*muni*-cation.

To make the point, Nancy insists that *Dasein* is, by definition, self-exposure. "To be itself [*Dasein*] is to expose *itself*"[84]—that is, to *be* the *with* that defines being as *being-with*. *Mitdasein*, in distinction from Heidegger's *Mitsein*, is intended to do the philosophical work of calling our awareness to the *with*, or the *co-* of co-extensiveness, or put yet another way, the *in* of being-in-common. *Mitdasein* means neither with-*there-being* (*Mit-da-Sein*) nor being-*there-with*, as we may find ourselves together in a room. Rather, it means being-with-*there*—that is, not merely being ahead of oneself (*Da-sein*) but being with the open, ex-*sisting* (standing out, but not taken out, ex-*capere*), being exposed.[85] *Mitdasein* in short, must be understood as *being-with* the exposure of being, of being "open to the *with*," Nancy says, "while being with or in the open."[86]

Taken in that light, all of this matters as perspective on the task of thinking about community and human communication, which is nothing less than a task, or challenge, of thinking about existence as co-existence, of common as being *in*-common. It is a philosophy of "communication" as the embodied relation that we are and have in common. "The self does not simply stand *in* relation," Raffoul explains, "it *is* that very relation. The self *is* the 'in' of Being-in-common."[87] For Nancy, the task of thinking, which, to repeat, is ours together and not only a task of philosophy, is to think the *with* "as" the relation (the *this is*) that we are, that we have to be, and within which we are exposed (in-common), each one of us to another. He writes, "Thinking the in-common means thinking it beyond those who are in this in-common; the community is not simply the 'collection' of the communicators, nor is it a function of them. It is the interval between them, and this interval is irreducible to its 'components.'"[88] Such a task—of being, thinking, and writing with it in mind—protects the space of the interval between us (the fact of being only by way of being-with one another in a relation of potential action) by keeping it open (in awareness of our shared exposure) rather than stitching it up, say, by mythologizing community, or essentializing identity. It remains a challenge for the coexistence of beings "among which," Nancy says, "the possibility of sense circulates indefinitely."[89]

To be sure, for Nancy "open" is not intended to mean receptive, warmly welcoming, or worse, merely tolerant. Rather, it is the ontological condition, and at times the terror, of human being's world exposure.[90] If "the open" or openness is the lived-through effect of being-in-common, and for that reason exposure to others who share in that opening as a basic ontological condition of being human (i.e., of community as the experience and meaning of not sameness but rather difference), then thinking about that condition is an urgent feature of being human. "Not only are people strange," Nancy reminds us, "but they do not recognize one another and approach one another only with difficulty, obliged to overcome at least a certain mistrust, and sometimes a fear or even repulsion."[91] It is in this precise, critical sense that the task of being aware of being-with must be understood as an ontological obligation first, and only later—much later—a so-called ethical obligation.[92] It is in fact a "pre-ethical condition" about which we are tasked with thinking.[93] The task of thinking and writing about community derives from the very condition of being together, the ontological fact of our being-with *as* open to one another.

How can such a perspective apply to daily life, to subjectivity, to community and/or to human communicating? Is this merely a call for charity? To answer the second question, I would say it is not. But if it is, then perhaps by "charity" what we must bear in mind is donation, a giving of oneself for community (cum-*munus*), a self-giving not simply out of grace or moral obligation, but for life, for having-to-be in defense of the space and time (the openness) for difference, disagreement, and for speech, even if not to be heard. It is a giving for interaction, even if not to achieve agreement, to say nothing of affinity. Nancy offers perspective on being-with *as* the open and *with* as its sign, a sign of the relation that each one of us is, holds in common, and through which sense is made.

In light of the *there* within which the being-in-common of human being is exposed (we are all exposed in mutual contact with our world environment and with one another), *being-with* calls attention to the spacing-timing of being that shapes human experience by way of cutting into and interrupting its consistency. It calls attention to *we* as our basic ontological condition and shared context—banal as that is. What Nancy's philosophy helps us recognize is how discourses on community are no more, and yet no less, than discourses about an opening, a world opening, a relation of potential that cannot be closed, an exteriorization of interiority that cannot be got rid of no matter how hard we try to explain it away—a wound, in other words, that is inoperable.[94] Being in contact and communication (Cicero's *conloquium evocare*), and being tasked with preserving the *with* of that condition (being with and *in* the open), we are exposed and abandoned, exposed in our abandonment, not only to language and the discourses it enables but also as the embodied openings through which sense and meaning circulate.[95]

With regard to the question of applying this perspective to daily life, we can say that philosophy is a practical way to think about the world. With regard to thinking about human communication, community, and embodied being, the contemporary continental philosophy advanced here connects directly with several communication, sociology, and anthropology discipline-based concerns that receive scholarly attention as topical studies of places of community, membership in community, and practices and experiences of building community. These include identity and difference, proximity and distance, group discourse and conflict, meaning-making and misinformation, and so on. What contemporary continental philosophy offers to human communication study is perspective with which to work through conceptual horizons that structure ways of thinking about difference, identity, corporeality and so on as relations of *communication*. It is against the backdrop of struggles to realize community that we are reminded that community is always experienced in and through communication, which not only precedes each of us ontologically but also is experienced in the vocabulary we use routinely, sometimes unreflectively, to bring structure and meaning (sense) to our communities.[96]

The importance of contemporary continental philosophy of communication cannot be understated. In one respect, attending to the language and embodied experience of being-with builds on philosophical efforts to question the certainty of modern communication theory's humanist, self-identical, preformed subject.[97] Relevant to those philosophical efforts, a relational ontology, exemplified by a philosophy of *being-with*, broadens thinking about community as that which is organized by conflicting perspectives about what goes where, who's in, who's out, and why—discourses that struggle to seal openings and close boundaries, whose foundations are, as Derrida says, "sealed within a philosophy of the subject."[98] Although debates about community can be highly polarized between appeals to higher goods for the collective versus individual freedom, a contemporary continental philosophical perspective sheds light on their point of commonality: namely, the open (*munus*, coexistence) of both community and the individual. Exposing human being as essentially an exposure that lacks a closed identity (is interdependent in its being-with a world with other beings), helps us, in turn, keep sight of the opening, wound, or lack that remains at the heart of any community and all communication.

Epilogue

This book engages the work of Giorgio Agamben, Roberto Esposito, Jean-Luc Nancy, and Lacanian psychoanalysis as perspectives on relation—that is, of *communication*. When considered together, the orientation in thinking about human consciousness, embodiment, and co-being invited by these perspectives demonstrates what human communication inquiry can look like, and accomplish, in a contemporary continental philosophical key. To support that argument, themes addressed throughout this book include language and the formation of the communicative subject; the uncertainty of communication and the limits of language (chapter 1); the law and order of communication and the injunction of noncommunication; the sovereignty and self-reference of language in instances of speech; the abandonment of human being to language and the obligation to communicate (chapter 2); the taking place of community in communication as contact and contagion; the threat and protection of identity boundaries by communication and-as immunization (chapter 3); body as an index of human coexistence and medium of coexposure (chapter 4); and *being-with* as a sign of the breaking-through of the lived world in human communication (chapter 5). Thinking about communication, embodiment, and community in terms of the experience of language, abandonment, immunization, and dis-integration, this monograph challenges many common assumptions, constructs, and problems of human communication while stimulating new questions for future inquiry.

I want to return here to the distinction drawn between communication and noncommunication, the examination of which I hope readers will appreciate as a new point of entry for contemporary continental philosophical investigation of the role played by language in the constitution of the communicative subject. In contrast to a transmission model, which runs the risk of presupposing an already existing sender-subject and measures communication in terms of the success, failure, or clarity of transmission,[1] I applied a nondichotomous logic of inclusive exclusion to that distinction—logic that blurs the clarity of distinctions and the hierarchical organization of conceptual pairings such as self/other, us/them, home/foreign, interiority/exteriority, and communication/noncommunication. Doing so shifts attention to the ordered domain (the *nomos*) instituted by media of communication, which shapes and is shaped by subjects in mutual exposure within it, and adds perspective on the semiotic function of language as it mediates contexts of human interaction (communities) and the embodied cultural meanings that are made of life through it. Language provides an apparatus that preserves these contexts by helping resolve conflict within them (its jurisdiction). It is constitutive of the subjects to whom it is addressed, which is the outcome of its application—that is, its use in/as communication.

This raises a critical question: Is all human communication intentional? If communication is defined narrowly, and conservatively, as the intentional transfer of content—whether ideas, information, or forged documents among agents—then we may certainly assume that one *can* not communicate (chapter 2): I have nothing more to say; he chose not to write bad checks; she had nothing to share in the first place; your number has been blocked; my account has been deleted, and so on.[2] However, if the sense of communication as transfer/transmission is broadened to include affinity/association, exposure, contact and contagion, and "the expressive capacities of the human body, other bodies, and indeed of the world itself,"[3] as advanced in this book, then thinking about human communication shifts toward thinking about it as a process that shapes social relations, attitudes, beliefs, and the conditions for individual and group expression, agreement and disagreement, identity, difference, conflict and harmony (chapter 3). Focus also shifts, quite heavily, to the ontological condition of being enmeshed in social and economic institutions such as kinship and discourses of the market, race, gender, and sexuality[4] that address us, that we negotiate, and through which human-world interaction is made meaningful (chapter 1). Being with one another, which is to be enmeshed in a community semiotic matrix rather than isolated points in a transmission chain, means that in some circumstances some communication may be unintentional rather than explicitly motivated—in cold blood, as it were.[5]

Still, this is banal. The much-maligned transfer model of communication typically orients questions of human communicating to understanding, as with the uttering of "inner content" (message/encoding) from a pregiven location (sender-subject) to another (receiver/decoding).[6] However, it is in contrast to the subject/object, inner/outer dualisms of modern thought reflected in such models that Agamben, Esposito, Nancy, and contemporary Lacanian perspectives help inform thinking about human communication. For them, communication is relation, exposure, and contact among agents whose singular opening (a lack) functions as an invitation to community, a possibility of "contamination" inside rather than external and prior to an imagined purity of environments of interaction, expression/perception, sense/sensing, and meaning-making. The possibility of human communication opened by and against which communication protects (chapter 3) is a fundamental condition of intersubjective existence, an expressive life structured by social relations that are enabled, preserved, extended, and filled with meaning *by way of communicating* (language use in/as interaction). Nonintentional communication—which may include words taken out of context, slips of tongue, facial expression, bodily posture, tone of voice, and so on, the sense and contextual impact of which, psychoanalysis tells us, an agent may be unaware—offers support to the presupposition of the impossibility of noncommunication (chapter 2). Human being is by definition co-being, an expressive, perceptive, and embodied semiotic being, and subjectivity is intersubjectivity constituted by, rather than existing outside of, processes of communication. It is for that reason that we can say that human being is always *in* communication (in relation, contact), and therefore has *already* communicated, a condition of being both exposed to and guarded by communication's identity-breaking potential.[7]

Agamben's perspective in this regard makes clear that what is at stake in language as a basic ontological condition of human being's having-to-be is not merely communication as transmission but as affinity, the having-to-be-with others (com-*muni*-cation) in community. From this perspective, the imperative of communication—"one cannot not communicate"—may be understood as an injunction or command of being, of having-to-be-with one another in our abandonment to and by language. It is a command (what I call a ban) to which one gives oneself over in obligation, in one's making sense of *how* to be. That said, if we are willing to accept, or at least entertain, the perspective advanced in this book that one of the primary operative functions of communication is immunization (chapter 3), then we may understand better how communication operates with a law-like function (chapter 2), both protecting and threatening by enabling and limiting human expressive and perceptive agency.

As an immunizing function, human communication can be understood, once again, as process and as affinity—and not only or exclusively, and reductively, as message transfer (that's information theory). Human communication may occur within contexts opened by shared resources of expression and perception, including languages, media technologies of mass communication, and the bodies of beings that constitute expressive media in their own right (chapter 4). Subjects do not preexist communication but are inscribed, exposed, and shaped within domains opened or instituted by expressive media. With regard to human embodied being, it is from the outside inside (the foreignness at home of being a lived human body, an outside that is not the simple inverse of an inside) that existence shows itself and is sensed, both as psyche and as body—as life. Coexposure, of humans as well as other beings, is the embodied condition that invites what we call "community" (chapter 5). For its part, the inclusive-exclusionary logic described in this book brings a nondichotomous perspective to thinking about the order of human com-*muni*-cation (chapter 2), its opening and both negative and affirmative immunizing properties (chapter 3), which circumscribe and justify raising academic questions about intersubjectivity and intercorporeality (chapter 5) rather than presuppose them. This foregrounds basic, communication discipline-specific questions of transmission, reception, and interpretation as well as affinity/community, interactivity, and commonality that continue to guide modern com-muni-*cation* inquiry.

In one important respect, the philosophical perspective advanced in this book turns our attention to discourses as they compete in social formations. Discourses can be forged, promoted, and can spread—they are possible—within an order of human communication, out of which social-political identities emerge, articulate, change, can gain momentum, may alter public perception, and/or falter and fade. Thinking about communication as the threat of discord, disagreement, misinformation, and misunderstanding is not simply to characterize its effects (which are discursive, both identity breaking and shaping) as imminently destructive, as if communication is an external power through which one is embroiled in an eternal crisis of conflict due to the presence of others, whether foreigners, strangers, or neighbors. Rather, and in contrast, human communicating may be understood constructively, as that which restricts and enables, as threat and defense, as exposure and shoring up, as contamination and protective immunization—a relation mediating what modern philosophy posits as inner-outer, subject-object dualities. The contemporary continental philosophical perspective offered here not only calls into question the identity-making distinctions that underpin modern impulses (dreams and/or nightmares) to dominate whatever is judged as foreign, outside, and other but also helps blur and thereby unsettle the stability of those very distinctions in an effort to keep them open.

In this regard, Esposito's perspective is especially important because it explains how communication may protect individuals and communities from not only the threat of unraveling into states of disconnection, misunderstanding, and conflict but also the potentially more threatening problem of overprotection. Too much immunization of communication—that is, the domination of communication by containing and curbing differences of viewpoint, opportunities for expression, and freedom of interpretation that closes identity borders and draws one back into itself—threatens the potential for ongoing, open, and productive communication. Such a condition demands a protective response from immunizing protection itself, autoimmunization. Responding to the threat of too much protection by communication—accomplished, Esposito tells us, by a return to thinking the *munus* that opens community and communication—can secure the fact of human coexposure as an invitation to the common, the different, and the community. Opening self to other, communication (com-*muni*-cation) calls for practices of interaction, dialogue, and sharing (com-muni-*cation*) that can protect the possibility for information sharing, mutual understanding, agreement, learning, and affinity, and in doing so, retain the healthy threat of human coexposure that gives rise to uncertainty, new interpretation, interpersonal and intergroup disagreement, and thereby, perhaps, ongoing communication.

This book offers perspective on the openness of human communication and community indicated by bodies—the material, front line of communication—not merely as integrated and unified identities but as collections of parts, sensations, functions, and relations. As an index of existential relations, a body signifies openings to new, and different, configurations, connections, and communities. To think of a body as an index of co-existential relation also broadens perspective on communication: *community* is a sign of what (without being a "what") is lived meaningfully, in part, by way of the shared values that define it and that may be unwritten but are nevertheless embodied—that is, practiced in communication. Nancy's perspective matters in this regard because it shows how, despite the categories into which bodies are placed and through which meaning is made of them, a body is in fact fluid. That is, its internal functions can disrupt and betray the external (conscious) sense of a stable, independent, and fully integrated identity, whether that identity is individual or collective, thereby demonstrating that the experience of a body, a singular existence, is always plural.

Questioning modern philosophical suppositions about bodily wholeness and integrity by offering perspective on how a body is both integrated and dis-integrating helps confirm the concrete, material fact that *every body* is a body in relation, in contact coexistentially—a body that is ontologically already communicative. In that regard, what remains to be thought in Western philosophical discourse, according to Nancy, is the *co-* or *with* of human co-existence, co-exposure, and co-being—thought, that is, in terms (signs) other than *subjectivity*, *identity*, or *community*. The slow turn of contemporary continental philosophy from poststructuralism's linguistic paradigm to thought of the material, embodied world, which Nancy, Esposito, and Agamben's writings exemplify, meets with communication discipline-specific efforts that have for decades attended to the intersection of human consciousness, embodiment, language, and rhetoric as a proper interdisciplinary domain of communication philosophy. Emphasizing the embodied experience of human communication as contact, touch, co-being, and coexposure—and not only as the transfer and transport of ideas, knowledge, messages, and meanings—these intellectual efforts are now broadened in their contact, relation, and coexposure with the perspectives advanced in this book. The outcome is an example for contemporary philosophical thinking about communication, embodiment, and our communities to come.

NOTES

Introduction

1. Eugene Allen Gilmore and William Charles Wermuth, *Modern American Law: A Systematic and Comprehensive Commentary on the Fundamental Principles of American Law and Procedure*, vol. 3 (Chicago: Blackstone Institute, 1914), 251.

2. William Lawrence Clark and William Lawrence Marshall, *A Treatise on the Law of Crimes*, 2nd ed. (St. Paul, MN: Keefe-Davidson, 1905), 593; John M. Scheb and John M. Scheb II, *Criminal Law and Procedure*, 5th ed. (Belmont, CA: Wadsworth, 2008), 181; Albert H. Putney, *Criminal Law, Criminal Procedure, Wills, Administration*, vol. 10, *Examining Questions*, Popular Law Library (Minneapolis: Cree, 1908), 102.

3. Signature retroactively constitutes the institutional legitimacy, and thereby the effect, of law. See Roberto Esposito, *Immunitas: The Protection and Negation of Life* (Cambridge, UK: Polity, 2011), 34–35; Giorgio Agamben, *The Sacrament of Language: An Archaeology of the Oath*, trans. Adam Kotsko (Stanford, CA: Stanford University Press, 2011).

4. This is why crimes against financial institutions, such as the manufacture and circulation of counterfeit money, or bank robbery, carry severe penalties. These are considered to be moral crimes, intentional violations of the belief in a system of accumulation that formally underpins and sustains the hopes and dreams of millions of people.

5. Schutz calls this act "reflective attending." Alfred Schutz, *Phenomenology of the Social World*, trans. George Walsh and Fredrick Lehnert (Evanston, IL: Northwestern University Press, 1967), 102.

6. "*Guilt refers not to transgression, that is, to the determination of the licit and the illicit, but to the pure force of the law, to the law's simple reference to something.*" Giorgio Agamben, *Homo Sacer: Sovereign Power and Bare Life*, trans. Daniel Heller-Roazen (Stanford, CA: Stanford University Press, 1998), 27. Emphasis in all quotations is in the original unless indicated otherwise.

7. Putney, *Criminal Law*, 102.

8. *Oxford English Dictionary*, s.v. "communication," accessed July 2, 2018, http://www.oed.com/view/Entry/37309. I choose the *OED* as a reference point—rather than, for instance, a psychology or communication handbook—because of the perspective opened by its record of the historical usage of *communication* as a common term, a usage that has remained remarkably stable for centuries.

9. Raymond Williams, "Communication," in *Keywords: A Vocabulary of Culture and Society* (New York: Oxford University Press, 2014), 72–73.

10. I group the theories, models, and histories of communication together and refer to them generally as "modern theory of communication" or "modern communication theory," the corpus of which is enormous. A few North American exemplars of modern thinking about communication include the following: Edward Sapir, "Communication," in *Encyclopedia of the Social Sciences*, ed. Edwin R. A. Seligman (New York: Macmillan, 1930), 4:78–81; Harold D. Lasswell, "The Structure and Function of Communication in Society," *The Communication of Ideas* 37 (1948): 215–28; Claude E. Shannon and Warren Weaver, *Mathematical Theory of Communication* (Champaign: University of Illinois Press, 1949); Carl Iver Hovland, Arthur A. Lumsdaine, and Fred D. Sheffield, *Experiments in Mass Communication* (Princeton, NJ: Princeton University Press, 1949); Harold Adams Innis, *The Bias of Communication* (Toronto: University of Toronto Press, 1999); Harold Adams Innis, *Empire and Communications* (Toronto: University of Toronto Press, 2008); Wilbur Schramm, "How Communication Works," in *The Process and Effects of Mass Communication* (Champaign: University of Illinois Press, 1954), 3–26; George Gerbner, "Toward a General Model of Communication," *Audio Visual Communication Review* 4, no. 3 (1956): 171–99; Elihu Katz, "The Two-Step Flow of Communication: An Up-to-Date Report on an Hypothesis," *Public Opinion Quarterly* 21, no. 1 (1957): 61–78; David K. Berlo, *The Process of Communication: An Introduction to Theory and Practice* (New York: Holt, Rinehart and Winston, 1960); Joseph Klapper, *Effects of Mass Communication* (Glencoe, IL: Free Press, 1960); Paul Felix Lazarsfeld, Bernard Berelson, and Hazel Gaudet, *The People's Choice: How the Voter Makes Up His Mind in a Presidential Campaign* (New York: Duell, Sloan, and Pearce, 1944); Elihu Katz and Paul Felix Lazarsfeld, *Personal Influence: The Part Played by People in the Flow of Mass Communications* (New Brunswick, NJ: Transaction, 2009); Gregory Bateson, "Cybernetic Explanation," in *Steps to an Ecology of Mind: Collected Essays in Anthropology, Psychiatry, Evolution, and Epistemology* (Chicago: University of Chicago Press, 1972), 405–15; Paul Watzlawick, Janet H. Beavin, and Donald D. Jackson, *Pragmatics of Human Communication: A Study of Interactional Patterns, Pathologies and Paradoxes* (New York: Norton, 1967); Herbert Schiller, *Mass Communications and American Empire* (Boulder, CO: Westview Press, 1992); Maxwell E. McCombs and Donald L. Shaw, "The Agenda-Setting Function of Mass Media," *Public Opinion Quarterly* 36, no. 2 (1972): 176–87; Anthony Wilden, *System and Structure: Essays in Communication and Exchange* (London: Tavistock, 1984); Jay G. Blumler and Elihu Katz, *The Uses of Mass Communications: Current Perspectives on Gratifications Research* (Beverly Hills, CA: SAGE, 1974); Raymond Williams, "Communications as Cultural Science," *Journal of Communication* 24, no. 3 (1974): 17–25; Edmund Leach, *Culture and Communication: The Logic by Which Symbols Are Connected; An Introduction to the Use of Structuralist Analysis in Social Anthropology* (Cambridge, UK: Cambridge University Press, 1976); Michael J. Reddy, "The Conduit Metaphor: A Case of Frame Conflict in Our Language about Language," in *Metaphor and Thought* (Cambridge, UK: Cambridge University Press, 1993), 164–201; Dallas Walker Smythe, *Dependency Road: Communications, Capitalism, Consciousness, and Canada* (Norwood, NJ: Ablex, 1981); John Fiske, *Introduction to Communication Studies* (London: Routledge, 1990); Dennis McQuail, *Mass Communication Theory: An Introduction* (Thousand Oaks, CA: SAGE, 1994); Jürgen Habermas, *Theory of Communicative Action*. Vol. 1, *Reason and the Rationalization of Society* (Boston: Beacon Press, 1984); and James Carey,

Communication as Culture: Essays on Media and Society (New York: Routledge, 1989). For recent theory, see Gregory J. Shepherd, Jeffrey St. John, and Theodore G. Striphas, eds., *Communication As . . . Perspectives on Theory* (Thousand Oaks, CA: SAGE, 2006); and Gary Genosko, *Remodeling Communication: From WWII to the WWW* (Toronto: University of Toronto Press, 2012). For intellectual history, see Jesse Delia, "Communication Research: A History," in *Handbook of Communication Science*, ed. Charles R. Berger and Steven H. Chaffee (Beverly Hills, CA: SAGE, 1987), 20–98; Michael Dues and Mary Louise Brown, *Boxing Plato's Shadow: An Introduction to the Study of Human Communication* (New York: McGraw-Hill, 2004); Hanno Hardt, *Critical Communication Studies: Essays on Communication, History and Theory in America* (London: Routledge, 2008); Armand Mattelart and Michèle Mattelart, *Theories of Communication: A Short Introduction* (London: SAGE, 1998); Wendy Leeds-Hurwitz, "Crossing Disciplinary Boundaries: The Macy Conferences on Cybernetics as a Case Study in Multidisciplinary Communication," *Cybernetics* 37, nos. 3–4 (1994): 349–69; and John Durham Peters, "Democracy and Mass Communication Theory: Dewey, Lippmann, Lazarsfeld," *Communication* 11, no. 3 (1989): 199–220.

11. Leonard Lawlor, *Early Twentieth-Century Continental Philosophy* (Bloomington: Indiana University Press, 2012).

12. Briankle G. Chang and Garnet C. Butchart, "Introduction," in *Philosophy of Communication* (Cambridge, MA: MIT Press, 2012), 2.

13. Critique of modern philosophy's completely unified subject corresponds to a critique of essentialism, which Ian Angus defines as "a critical term referring to the pre-discursive notion that an expression has an internal meaning that could be determined without reference to the actual discursive formation in which it occurs." In the "discursive turn" of twentieth-century humanities, Angus explains, "human 'subjects' are thus redefined as subject-*positions*, as places within the field from which characteristic utterances originate. The field defines possible speakers through these subject-positions, as well as expressions, and the current critique of the 'essentialist subject' is a rejection of the notion that the subject exists prior to expression and 'enters into' language as a formed unity. Rather, it is suggested, the discursive formation itself encompasses expressions, speakers, and a field of discourse." Ian Angus, *Primal Scenes of Communication: Communication, Consumerism, and Social Movements* (Albany: SUNY Press, 2000), 9.

14. See, for example, Philippe Lacoue-Labarthe and Jean-Luc Nancy, *The Title of the Letter: A Reading of Lacan* (Albany: SUNY Press, 1992); Eduardo Cadava, Peter Connor, and Jean-Luc Nancy, eds., *Who Comes after the Subject?* (New York: Routledge, 1991); and Jean-Luc Nancy, *The Birth to Presence*, trans. Brain Holmes et al. (Stanford, CA: Stanford University Press, 1993).

15. Giorgio Agamben, *Language and Death: The Place of Negativity*, trans. Karen E. Pinkus with Michael Hardt (Minneapolis: University of Minnesota Press, 1991); Giorgio Agamben, *State of Exception*, trans. Kevin Attell (Chicago: University of Chicago Press, 2005); Agamben, *Homo Sacer*.

16. Roberto Esposito, *Communitas: The Origin and Destiny of Community*, trans. Timothy C. Campbell (Stanford, CA: Stanford University Press, 2010); Roberto Esposito, *Bíos: Biopolitics and Philosophy*, trans. Timothy C. Campbell (Minneapolis: University of Minnesota Press, 2008); Esposito, *Immunitas*.

17. In the introduction to *New French Philosophy*, Ian James confirms that all of the thinkers in that category (namely, new

French philosophy) "have come to reaffirm what one might call the 'materiality of the real' in the wake of the preceding generation's focus on language and signification." Ian James, *New French Philosophy* (Malden, MA: Polity, 2012), 7.

18. Some scholars have gone as far as to name the end of phenomenology "object oriented ontology." See Tom Sparrow, *The End of Phenomenology: Metaphysics and the New Realism* (Edinburgh: Edinburgh University Press, 2014).

19. James, *New French Philosophy*, 9.

20. On the one hand, it may seem odd and even inaccurate to include Lacan in the category of contemporary continental philosophy for the obvious reasons that his writings stand as a central movement in mid-twentieth-century European philosophy and that his work exemplifies the linguistic structuralism from which contemporary continental philosophers are slowly moving away. On the other hand, however, Lacanian psychoanalysis continues to develop in the current period of scholarship, and for that reason, the inclusion of it as contemporary continental philosophy is completely justified. See, for example, Derek Hook, *Six Moments in Lacan: Communication and Identification and Psychoanalysis* (New York: Routledge, 2018); Bruce Fink, *The Lacanian Subject* (Princeton, NJ: Princeton University Press, 1996); Lorenzo Chiesa, *Subjectivity and Otherness: A Philosophical Reading of Lacan* (Cambridge, MA: MIT Press, 2007); Slavoj Žižek, *The Plague of Fantasies* (New York: Verso, 1997); and Annie G. Rogers, *The Unsayable: The Hidden Language of Trauma* (New York: Random House, 2006), to name only a few sources of contemporary Lacanian psychoanalytic theory and research.

21. The philosophy of communication tradition that explicitly merges rather than detaches semiotics and phenomenology is recognized under the discipline name *communicology*. For scholars working within this discipline, "semiotic phenomenology" is the name of a method of communication inquiry that "locates the system of semiosis (expression) as a conjunction with the process of phenomenology (perception)." Richard Lanigan, "Television: The Semiotic Phenomenology of Communication and the Image," in *Semiotics of the Media: State of the Art, Projects, and Perspectives*, ed. Winfried Nöth (New York: Walter de Gruyter, 1997), 383. Central to the philosophy of communication defined by this method is the work of Lanigan, an American scholar whose corpus of writing on human speech, rhetoric, grammar, embodiment, and media of human communication, drawing from German and French as well as American philosophical traditions, is foundational to the relevance and institutional legitimacy of continental philosophy of communication in North America. As I argue in the final chapter of this volume, Nancy exhibits tendencies in his philosophy that align him closely with the spirit and intellectual aim of semiotic phenomenology *à la* Lanigan—namely, the creation of a vocabulary that helps address problems that modern philosophy has difficulty articulating: subject/object dualisms, the embodiment of language, and communication in/and as community.

22. See Chang's analysis of the "subjectivist thesis" of communication theory, what he calls "the ideology of the communicative." Briankle G. Chang, *Deconstructing Communication: Representation, Subject, and Economies of Exchange* (Minneapolis: University of Minnesota Press, 1996), xi, 17, 69–111.

23. Watzlawick, Beavin, and Jackson, *Pragmatics*.

24. Agamben, *Homo Sacer*, 29.

25. For example, in linguistics, "Every cultural pattern and every single act of social behavior involves communication in either an explicit or implicit sense," Edward Sapir, *Selected Writings in*

Language, Culture and Personality, ed. David Goodman Mandelbaum (Berkeley, CA: University of California Press, 1949), 104; in semiotics, "Any aspect of human activity carries the potential for serving as, or becoming a sign," Terence Hawkes, *Structuralism and Semiotics* (Berkeley, CA: University of California Press, 1977), 134; in phenomenology, "Man shows himself as the entity which talks," Martin Heidegger, *Being and Time*, trans. John Macquarrie and Edward Robinson (New York: HarperCollins, 1962), 208; in modern social theory, "Behavior does not 'contain' meaning intrinsically; rather, it is found to be meaningful by an act of interpretation," Anthony P. Cohen, *The Symbolic Construction of Community* (New York: Routledge, 2001), 17.

26. See Michael T. Motely, "On Whether One Can(not) Not Communicate: An Examination via Traditional Communication Postulates," *Western Journal of Speech* 54, no. 1 (1990): 1–20. See also Chang and Butchart, eds., *Philosophy of Communication*, 1–10.

27. "The presence of an embodied consciousness to itself is from the beginning its co-presence to a similarly embodied consciousness suspended in language whereby each explores its own horizon and overlap of spatial and temporal orientation in a world of things and persons, identities and purposes that are mine and thine." John O'Neill, *The Communicative Body: Studies in Communicative Philosophy, Politics, and Sociology* (Evanston, IL: Northwestern University Press, 1989), 10.

28. "Risk and protection strengthen each other reciprocally." Timothy C. Campbell, "*Bíos*, Immunity, Life: The Thought of Roberto Esposito," translator's introduction to *Bíos: Biopolitics and Philosophy*, by Roberto Esposito (Minneapolis: University of Minnesota Press, 2008), xviii.

29. "Systems function not by rejecting conflicts and contradictions, but by producing them as necessary antigens for reactivating their own antibodies." Esposito, *Bíos*, 49.

30. As Esposito explains, whoever is exempt from the obligation to others "places himself or herself outside the community," is alone because immune to what puts everyone else in common. Esposito, *Immunitas*, 6.

31. See, for example, Michel Foucault, *The Birth of Biopolitics: Lectures at the Collège de France, 1978–1979*, ed. Arnold I. Davidson, trans. Graham Burchell (New York: Palgrave Macmillan, 2008); Michael Hardt and Antonio Negri, *Multitude* (New York: Penguin, 2004); Agamben, *Homo Sacer*; and Timothy C. Campbell, *Improper Life: Technology and Biopolitics from Heidegger to Agamben* (Minneapolis: University of Minnesota Press, 2011); as well as Jean-Luc Nancy, *Being Singular Plural*, trans. Robert Richardson and Anne O'Byrne (Stanford, CA: Stanford University Press, 2000).

32. Esposito, *Immunitas*, 113. Cf. Henry: "Let us give a name right away to this single and essential reality of the community and its members: life. So, we can already say that the essence of community is life; every community is a community of living beings." Michel Henry, *Material Phenomenology*, trans. Scott Davison (New York: Fordham University Press, 2008), 119.

33. Esposito, *Immunitas*, 113.

34. Ibid., 17, 124.

35. "If in the past philosophy had the meaning of contemplating and gazing [*fissare*], today it means to open the eyes, eyes which had until now remained shut." Nancy, quoted in Roberto Esposito, Jean-Luc Nancy, and Timothy Campbell, "Dialogue on the Philosophy to Come," *Minnesota Review*, no. 75 (Fall 2010): 74.

36. As will be explained throughout this book, what holds us together is the "defect" that constitutes every one of us: human being is, by definition,

co-being, being-with-one-another. No individual being exists outside of its coexistence, its being with other beings. Human beings are, in that sense, lacking completion. Therefore, community is necessary. Community already *is*, however, because existence is by definition coexistence. For that reason, as Esposito argues, community is unrealizable. See Esposito, *Communitas*.

37. Campbell, "*Bíos*, Immunity, Life," xii.

38. Secondary literature on the philosophers discussed in this book is large, and growing. Some of the most helpful sources I have found devoted to Nancy are Ian James, *The Fragmentary Demand: An Introduction to the Philosophy of Jean-Luc Nancy* (Stanford, CA: Stanford University Press, 2006); Benjamin Hutchens, ed., *Jean-Luc Nancy: Justice, Legality and World* (New York: Bloomsbury, 2012); B. C. Hutchens, *Jean-Luc Nancy and the Future of Philosophy* (Montreal: McGill-Queen's University Press, 2005); Marie-Eve Morin, *Jean-Luc Nancy* (Malden, MA: Polity, 2012); and Christopher Watkin, *Phenomenology or Deconstruction? The Question of Ontology in Maurice Merleau-Ponty, Paul Ricoeur and Jean-Luc Nancy* (Edinburgh: Edinburgh University Press, 2009). Helpful secondary sources on Agamben include Leland de la Durantaye, *Giorgio Agamben: A Critical Introduction* (Stanford, CA: Stanford University Press, 2009); and Alex Murray and Jessica Whyte, eds., *The Agamben Dictionary* (Edinburgh: Edinburgh University Press, 2011). For secondary sources on Esposito, see Campbell, *Improper Life*; and Peter Langford, *Roberto Esposito: Law, Community and the Political* (New York: Routledge, 2015). Some of the most accessible volumes on the category of continental philosophy include David West, *Continental Philosophy: An Introduction* (Malden, MA: Polity, 2010); Richard Kearney, *Modern Movements in European Philosophy: Phenomenology, Critical Theory,* *Structuralism* (Manchester: Manchester University Press, 1994); and Lawlor, *Early Twentieth Century*.

39. Simon Glendinning, "What Is Continental Philosophy?," in *The Edinburgh Encyclopedia of Continental Philosophy*, ed. Simon Glendinning (Edinburgh: Edinburgh University Press, 1999), 5.

40. Exemplars of continental philosophy of communication, in Anglo-American contexts, that opened the possibility for the kind of perspective developed in the present volume, and with which the present research is aligned, include Richard Lanigan, *Speaking and Semiology: Maurice Merleau-Ponty's Phenomenological Theory of Existential Communication* (The Hague: Mouton, 1972); Chang, *Deconstructing Communication*; Vivian Sobchack, *The Address of the Eye: A Phenomenology of Film Experience* (Princeton, NJ: Princeton University Press, 1992); and Ramsey Eric Ramsey, *The Long Path to Nearness: A Contribution to a Corporeal Philosophy of Communication and the Groundwork for an Ethics of Relief* (Atlantic Highlands, NJ: Humanities Press, 1998).

Chapter 1

1. Chang, *Deconstructing*, 38–49. Other perspectives on human communication informed by continental philosophy include Angus, *Primal Scenes*; Frank J. Macke, *The Experience of Human Communication: Body, Flesh, and Relationship* (Lanham, MD: Fairleigh Dickinson University Press, 2015); and Isaac E. Catt, *Embodiment in the Semiotic Matrix: Communicology in Peirce, Dewey, Bateson, and Bourdieu* (Lanham, MD: Fairleigh Dickinson University Press, 2017).

2. Further detail on psychoanalysis as related to communication inquiry may be found in Jacques Lacan, *The Language of*

the Self: The Function of Language in Psychoanalysis, trans. Anthony Wilden, 2nd ed. (Baltimore: Johns Hopkins University Press, 1981); Anthony Wilden, *The Rules Are No Game: The Strategy of Communication* (New York: Routledge, 1987); Wilden, *System and Structure*, a landmark contribution to modern communication theory; and Wilden's 1968 translation of Lacan's "Rome Discourse," in *The Language of the Self*, a work overshadowed by translations by Alan Sheridan, *Écrits: A Selection* by Jacques Lacan (New York: Norton, 1977); Bruce Fink, *Écrits: A Selection* by Jacques Lacan (New York: Norton, 2002); and *Écrits: The First Complete Edition in English* by Jacques Lacan (New York: Norton, 2007) but brimming nevertheless with insight into Lacan's relevance to communication philosophy. For a pragmatic application of the theory of transference to the study of rhetoric, Loyd S. Pettegrew's article, "Psychoanalytic Theory: A Neglected Rhetorical Dimension," *Philosophy & Rhetoric* 10, no. 1 (1977): 46–59 offers a lucid introduction; Michael J. Hyde, "Jacques Lacan's Psychoanalytic Theory of Speech and Language," *Quarterly Journal of Speech* 66, no. 1 (1980): 96–118 offers an excellent overview of structuralist concerns of Lacan's theory of language and the phenomenological and hermeneutic goals of the analytic interview.

3. Jacques Lacan, "Seminar on 'The Purloined Letter,'" trans. Jeffrey Mehlman, *Yale French Studies* no. 48 (1972): 39–72; Jacques Lacan, *The Seminar of Jacques Lacan, Book I: Freud's Papers on Technique, 1953–1954*, trans. John Forrester (New York: Norton, 1991); Jacques Lacan, *The Seminar of Jacques Lacan: The Four Fundamental Concepts of Psychoanalysis*, ed. Jacques-Alain Miller, trans. Alan Sheridan (New York: Norton, 1998); Lacan, *Écrits*, trans. Bruce Fink (2007); Lacan, *Language of the Self*.

4. Lacan, *Écrits*. I use the 2007 Fink translation for this and future references to *Écrits*.

5. Aloysius P. Martinich, *Communication and Reference* (Hawthorne, NY: Walter de Gruyter, 1984).

6. Wilden, *Rules*, 132.

7. Ibid.

8. Ana-María Rizzuto, "The Talking Cure and the Analyst's Intentions," *Psychoanalytic Review* 95, no. 5 (2008): 736.

9. Wilden, *Rules*, 132.

10. For a comprehensive summary of these registers, see Chiesa, *Subjectivity and Otherness*.

11. See Lacan's "Purloined Letter" and *Freud's Papers on Technique*.

12. Richard Kearney, *Modern Movements*, 276.

13. See Walter Benjamin on the messianic quality of language: "All language communicates itself." Walter Benjamin, *Reflections: Essays, Aphorisms, Autobiographical Writings*, ed. Peter Demetz (New York: Harcourt Brace Jovanovich, 1978), 316.

14. In addition to what Watzlawick, Beavin, and Jackson, *Pragmatics*, identify as the report and command functions of a statement, what is also communicated by a statement is the *fact* of language, its presence. Language says, this is language and not something else. Cf. Heidegger: "Whenever something is communicated in what is said-in-the-talk, all talk about anything has at the same time the character of *expressing itself*," and "Discourse which expresses itself is communication." Heidegger, *Being and Time*, 205, 211.

15. See Watzlawick, Beavin, and Jackson, *Pragmatics*; Wilden, *System and Structure*; Richard Lanigan, *Phenomenology of Communication: Merleau-Ponty's Thematics in Communicology and Semiology* (Pittsburgh: Duquesne University Press, 1988); and Jacqueline M. Martinez, *Communicative Sexualities* (Lanham, MD: Lexington Books, 2011), to name only a few.

16. See Rogers, *The Unsayable*; Ana-María Rizzuto, "Speech Events, Language Development, and the Clinical Situation," *International Journal of Psychoanalysis* 83, no. 6 (2002): 1325–43; Rizzuto, "Talking Cure."

17. Joseph D. Lichtenberg, Frank M. Lachmann, and James L. Fosshage, *A Spirit of Inquiry: Communication in Psychoanalysis* (Hillsdale, NJ: Analytic Press, 2002): 126.

18. Alexandre Stevens, "Lacanian Interpretation," *Hurly-Burly: The International Lacanian Journal of Psychoanalysis* 1 (2009): 58.

19. Rizzuto, "Speech Events," 1326.

20. "What the person has not said, but is frequently insinuated or clearly audible in the pronunciation of the communication and the type of words selected, points to other representational realms and feelings that cannot be explicitly revealed, but that are nonetheless present nonconsciously in the speaker's mind." Rizzuto, "Talking Cure," 738.

21. Kearney, *Modern Movements*, 277.

22. Rizzuto, "Speech Events," 1326.

23. Stevens, "Lacanian Interpretation."

24. See Mignon Nixon, "On the Couch," *October* 113 (2005): 39–76.

25. Lacan famously locates the analyst as follows: "It is to the Other beyond the other that the analyst cedes place . . . , and if he keeps silent, it is to let the Other speak." Lacan, *Language of the Self*, 140.

26. Lichtenberg, Lachmann, and Fosshage, *Spirit of Inquiry*.

27. In the discipline of contemporary rhetorical studies, Gunn has examined the significance of "what is being spoken and how it has been said over a lifetime" in the analysis of "fantasy," a psychoanalytic concept linking desire and communication to the process through which lived experience is made meaningful by the subject in its entry into culture. He defines fundamental fantasy as "the narrative that a subject has internalized to explain to herself the cause of her desiring. [It] protect[s] the subject from the Real of her division, enabling a sense of agency." Joshua Gunn, "Refitting Fantasy: Psychoanalysis, Subjectivity, and Talking to the Dead," *Quarterly Journal of Speech* 90, no. 1 (2004): 10–11. In response to Gunn's article, Lundberg calls attention to the missing importance of "the status of the Other as the Symbolic." See Christian Lundberg, "The Royal Road Not Taken: Joshua Gunn's 'Refitting Fantasy: Psychoanalysis, Subjectivity, and Talking to the Dead' and Lacan's Symbolic Order," *Quarterly Journal of Speech* 90, no. 4 (2004): 499, a position similar to my understanding of Lacan's theory of subjectivity as relevant to human communication inquiry. Later, I address the division of the subject in language and its potential for expressive agency. However, the point here is to bring to philosophical conversations about communication (of which the rhetorical theory identified here is part) a critical focus on the possibility and uncertainty of this phenomenon as shown by psychoanalysis.

28. Lacan, *Écrits*, 257.

29. See Hyde for a clear discussion of the hermeneutic process of determining "how the patient used language at crucial moments to move from prephenomenal experience to phenomenal experience wherein the symptom [of his or her suffering] became apparent." Hyde, "Jacques Lacan," 107.

30. For a critique of the certainty of communication posited by social scientific approaches to its study, see Isaac E. Catt, "Communication Is Not a Skill: Critique of Communication Pedagogy as Narcissistic Expression," in *Communicology: The New Science of Embodied Discourse*, ed. Deborah Eicher-Catt and Isaac E. Catt (Lanham, MD: Fairleigh Dickinson University Press, 2010), 144. In an essay on Bateson, Catt argues that "communication is neither message nor code. Context

serves the communicative function of illuminating meaning. That which creates context is neither sign nor semiotics but, rather, the phenomenology of the sign. . . . Discourse is often visible but communication is not." Isaac E. Catt, "Gregory Bateson's 'New Science' in the Context of Communicology," *American Journal of Semiotics* 19, no. 1 (2003): 167–68.

31. Angus, *Primal Scenes*, 70.

32. Jean-Luc Nancy, *Corpus*, trans. Richard A. Rand (New York: Fordham University Press, 2008), 65.

33. The full quote is as follows: "If my voice is mine because it comes from me, it can only be known as mine because it also *goes from me*. My voice is, literally, my way of taking leave of my senses. What I say goes." Steven Connor, *Dumbstruck: A Cultural History of Ventriloquism* (Oxford: Oxford University Press, 2000), 7.

34. For example, Hacking, in his book *Rewriting*, examines how psychiatric classification of emotional disorders has the power to impact the behavior and self-conceptions of people who interpret their experiences through such classifications. He calls this phenomenon "semantic contagion," the public description of a disorder (its symbolic reification in diagnostic manuals and measures, as well as treatments, such as therapy and support groups), which offers the means for the lived embodiment of the disorder to spread. Ian Hacking, *Rewriting the Soul: Multiple Personality and the Sciences of Memory* (Princeton, NJ: Princeton University Press, 1998).

35. Agamben, *Language and Death*, 44.

36. Lacan, *Écrits*, 83.

37. "To listen is to be straining toward a possible meaning, and consequently one that is not immediately accessible." Jean-Luc Nancy, *Listening*, trans. Charlotte Mandell (New York: Fordham University Press, 2007), 6.

38. "*Entendre*, 'to hear,' also means *comprendre*, 'to understand,' as if 'hearing' were above all 'hearing say' (rather than 'hearing sound'), or rather, as if in all 'hearing' there had to be a 'hearing say,' regardless of whether the sound perceived was a word or not." Ibid.

39. The "how" of a message in its delivery is its co-called report function, a comment on the nature of the relation between speakers. For example, the simple request to "pass the salt" may be received, or intended, to indicate disdain for the person who prepared the meal.

40. Ferdinand de Saussure, *Course in General Linguistics*, ed. Charles Bally, Albert Sechehaye, and Albert Riedlinger, trans. Wade Baskin (New York: McGraw-Hill, 1966), 141–68.

41. John P. Muller and William J. Richardson, *The Purloined Poe: Lacan, Derrida & Psychoanalytic Reading* (Baltimore: Johns Hopkins University Press, 1988), 98.

42. Jonathan Culler, *Ferdinand de Saussure* (Ithaca, NY: Cornell University Press, 1986), 39.

43. Ibid., 39.

44. Bruce Fink, *Lacan to the Letter: Reading "Écrits" Closely* (Minneapolis: University of Minnesota Press, 2004), 7.

45. Drawing on studies of sensory stimulation of infants, Rizzuto argues that patients who accept psychoanalytic treatment do so out of hope: "The experience of having been contacted as a self by the maternal voice bestows upon the spoken word a sense of hope about the voice and words of the mother, and later of other people, the hope that one can be found psychically when one is lost and can be helped when in need." Rizzuto, "Talking Cure," 735. What is shown by this idea of the hope of finding oneself in contemporary psychoanalysis is the absence of any guarantees of being understood, recognized, or heard in the process of communication.

46. Ibid., 745.

47. Sigmund Freud, "Psychical (or Mental) Treatment," in *A Case of Hysteria:*

Three Essays on Sexuality and Other Works, trans. James Strachey (1953; repr., London: The Hogarth Press, 1975), 283.

48. Ibid., 292.

49. Nixon, "On the Couch," 68.

50. "I identify myself in language, but only by losing myself in it like an object." Lacan, *Écrits*, 84. See also Heidegger: "Everyone is the other, and no one is himself." Heidegger, *Being and Time*, 165. See also Gusdorf: "To speak is to alienate oneself in order to mingle with others." Georges Gusdorf, *La parole*, trans. Paul T. Brockelman (Evanston, IL: Northwestern University Press, 1965), 81.

51. Lundberg, "Royal Road," 308.

52. Lacan, *Four Fundamental Concepts*, 207.

53. Lacan, *Écrits*, 156.

54. Rizzuto, "Speech Events," 1337.

55. Macke, in *Experience*, examines the significance of attachment and anxiety to the embodied experience of communication. Of particular import is his nuanced discussion of the interplay of the "I" and "me" in that intrapersonal experience.

56. Ghyslain Levy, "Un patient est remboursé; ou, Variations sur le thème du paiement et de ses diverses alternatives dans la situation analytique," *Psychanalystes: Revue du Collège des Psychanalystes* 20 (1986): 21.

57. Slavoj Žižek, *For They Know Not What They Do: Enjoyment as a Political Factor* (New York: Verso, 2002), xxxix.

58. Rizzuto, "Talking Cure," 734.

59. For a fascinating case of a client who undertook a lengthy course of psychotherapy only to discover, to her horror, that the image she had of herself (the love object of another man) was never there to begin with, see Irvin D. Yalom, *Love's Executioner and Other Tales of Psychotherapy* (New York: Perennial, 2000).

60. Lacan, *Freud's Papers*, 3.

61. Stevens, "Lacanian Interpretation," 57.

62. Lacan, *Écrits*, 44.

63. Ibid., 91.

64. Jacques Lacan, *Television: A Challenge to the Psychoanalytic Establishment*, trans. Denis Hollier, Rosalind Krauss, Annette Michelson, and Jeffrey Mehlman (New York: Norton, 1990), 3.

65. "All of one's lived experiences are not meaningful.... Only those experiences can be remembered and made meaningful that occur after the symbolic entry into language. Only those lived experiences wherein one had the potential to think can be recalled by thought; for thought is constrained by that which it is, language. Thought cannot think in terms of that which it is not." Hyde, "Jacques Lacan," 105.

66. Wilden, *System and Structure*, 186.

67. Angus, *Primal Scenes*, 70.

68. For a corresponding critique of the inner/outer distinction of expression in Husserl's phenomenology of communication, see Angus, *Primal Scenes*, 67–74. With regard to the here and now of expression, or what he calls a "primal scene" of communication, Angus argues that an "utterance is not concerned with 'internal' meaning, but with the 'lateral' construction of social relations through the indication of the content of other minds and the evaluative accent given to a certain way of life." Angus, *Primal Scenes*, 74.

69. Frank J. Macke, "Intrapersonal Communicology: Reflection, Reflexivity, and Relational Consciousness in Embodied Subjectivity," *Atlantic Journal of Communication* 16, no. 3–4 (2008): 133.

Chapter 2

1. *Language* here is broadly construed, including spoken and written language, nonverbal language, the language of art

and electronic media, fashion as a language, and so on.

2. See chapter 1 of the present volume for psychoanalytic studies of communication; for a deconstructive perspective on the authority of language and discourse in organizations, one that communicates through, and animates, speaking agents, see François Cooren, "Communication Theory at the Center: Ventriloquism and the Communicative Constitution of Reality," *Journal of Communication* 62, no. 1 (2012): 1–20. For pioneering work in continental communication philosophy of language, speech, and speaking, see Lanigan, *Speaking and Semiology*; Lanigan, *Phenomenology*; and Richard Lanigan, *The Human Science of Communicology: A Phenomenology of Discourse in Foucault and Merleau-Ponty* (Pittsburgh: Duquesne University Press, 1992). For recent semiotic phenomenology of human communication, see Macke, *Experience*; and Martinez, *Communicative Sexualities*.

3. Watzlawick, Beavin, and Jackson, *Pragmatics*.

4. *Injunction* is to be understood in the same sense that Fynsk brings to Heidegger's notion of *Geheiss* [G. order, command]: "An injunction that sounds as language gives itself in its essence as the opening of a relation to what it is. The injunction is that all should respond (to the injunction); in its historical character . . . it is at the origin of community." Christopher Fynsk, "A Note on Language and the Body," *Paragraph* 16, no. 2 (1993): 192. Cf. Chang, for what he calls the "imperative of communication." Chang, *Deconstructing*, 226.

5. "It is a speaking man whom we find in the world, a man speaking to another man, and language provides the very definition of man." Émile Benveniste, *Problems in General Linguistics*, ed. Mary Elizabeth Meek (Miami: University of Miami Press, 1973), 224.

6. Agamben, *Language and Death*, 29.

7. These questions reflect the preoccupation of Benveniste in his classic essay, "Subjectivity in Language," where he asks, "By what right does language establish the basis of subjectivity? As a matter of fact, language is responsible for it in all of its parts." Benveniste, *Problems*, 225.

8. I am not the first to have identified the inside-outside problematic of communication. See Angus, *Primal Scenes*, 23–26.

9. For example, Shannon and Weaver, *Mathematical Theory*, 109.

10. "In regarding the production of 'noise' as extrinsic to the content of a medium, the transportation model conceals its politics. . . . There is a contradiction inherent in the transmission model such that the introduction of extrinsic noise appears as equivalent to the production of new information. In a manner characteristic of ideological thought, this contradiction is neither addressed or resolved within the transmission model, but is simply arbitrarily and stipulatively removed." Angus, *Primal Scenes*, 128.

11. Chang, *Deconstructing*, 33–67.

12. On the self-announcement of noise, see Greg Hainge, "Of Glitch and Men: The Place of the Human in the Successful Integration of Failure and Noise in the Digital Realm," *Communication Theory* 17, no. 1 (2007): 91–114.

13. The phrase "gearing into" is used by Donald A. Landes, *Merleau-Ponty and the Paradoxes of Expression* (New York: Bloomsbury, 2013).

14. Wilden, *System and Structure*, 187.

15. Agamben, *Homo Sacer*, 17–18.

16. Agamben explains, "The state of exception is thus not the chaos that precedes order but rather the situation that results from its suspension. In this sense, the exception is truly, according to its etymological root, *taken outside* (*ex-capere*), and not simply excluded." Ibid., 18.

17. "The 'outside' we are talking about must be situated inside while continuing

to be an outside, introjected as such, in a form that simultaneously eliminates and maintains the outside by leaving it external to that which it is nevertheless inside." Esposito, *Immunitas*, 30.

18. Agamben calls this a "zone of exception," or "zone of indifference," a location "where inside and outside do not exclude each other but rather blur with each other." Agamben, *Homo Sacer*, 23. He explains, "*The exception is what cannot be included in the whole of which it is a member and cannot be a member of the whole in which it is always already included.* What emerges in this limit figure is the radical crisis of every possibility of clearly distinguishing between membership and inclusion, between what is outside and what is inside, between exception and rule." Ibid., 25.

19. On grammar, logic, and rhetoric, see Richard Lanigan, "Information Theories," in *Theories and Models of Communication*, ed. Paul Cobley and Peter Schultz (Boston: De Gruyter Mouton, 2013), 61.

20. As Landes explains this basic semiotic principle, "Constituted language is not a pure set of meanings associated with signs, but the residue of a countless number of past expressive gestures that have sedimented into a structure of merely *relatively* stable acquired significations that themselves will be reshaped with each new repetition." Landes, *Merleau-Ponty*, 14.

21. For example, Saussure explains,

> Language is a well-defined object in the heterogeneous mass of speech facts. It can be localized in the limited segment of the speaking-circuit where an auditory image becomes associated with a concept. It is the social side of speech, outside the individual who can never create nor modify it by himself; it exists only by virtue of a sort of contract signed by the members of a community. Moreover, the individual must always serve an apprenticeship in order to learn the functioning of language; a child assimilates it only gradually. It is such a distinct thing that a man deprived of the use of speaking retains it provided that he understands the vocal signs that he hears. (Saussure, *Course*, 14)

22. Agamben, *Homo Sacer*, 21; original emphasis.

23. "If the exception is the structure of sovereignty, then sovereignty is not an exclusively political concept, an exclusively juridical category, a power external to law (Schmitt), or the supreme rule of the juridical order (Hans Kelsen): it is the originary structure in which law refers to life and includes it in itself by suspending it." Ibid., 28.

24. Benveniste, *Problems*; Benjamin, "On Language as Such and on the Language of Man," in *Reflections*.

25. "If, on the one hand, language merely shows, on the other discourse denotes, and this passage and relation are mediated by the potentiality of humans who are naturally able to progress, as well as individually capable of manipulating language." Paolo Bartolini, "Benveniste, Émile," in *The Agamben Dictionary*, ed. Alex Murray and Jessica Whyte (Edinburgh: Edinburgh University Press, 2011), 35.

26. De la Durantaye, *Giorgio Agamben*, 218.

27. Cf. Hall: "This 'subject' is not to be confused with lived historical individuals. It is the category, the position where the subject—the I of ideological statements—is constituted." Stuart Hall, "Signification, Representation, Ideology: Althusser and the Post-structuralist Debates," *Critical Studies in Media Communication* 2, no. 2 (1985): 102.

28. Benveniste, *Problems*, 226.

29. "It is in and through language that man constitutes himself as a *subject*,

because language alone establishes the concept of 'ego' in reality, in *its* reality which is that of the being." Ibid., 224.

30. "*Deixis*, or indication—with which their peculiar character has been identified, from antiquity on—does not simply demonstrate an unnamed object, but above all the instance of discourse, its taking place. The place indicated by the *demonstratio*, and from which only every other indication is possible, is a place of language. Indication is the category within which language refers to its own taking place." Agamben, *Language and Death*, 25.

31. "The passage from *langue* to *parole*, or from the semiotic to the semantic, is not a logical operation at all; rather, it always entails a practical activity, that is, the assumption of *langue* by one or more speaking subjects and the implementation of that complex apparatus that Benveniste defined as the enunciative function." Agamben, *State of Exception*, 39.

32. Agamben, *Language and Death*, 25.

33. In addition to works of Derrida, see also Chang, *Deconstructing*.

34. In chapter 5 of the present volume, I address the concept of *exscription*, a term Jean-Luc Nancy coins to question the relation between writing and its outside—namely, a body.

35. Benveniste, *Problems*, 226.

36. Werner Hamacher, "Ou, séance, touche de Nancy ici," *Paragraph* 16, no. 2 (1993): 218. See also Heron: "Once in language in the strictest sense it [the subject] cannot speak. It is neither inside nor outside language, but constitutes *the* outside *of* language, the pure fact that language exists." Nicholas Heron, "Subject," in *The Agamben Dictionary*, ed. Alex Murray and Jessica Whyte (Edinburgh: Edinburgh University Press, 2011), 188.

37. "Language is accordingly the possibility of subjectivity because it always contains the linguistic forms appropriate to the expression of subjectivity, and discourse provokes the emergence of subjectivity because it consists of discrete instances. In some way language puts forth 'empty' forms which each speaker, in the exercise of discourse, appropriates to himself and which he relates to his 'person,' at the same time defining himself as *I* and a partner to *you*. The instance of discourse is thus constitutive of all the coordinates that define the subject." Benveniste, *Problems*, 227.

38. Agamben, *Sacrament*, 71.

39. Benveniste, *Problems*, 229.

40. "The utterance *I swear* is the very act which pledges me, not the description of the act that I am performing. In saying *I promise, I guarantee*, I am actually making a promise or a guarantee. The consequences (social, judicial, etc.) of my swearing, of my promise, flow from the instance of discourse containing *I swear, I promise*. The utterance is identified with the act itself. But this condition is not given in the meaning of the verb, it is the 'subjectivity' of discourse which makes it possible." Ibid.

41. Agamben, *Sacrament*, 33.

42. Benveniste, *Problems*, 229.

43. Agamben, *Sacrament*, 55–56.

44. "In order for speech to be a vehicle of 'communication,' it must be so enabled by language, of which it is only the actualization." Benveniste, *Problems*, 224.

45. It is appropriate to note the qualification by Saussure, offered late in the *Course*, on the contract of language: "No longer can language be identified with a contract pure and simple, and it is precisely from this viewpoint that the linguistic sign is a particularly interesting object of study; for language furnishes the best proof that a law accepted by a community is a thing that is tolerated and not a rule to which all freely consent." Saussure, *Course*, 71.

46. Benveniste, *Problems*, 224.

47. "The particular structure of law has its foundation in [the] presuppositional structure of human language. It expresses

the bond of inclusive exclusion to which a thing is subject because of the fact of being in a language, of being named. To speak [*dire*] is, in this sense, always to 'speak the law,' *ius dicere*." Agamben, *Homo Sacer*, 21.

48. "Law has no existence for itself; rather, its essence lies, from a certain perspective, in the very life of men." Friedrich Karl von Savigny, quoted in ibid., ix. See also de la Durantaye, *Giorgio Agamben*, 203.

49. Agamben, *Homo Sacer*, 50. Agamben's thinking about language and law is informed by Nancy's writing on abandonment: "Abandoned being finds itself . . . remitted, entrusted, or thrown to this law that constitutes the law, this other and same, to this other side of all law that borders and upholds a legal universe: an absolute, solemn order, which prescribes nothing but abandonment. Being is not entrusted to a cause, to a motor, to a principle; it is not left to its own substance, or even to its own subsistence. It is—in abandonment." Nancy, *Birth*, 44.

50. "What has been banned is delivered over to its own separateness and, at the same time, consigned to the mercy of the one who abandons it—at once excluded and included, removed and at the same time captured." Agamben, *Homo Sacer*, 109–10.

51. Ibid., 50.

52. Ibid. Cf. Hamacher: "The banishment which enthralls—so, connexion, community, society, however they may be defined, whether as moral, hermeneutic or political, the law, whether of discussion, or conversation, or mere presence—this law, this enthralling, is an excommunication." Hamacher, "Ou, séance," 217.

53. "He who is banned is not, in fact, simply set outside the law and made indifferent to it but rather *abandoned* by it, that is, exposed and threatened on the threshold in which life and law, outside and inside, become indistinguishable. It is literally impossible to say whether the one who has been banned is outside or inside the juridical order." Agamben, *Homo Sacer*, 28–29.

54. Francois Raffoul, "Abandonment," in *Jean-Luc Nancy: Justice, Legality and World*, ed. B. C. Hutchens (New York: Continuum, 2012), 65–81.

55. Ibid., 73.

56. Ibid., 74. See also Nancy: "The origin of 'abandonment' is a putting at *bandon*. Bandon (*bandum, band, bannen*) is an order, a prescription, a decree, a permission, and the power that holds these freely at its disposal. To *abandon* is to remit, entrust, or turn over to such a sovereign power, and to remit, entrust, or turn over to its ban, that is, to its proclaiming, to its convening, and to its sentencing. One always abandons to a law." Nancy, *Birth*, 43–44.

57. Raffoul, "Abandonment," 74. He continues, "Dasein exists only in such a way that it projects itself towards possibilities in which it is thrown. What is has to be, then, what it has to assume and be responsible for, is precisely its being-thrown and abandonment as such." Ibid., 75.

58. For Agamben, the upshot of human being's ontological foundation in language—its experience of language's ban, or what I call the law of communication—is shame, or guilt. But it is not moral guilt: "The cipher of this capture of life in law is not sanction . . . but guilt (not in the technical sense that this concept has in penal law but in the originary sense that indicates a being-in-debt: *in culpa esse*). . . . *Guilt refers not to transgression, that is, to the determination of the licit and the illicit, but to the pure force of the law, to the law's simple reference to something*. This is the ultimate ground of the juridical maxim, which is foreign to all morality, according to which ignorance of the rule does not eliminate guilt." Agamben, *Homo Sacer*, 27.

59. "Abandonment respects the law; it cannot do otherwise. That does not mean that there is any question of a forced respect, one consequently deprived of the characteristic value of respect. That 'it cannot do otherwise' means it cannot be otherwise, it is not otherwise." Nancy, *Birth*, 44.

60. Agamben, *Language and Death*, 31–37. See also Nancy: "One abandons to a law, which is to say, always to a voice. . . . But here the voice is no longer an acoustic medium or the articulation of a discourse. The voice *constitutes* the law, to the extent that it orders; and, to that extent, the law *is* the voice." Nancy, *Birth*, 45.

61. "The utterance and the instance of discourse are only identifiable as such through the voice that speaks them . . . ," voice, that is, "as an intention to signify and as a pure indication that language is taking place." Agamben, *Language and Death*, 34.

62. "One must recognize that language is both the instrument and the product of speaking. Language in speaking can be existential by constituting meaning, or language can settle into a sediment after being spoken which is an essential meaning." Lanigan, *Speaking and Semiology*, 161. The notion of a "dead language," that which is no longer spoken, is relevant here.

63. Body image is at a spatial and temporal distance from bodily experience. It is this spatial-temporal gulf (the image is not here, it is out there, ahead of the body) that can never be overcome. It propels the subject to chase its image (a sign) for the remainder of its time.

64. Lacan, *Four Fundamental Concepts*, 207.

65. "Socially, we define ourselves with the law as go-between. It is through the exchange of symbols that we locate our different selves in relation to one another." Lacan, *Freud's Papers*, 140.

66. The point that the other is always another *self* is important. In the classic essay "The Problem of Society," Mead says, "Thinking is a process of conversation with one's self when the individual takes the attitude of the other, especially when he takes the common attitude of the whole group, when the symbol that he uses is a common symbol, so that it has a meaning common to the entire group, to everyone who is in it and anyone who might be in it." George Herbert Mead, "The Problem of Society: How We Become Selves," in *Movements of Thought in the Nineteenth Century*, ed. Merritt H. Moore (Chicago: University of Chicago Press, 1972), 366. As Merleau-Ponty puts it, "There is, then, a taking up of others' thought through speech, a reflection in others, an ability to think *according to others which* enriches our own thoughts." Maurice Merleau-Ponty, *Phenomenology of Perception*, trans. Colin Smith (New York: Routledge, 2004), 208.

67. Schutz, *Phenomenology*, 115. Landes describes the tension between the constraints and freedom of communication:

> The body is a natural power of expression that allows the child to see the other's gestures as immediately resonating with her own body. This fundamental *communication* provides the basis for being in the world together and for the origin of language itself. We enter into dialogue, we express more than either of us could have ourselves imagined on our own. And yet, we ultimately fall back into our own trajectories. . . . As soon as we break communication, the conversation settles into our respective pasts, and how we understand its significance or how it sediments such as to influence our potential future actions or speech acts will be different. We immediately begin to accumulate different experiences, which can reshape the sense of the

dialogue for each of us in dramatically different ways. The contingency of expression cannot be removed, the task is never completed, and so the responsible thing to do would be to embrace expression and communication as the constant task with no end at the open source of human existence in the shared world. (Landes, *Merleau-Ponty*, 98)

68. Susan Petrilli, "For a Critique of the Subject," *Southern Semiotic Review* 1, no. 1 (2013): para. 23. See also Gasché: "A name is the proper name, so to speak, of things' intention or mode of signification. In other words, in thus calling by their name the each-time-singular mode in which things yearn to speak, man completes language as communication *in actu*, by naming it. The name names language's each-time-particular mode of communicating, its mode of expression." Rodolphe Gasché, *Of Minimal Things: Studies on the Notion of Relation* (Stanford, CA: Stanford University Press, 1999), 72.

69. "The lived-body experience which is perception becomes the *matrix* from which existential speaking issues to create the *Lebenswelt* reflected in sedimented speech." Lanigan, *Speaking and Semiology*, 167.

70. Susan Petrilli, *The Self as a Sign, the World, and the Other: Living Semiotics* (New Brunswick, NJ: Transaction, 2013), 30.

71. Martinez, *Communicative Sexualities*, 72.

72. Benveniste, *Problems*, 230.

73. Angus, *Primal Scenes*, 55. See also Martinez: "Sign systems—of which language is the prime example—provide us with meaning structures that set particular kinds of limits and possibilities of human expression and perception that are connected directly to the structures and features of *spoken* language." Martinez, *Communicative Sexualities*, 59.

74. Landes, *Merleau-Ponty*, 21. It does so as "an incarnate entity, incorporeal and intersubjective sign materiality that not only relates to external bodies and signs but is itself a body in semiosis, a body-sign." Petrilli, *Self as Sign*, 7. As Kearney puts it, "expression does not exist apart from the body and the body does not exist apart from expression." Richard Kearney, "The Wager of Carnal Hermeneutics," in *Carnal Hermeneutics*, ed. Richard Kearney and Brian Treanor (New York: Fordham University Press, 2015), 41. See also Landes: "Perception is already *communication*, and being in the world is already *expression*." Landes, *Merleau-Ponty*, 97. See also Angus, *Primal Scenes*, 190.

75. Agamben, *Sacrament*, 68.

76. Martinez, *Communicative Sexualities*, 100.

77. "The world is humanity's exterior, but it is an exteriority also in me and to which I am exposed." Diane Perpich, "*Corpus Meum*: Disintegrating Bodies and the Ideal of Integrity," *Hypatia* 20, no. 3 (2005): 80.

78. What makes human language specific to human being, Agamben argues, is the fact that "man is not limited to acquiring language as one capacity among others that he is given but has made of it his specific potentiality; *he has, that is to say, put his very nature at stake in language*. Just as, in the words of Foucault, man 'is an animal whose politics places his existence as a living being in question,' so also is he *the living being whose language places his life in question*." Agamben, *Sacrament*, 68–69.

79. Martinez, *Communicative Sexualities*, 58.

80. Landes, *Merleau-Ponty*, 20.

81. "*Ontologically, communication has always and already occurred*. Communication precedes existence—*to be is to communicate*. . . . 'You cannot not communicate' does not simply mean that whatever one does carries meaning or that one's actions (including non-action)

will always be interpreted by (and hence mean something to) others. Rather, it voices the deeper ontological truth that one's very existence *is communication* between self and others, between self and world. Ontologically speaking, communication communicates; ontic exchanges of meaning between subjects, of information between machines, and so on are mere alibis of the event, the *taking-place*, of communication." Chang, *Deconstructing*, 110.

82. "*I* requires a mouth that opens, it requires me to have dragged myself, hurled myself, outside me beforehand, to have abandoned myself." Nancy, *Birth*, 38.

83. Irving Goh, *The Reject: Community, Politics, and Religion after the Subject* (New York: Fordham University Press, 2014), 244.

84. For a critique of this position, see Petrilli, *Self as Sign*.

Chapter 3

1. This chapter draws primarily from Esposito, *Communitas* and *Immunitas*. *Communitas* is devoted to the idea of community in the major works of Hobbes, Rousseau, Kant, Nietzsche, Heidegger, and Bataille, while *Immunitas* is thematically oriented toward explaining the philosophy and political implications of immunity. In the latter, Esposito addresses the works of Gigard, Luhmann, Haraway, and others while synthesizing his perspective with that of Benjamin (on violence and law), Foucault (on biopolitics), and Nancy and Agamben (on co-being and law). See also Roberto Esposito, *Third Person: Politics of Life and Philosophy of the Impersonal*, trans. Zakiya Hanafi (Cambridge, UK: Polity, 2012); Roberto Esposito, *Terms of the Political: Community, Immunity, Biopolitics*, trans. Rhiannon Noel Welch (New York: Fordham University Press, 2013); Roberto Esposito, *Living Thought: The Origins and Actuality of Italian Philosophy*, trans. Zakiya Hanafi (Stanford, CA: Stanford University Press, 2012); and Roberto Esposito, *Persons and Things: From the Body's Point of View* (Malden, MA: Polity, 2015).

2. Esposito, *Immunitas*, 1, 2.

3. Ibid., 2.

4. The temporal structure of information exchange makes prediction the chief concern of cybernetics and communication systems inquiry. As Halpern explains, "Information theory as emerging from cybernetics thus aspires to the future tense, while existing in a heterogeneous temporal state where the control of this future comes through the abstraction of processes from historical data to produce preprogrammed, self-contained conditions." Orit Halpern, "Dreams for Our Perceptual Present: Temporality, Storage, and Interactivity in Cybernetics," *Configurations* 13, no. 2 (2005): 290.

5. The research tradition of communicology has brought together the seemingly opposed intellectual traditions of semiotics and phenomenology under the name *semiotic phenomenology*, a methodology for human communication inquiry that "conceives of signs as the boundary media of consciousness." Isaac E. Catt, "Communicology and Human Conduct: An Essay Dedicated to Max," *Semiotica*, no. 204 (2015): 357.

6. Esposito, *Terms*, 18.

7. Ibid., 14.

8. Vanessa Lemm, "Biopolitics and Community in Roberto Esposito," introduction to Esposito, *Terms*, 3.

9. "The essence of community is not something that is; instead, it is that which (*cela*)—not being a that (*ça*)—occurs as the relentless arrival of life into oneself and thus the arrival of each one into itself." Henry, *Material Phenomenology*, 133.

10. Esposito, *Communitas*, 139.

11. "As impossible as it is, the community is necessary. It is our *munus* in the exact sense that we deeply carry responsibility for community." Ibid., 49. See also Henry: "Communities are multiple. The study of them is indispensable if one treats each one of them as being a variation of the *eidos* of community, a variation that would allow hitherto unperceived features to be conferred to this essence." Henry, *Material Phenomenology*, 134.

12. Esposito shares Nancy's perspective on what the latter calls the "autoproductive" and "autodestructive" quality of community: "It has to appropriate the in-common in order to become 'community' in an operative sense, and simultaneously, it cannot appropriate the in-common, for it would stop being 'community.' In the end, it is left with the discovery that it can never control its in-common—never control 'itself.'" Jean-Luc Nancy and Laurens ten Kate, "'*Cum*' . . . Revisited: Preliminaries to Thinking the Interval," in *Intermedialities: Philosophy, Arts, Politics*, ed. Henk Oosterling and Ewa Plonowska Ziarek (Lanham, MD: Lexington Books, 2011), 39.

13. "The community is nothing but this group of living individuals." Henry, *Material Phenomenology*, 121.

14. See Esposito, *Communitas*, 21–61.

15. Ibid., 140.

16. Ibid.

17. Esposito, *Terms*, 123–34. See Lemm, "Biopolitics," 4.

18. Esposito, *Immunitas*, 8.

19. See Esposito, *Communitas*, 20–61.

20. Esposito argues that neither Hobbes nor Rousseau could resolve the problem of community because, for them, the subjects of their philosophies were posited as undivided rather than as lacking and alienated and thereby closed to the sense of being-with others. If the subject is merely self-interested and closed to itself, then there is no contact and thus no community. As Esposito says, "They couldn't resolve it because the individual subject, undivided, and far from being an unconscious part of the community, is what bars the way and in fact is defined exactly by its own incommunicability: what lives *in* and *of* the inexistence of the other; that exists, subsists, and persists as if the other didn't exist. In brief, that survives it." Ibid., 73.

21. Esposito, *Immunitas*, 9. See Esposito, *Communitas*, 63–111.

22. Campbell, "*Bíos*, Immunity, Life," xvi.

23. Esposito, *Immunitas*, 10.

24. Ibid., 25.

25. Esposito, *Terms*, 127.

26. Lemm, "Biopolitics," 4.

27. Esposito, *Terms*, 127. See Esposito, *Communitas*, 41–61 (on Rousseau and solitude) and 63–85 (on Kant and the moral imperative).

28. "What the members of the community have in common is not a something, this or that, such as a patch of land or a job. Instead, they have in common the way in which these things are given to them. How are they given to them? They are given in and through life. But, our question must then be reformulated: How are things given in and through life? How is life given?" Henry, *Material Phenomenology*, 119.

29. Cf. Nancy: "What is proper to community, then, is given to us in the following way: it has no other resource to appropriate except the 'with' that constitutes it, the *cum* of a co-appearance, wherein we do nothing but appear together with one another, co-appearing before no other authority than this 'with' itself, the meaning of which seems to us to instantly dissolve into insignificance." Nancy, *Being Singular Plural*, 63. See chapter 5 of the present volume for perspective on "with" not as an afterthought but as the essential trait of human community and communication.

30. "The *munus* that the *communitas* shares isn't a property or a possession. It

isn't having, but on the contrary, is a debt, a pledge, a gift that is to be given, and that therefore will establish a lack. The subjects of community are united by an 'obligation,' in the sense that we say 'I owe *you* something,' but not 'you owe *me* something.' This is what makes them not less than the masters of themselves, and that more precisely expropriates them of their initial property (in part or completely), of the most proper property, namely, their very subjectivity." Esposito, *Communitas*, 6–7.

31. Esposito, *Terms*, 49.

32. Esposito, *Communitas*, 140.

33. Esposito, *Immunitas*, 24.

34. "Community is both that toward which all efforts of men and women who deserve to be called as such are oriented and also that which, given their natural unsociability, they will never be able to fully realize." Esposito, *Terms*, 24.

35. The "inoperative" is Nancy's term. Jean-Luc Nancy, *The Inoperative Community* (Minneapolis: University of Minnesota Press, 1991). See also chapter 5 of this volume.

36. Esposito, *Terms*, 130.

37. Ibid., 130.

38. Campbell, "*Bíos*, Immunity, Life," xv.

39. Pregnancy offers a clear example of the autoimmunization process, where a body resists rejecting a foreign substance by suppressing its own protective mechanism and concealing the foreign element by making it indistinguishable from the host. Anne O'Byrne explains,

> From the point of view of the maternal immune system, how does the fetus escape detection and rejection as foreign? The answer appears to lie in the placenta, the point of contact between the blood streams of fetus and maternal body. The placenta is generated from the fetus's genetic material and is a place remarkably lacking in the markers that would alert the maternal body to the foreignness of what she is carrying. Thus the fetus is indeed differentiated by and from the maternal body but in such a way that immunologically speaking, the womb is a relatively neutral space where the fetus begins the work of learning identity in the original confusion of difference.

(Anne O'Byrne, *Natality and Finitude* [Bloomington: Indiana University Press, 2010], 144)

40. Esposito, *Terms*, 133.

41. "If by 'community' one understands the exteriorization of existence, its mythologization can be referred to as the interiorization of this exteriority." Esposito, *Communitas*, 60.

42. "What human beings share," Esposito explains in his reflection on Heidegger, "is just this impossibility to 'make' the community that they already 'are,' which is to say the ecstatic opening that destines them to a constitutive lack." Ibid., 95. He continues, "Common is only lack and not possession, property, or appropriation." Ibid., 139.

43. Lemm, "Biopolitics," 4.

44. Both the authority and the legality of the modern social order is secured by the threat of potential violence among community members, a potential for violence that, as with the sovereign in social contract theory, is absorbed by the legal system and used to maintain its power and force. As Esposito explains, "The immunitary function it performs for the community is all too evident: if violent means such as the police apparatus or even the death penalty are used to exclude violence external to the legitimate order, the legal system works by adopting the same thing it aims to protect against." Esposito, *Immunitas*, 29. See also Esposito, *Terms*, 123–34.

45. Lemm, "Biopolitics," 3.

46. Campbell, "*Bíos*, Immunity, Life," xxxi. See also Esposito: "If the *communitas* necessarily refers to something 'impersonal,' or even 'anonymous,' as Weil specifies, the immunitary principle of law places the person as the sole bearer of rights back into the picture." Esposito, *Immunitas*, 23.

47. Esposito explains that in order for individuals in the modern social order to exercise their agency, freedom, and ability to claim what is necessary for each to live without destroying one another, the weak debt/obligation relation (*munus*) that structures being-in-common must be removed. The "poisonous fruits" of the *munus*, as he calls it (*Communitas*, 14), must be taken away from the community. This is because at a personal level the decision would be vexing, and in no way binding, regarding how to repay the gift of existence (how much of one's freedom and time is enough to give up so that others may enjoy theirs?) while also protecting what is one's own from claims of other persons who must also decide, which amounts to a perception of threat to individuality by the community's lack of protective differentiation. In the modern social order, *munus* is therefore displaced from the private realm of personal judgment and is appropriated into the public realm of law. He writes, "Law does not seek to shelter the community from a risk external to it, but rather from something that is originally inherent to it, which constitutes it. To grasp this point, we need only turn our attention to the most radical significance of *munus* from which 'community' derives its own meaning: law seeks to protect the common life from a danger that can be seen in the relation that makes it what it is. Common life is what breaks the identity-making borders of individuals, exposing them to alteration—and thus potential conflict—from others. . . . The law responds to this unsustainable contamination by constituting the limits threatened by the connective power of the *munus*." Esposito, *Immunitas*, 22.

48. From its outset, Esposito says, law "was prescribed to preserve peaceful cohabitation among people naturally exposed to the risk of destructive conflict. Even before being put into codified forms, therefore, law is necessary to the very life of the community. This is the primal, radical sense of the immunizing role it performs: just as the immune system functions for the human organism, law ensures the survival of the community in a life-threatening situation." Ibid., 21. Paradoxically, however, although "law is absolutely necessary for the community to survive, it actually relates to the community through its inverse side: to keep community alive, it tears it away from its most profound meaning [*munus*]. By protecting it from the risk of expropriation—expropriation being community's most intrinsic, natural inclination—law empties community of its core meaning. One could even go so far as to say that law preserves community by making it destitute." Ibid., 22.

49. The full quotation is as follows: "This is precisely how law immunizes the social system as a whole: substituting uncertain expectations with problematic but secure expectations. That is to say, not by eliminating instability, but by establishing a stable relationship with it: better foreseeable uncertainties than insecure certainties." Ibid., 48.

50. "Only the constant return of the past can assure the present in the face of the uncertainty that bears down on it from the future. This reassuring figure is the most meaningful expression of legal immunization: what else does immunity imply if not assurance against a future risk, paid for by taking preventative, sustainable doses?" Ibid., 31.

51. *OED*, "communication."

52. Martinez, *Communicative Sexualities*, 72.

53. The *OED* defines communication as "interpersonal contact, social interaction, association, intercourse," and "the transmission or exchange of information, knowledge, or ideas, by means of speech, writing, mechanical or electronic media, etc." *OED*, "communication."

54. For a lucid critique of what he calls the "logic of deferral" operating in modern theories of communication, see Chang, *Deconstructing*, 43–55.

55. We can once again note a slippage in terms. *Communication* appears to disappear in modern theory definitions of it once transmission and understanding are installed as the defining problems of overcoming the separation of individuals or the differences of identities. In turn, *communication* is pressed into service as a solution to the problem of individual separation without acknowledging it (i.e., communication as the threshold relation between oneself and another, rendering both incomplete) as the cause of the problem (the want of and need for affinity, transfer, transmission) to which it (communication/communicating) is itself invoked as solution. See Chang, *Deconstructing*, 55–67, especially on the role of "intersubjectivity" as a modern theoretical solution to this fundamental human communication problem.

56. As previously mentioned, Hacking (*Rewriting*) examines how psychiatric classification of emotional disorders can impact the self-conceptions of people who interpret their experiences through such classifications, what he calls "semantic contagion," the public description of a disorder (its symbolization in diagnostic manuals, measures, treatments, therapy, and support groups), which offers the means for the lived embodiment of the disorder to spread. For a discussion of Bataille's perspective on the centrality of risk and/or threat to human communication, see Macke, *Experience*, 128–36. See also George F. Will, "Intellectual Viruses," *Pittsburgh Post Gazette*, January 30, 2017.

57. See chapter 3 of this volume for discussion of the order or *nomos* of communication.

58. O'Neill, *Communicative Body*, 80.

59. Although federal regulation in the United States no longer formally protects the free flow of ideas in mass communication, the mass media industries do typically self-regulate, mainly for commercial reasons, not necessarily for educational or informational purposes, offering a blend of topics and perspectives, as well as upholding the community standards of decency that are defined by the Federal Communication Commission.

60. Esposito, *Immunitas*, 47. Esposito draws on Luhmann. See Niklas Luhmann, *Social Systems*, trans. John Bednarz Jr. with Dirk Baecker (Stanford, CA: Stanford University Press, 1995).

61. For a discussion of cause as effect of communication—namely, *écriture*—see Chang, *Deconstructing*, 207.

62. See Briankle G. Chang, "Communication as Communicability," in *Communication As . . . Perspectives on Theory*, ed. Gregory J. Shepherd, Jeffrey St. John, and Ted Striphas (Thousand Oaks, CA: SAGE, 2006), 246; and Macke, *Experience*, 145. As Schutz argues, "The actual *communicating* is itself a meaningful act, and we must interpret that act and the way it is done as things in their own right." Schutz, *Phenomenology*, 129. In a similar vein, Angus identifies the "constitutive paradox of communication," which he argues "stems from the fact that every 'communication' as the meaning of an expression, or sense-content, is a metaphorical formation of the very possibility of 'communication' as shaping a form of connection by a medium, or institution. This paradox . . . undercuts the conventional account of truth as a correspondence between knower

and the known, as well as the concept of communication as transmission of content." Or, to put this in phenomenological terms, "every communication act is simultaneously a 'mundane' act within the given world-horizon and a 'transcendental' act of constitution of that horizon." Angus, *Primal Scenes*, 40.

63. Esposito, *Immunitas*, 50.

64. "Identity is equal to immunity." Nancy, *Corpus*, 167.

65. For example, Angus, *Primal Scenes*, 127–37.

66. Cf. Macke's discussion of lying, or keeping silent, as a cover of inner selfhood, a phenomenon that may be subject to interpretation but nevertheless, he argues, disguises and protects the private sanctum of the self. Macke, *Experience*, 126.

67. Philosophical reflection on the possibility of autoimmunization in communication has haunted the thinking of at least two scholars in the continental philosophical tradition other than Esposito. It is at the forefront of Jacques Derrida, *Monolingualism of the Other; or, The Prosthesis of Origin*, trans. Patrick Mensah (Stanford, CA: Stanford University Press, 1998), an investigation of the constitutive yet alienating experience of appropriating a language, and therefore a culture, that is not one's own (for Derrida, the experience of foreignness in his own mother tongue), and in Paul Ricoeur, *On Translation* (London: Routledge, 2006), albeit in a different register: namely, the burden of doing justice to a text in the process of transforming it into a different language to share it. For Derrida more than for Ricoeur, thinking about the autoimmunization of communication (i.e., the protection of a foreign element by attacking the domestic system designed to reject it) points directly to the fact of discourses that are shared within a community and within oneself, a thinking about the linguistic basis of identity and the impossibility of rejecting it as a personal defense system, to say nothing of the lifelong challenge of gaining awareness of the discourses one speaks.

68. There are numerous histories of communication study in the United States. Some of the most helpful are Dues and Brown, *Boxing*; Hardt, *Critical Communication Studies*; Mattelart and Mattelart, *Theories of Communication*; and Delia, "Communication Research."

69. "Communication goes hand in hand with the greater possibility of domination over beings." Campbell, *Improper Life*, 25.

70. Esposito, *Immunitas*, 170. For a critique of the instrumentalist teaching of communication in the United States, see Catt, "Communication Is Not a Skill."

71. Lemm, "Biopolitics," 6.

72. Jean-Luc Nancy, *The Evidence of Film: Abbas Kiarostami*, trans. Christine Irizarry and Verena Andermatt Conley (Brussels: Yves Gevaert, 2001), 42.

73. Watkin, *Phenomenology or Deconstruction?*, 116. According to Peters and Simonson, the Progressive-era philosopher Charles Horton Cooley similarly asserted that "communication is the means by which communities were made and sometimes the means by which they were destroyed." John Durham Peters and Peter Simonson, *Mass Communication and American Social Thought: Key Texts, 1919–1968* (Oxford: Rowman and Littlefield, 2004), 13.

74. "In other words, our task will be to defer the claim to what might be common to us, and to think the being-*in*-common, to think the *interval*." Nancy and Kate, "'*Cum*' . . . Revisited," 39.

75. John Dewey (1916), quoted in Peters and Simonson, *Mass Communication*, 13.

76. Williams, "Communication," 72–73.

77. Relevant here is Grossberg's focus on mediation in the discursive production of reality: "Discourse does not signify,

represent, or even mediate a reality that exists on a separate plane of reality. . . . In fact, discourse can produce many different kinds of mediations or effects, and these effects can then be articulated to many different uses, for example, nation-building, identity, education, and civilizing. Discourse is a milieu of possibilities, or, better, a virtual space of possibility and imagination if you will." Lawrence Grossberg, *Cultural Studies in the Future Tense* (Durham, NC: Duke University Press, 2010), 191–92.

78. Lasswell, "Structure and Function."

79. There are other assumptions concealed in the transfer model of communication, the full critique of which is not essential to the present research. For a full perspective, see Angus, *Primal Scenes*, 85. For communication theory assumptions about storage, memory, and retrieval in the sender-receiver process, see Orit Halpern, *Beautiful Data: A History of Vision and Reason Since 1945* (Durham, NC: Duke University Press, 2015), 60–66.

80. Esposito, *Immunitas*, 113.

81. "If the subject of community is no longer the 'same,' it will by necessity be an 'other'; not another subject but a chain of alterations that cannot ever be fixed in a new identity." Esposito, *Communitas*, 138.

82. Campbell, "*Bíos*, Immunity, Life," 202n83.

Chapter 4

1. Nancy, *Inoperative Community*; Jean-Luc Nancy, *The Sense of the World*, trans. Jeffery S. Librett (Minneapolis: University of Minnesota Press, 1997); Jean-Luc Nancy, *The Creation of the World or Globalization*, trans. François Raffoul and David Pettegrew (Albany: SUNY Press, 2007); Jean-Luc Nancy, *Corpus II: Writings on Sexuality*, trans. Anne O'Byrne (New York: Fordham University Press, 2013); Jean-Luc Nancy, *Being Nude: The Skin of Images*, trans. Anne O'Byrne and Carlie Anglemire (New York: Fordham University Press, 2014); Nancy, *Being Singular Plural*; Nancy, *Listening*; Nancy, *Evidence of Film*.

2. Nancy, *Corpus*, 83.

3. In the Catholic mass, *hoc est enim corpus meum* are words spoken by a priest in the ritual transformation of sacramental bread into the body of Christ.

4. Nancy, *Corpus*, 3. The spoken repetition of this phrase not only functions mnemonically to not forget the word of God but also adds immediacy, in a way that the written word does not, to the absent body of Christ.

5. Ibid., 5.

6. "The anxiety, the desire to see, touch, and eat the body of God, to *be* that body and *be nothing but that*, forms the principle of Western (un)reason." Ibid.

7. Ibid.

8. "The body keeps its secret, this nothing, this spirit that isn't lodged in it but spread out, expanded, extended all across it, so much so that the secret has no hiding place, no intimate fold where it might someday be discovered. The body keeps nothing: it keeps itself as a secret. That's why the body dies and is borne away, concealed, into the grave. Of its passage, hardly a few indices remain." Nancy, *Corpus*, 156.

9. Nancy, *Corpus II*, 6. As O'Byrne explains, "The incorporeal—for the Stoics, this consisted of the fourfold of space, time, emptiness, and the said—is what makes it possible for bodies to distinguish themselves; without it, there would be an undifferentiated mass." O'Byrne, *Natality*, 140.

10. Nancy, *Corpus II*, 7. He continues, "Put still another way, on the one hand, the relation and separation between subjects (things or persons) are one and the same thing, while, on the other, this same thing is sameness itself as different from

itself and deferring itself, or desiring itself, or loving itself, all of which is a single reality or a single movement that is as foreign to the logic of identity as it is to the symmetrical logic of constitutive lack or separation." Ibid., 8.

11. Nancy, *Corpus*, 53.
12. Ibid., 155.
13. Ibid., 156.
14. Ibid., 53.
15. Perpich, "*Corpus Meum*," 83.
16. Nancy, *Corpus*, 156.
17. Ibid., 157.
18. Thought of body as an active complex, extended spatially and temporally, is at the basis of Nancy's and Esposito's critiques of *community* as a substance and an accepted idea.
19. Albert Atkin, "Peirce's Theory of Signs," in *Stanford Encyclopedia of Philosophy*, Stanford University, 1997–, published October 13, 2006; last modified April 4, 2013, https://plato.stanford.edu/entries/peirce-semiotics/. See section 3.2.
20. Nancy, *Corpus*, 155.
21. Ibid., 113. See also Perpich: "Meaning happens or takes place when something appears *as* something, which is to say appears *as this* and not *that*. Meaning is thus plural and determinate at the same time: plural insofar as meaning could not exist were it a single or total meaning attached to a thing or to all of existence as a pure presence, and determinate insofar as the articulated structure or network in which meaning occurs entails always the existence of both sameness and difference—identity and singularity, alterity and plurality." Perpich, "*Corpus Meum*," 77.
22. The present chapter takes its turn and refers to Isaac E. Catt's article, "The Signifying World between Ineffability and Intelligibility: Body as Sign in Communicology," *Review of Communication* 11, no. 2 (2011): 122–44.
23. Nancy, *Corpus*, 75.
24. For Nancy, being is not knowledge (*cogito sum*), but becoming, a being moved (*some where*). Ibid., 140. He says, "Being is *there*, the being-place of a 'there,' a body." Ibid., 113.

25. Lanigan, *Speaking and Semiology*, 127.
26. Nancy, *Corpus*, 15.
27. Ibid.
28. "Existence, then, is a question of relation, the problem of the many, spatiality and spacing, (a)cosmology." Watkin, *Phenomenology or Deconstruction?*, 176.
29. "When we talk about the body we talk about something open and infinite, about the opening of closure itself, the infinite of the finite itself. . . . The body is the open." Nancy, *Corpus*, 122.
30. Ibid., 124.
31. Ibid., 135.
32. For *being-with* and the codes of communication, see chapter 5 of this volume.
33. Nancy, *Corpus*, 126.
34. Phenomenologically, the mode of givenness of the other is intentionality.
35. "The now itself, as boundary or limit, has itself the structure of an interval, and is therefore doubled: the now as a limit of the before, the now as limit of the after." François Raffoul, "The Logic of the With: On Nancy's *Être singulier pluriel*," *Studies in Practical Philosophy* 1, no. 1 (1999): 48.
36. Cf. Chang, *Deconstructing*, 159.
37. Henry explains,

The secret homogeneity of the transcendental experience of the other and the objective world insofar as they are constitutive of one another is what ultimately authorizes them to be placed side by side. The other is what is first given to me in the constitution of objective nature; the other precedes and founds objective nature. But this precedence quickly appears to be illusory and is overturned, if one notes that, if not the objective world, at least something like a world has already been opened so that this prior domain in which the ego is opened to the other may be accessed and experienced. It is indeed in a primordial world and thus within a world that the other appears. Additionally, this means that the other, even in its most archaic form, is necessarily given to an intentionality. (Henry, *Material Phenomenology*, 103)

38. Lanigan, *Speaking and Semiology*, 127.

39. Ibid.

40. For example, see Jean-Luc Marion, *In Excess: Studies of Saturated Phenomena*, trans. Robyn Horner and Vincent Berruad (New York: Fordham University Press, 2002); Jean-Luc Marion, *The Erotic Phenomenon*, trans. Stephen E. Lewis (Chicago: University of Chicago Press, 2007); Esposito, *Bíos*; Henry, *Material Phenomenology*; and Richard Kearney and Brian Treanor, eds., *Carnal Hermeneutics* (New York: Fordham University Press, 2015).

41. Nancy, *Corpus*, 155.

42. Perpich, "*Corpus Meum*," 85. O'Byrne illustrates the idea of a body as limit in terms of the infant/mother relation: "We are *ex-peaused*, skin to skin and flesh to flesh from the earliest moments of our existence when we begin to come to be as finite beings with and within another singular finite being. Those earliest moments happen in our mothers' bodies but in the mode of being with as well as within, *partes extra partes*. Our spatial, extended existence means that we are at a distance from one another. Even as our bodies will later reach out and touch and entwine, they will nonetheless remain in a relation of exteriority; our natal spacing is the fact that this is so right down to the touch of the fetus and the maternal body." O'Byrne, *Natality*, 138.

43. Nancy, *Corpus*, 132.

44. Ibid., 19.

45. Ibid. He also says, "The body is the return of the 'outside' that it is to this 'inside' that it isn't. Instead of being in extension, the body is in expulsion toward its own 'interior,' right to the very limit where the sign is abolished in the presence it represented." Ibid., 67.

46. "We need a corpus of entries into the body, dictionary entries, language entries, encyclopedia entries, all the body's introductory topoi, registers for all its articles, an index for all its places, postures, planes, and recesses. A corpus would be the registration of this long discontinuity of entries (*or* exits: the doors always swing both ways) . . . A body is the topic of its every access, its every here/there, its *fort/da*, its coming-and-going, swallowing-and-spitting, breathing in/breathing out, displacing and closing." Ibid., 55.

47. What is said here about the presence of bodies applies to what was said in previous chapters of the present volume about the presence of what is given in language: "*Here* is thus, before it can be here, exposed to an alteration, a modification or a pause which destroys the appearance not only of its sense certainty but also its linguistic certainty and which, as a linguistic alteration and as an alteration of the *here* and *now* of language can be called the law of its cessation, its ex-position or of its abandon. For *here* is always *here* or *there*, *here* or *here*." Hamacher, "Ou, séance," 219.

48. Lanigan, *Speaking and Semiology*, 128, 132.

49. Although the body-object is perceptible, and is understood to be inhabited by a psyche or consciousness, this psyche cannot be perceived in itself but only represented (i.e., appresented). Perception of the psyche of another would require the perceiver (a self) to be that other. Psyche transcends intentional perception. See Henry, *Material Phenomenology*, 110–13.

50. Perpich, "*Corpus Meum*," 85.

51. "Where am I? In my foot, my hand, my genitals, my ear? Where am I in this

face, these traits, traces, eccentricities, tremblings? Who am I on the contours of this mouth that says 'I'?" Nancy, *Corpus II*, 87.

52. Benveniste, *Problems*, 224. Lanigan defines the "foundational principle of Postmodernity" as follows: "Human being is a sign (Peirce); A human being is language (Hjelmslev, Heidegger); A human being is discourse (Foucault, Merleau-Ponty)." Lanigan, *Human Science*, 96.

53. Landes, *Merleau-Ponty*, 9.

54. Nancy, *Birth*, 175–76. Landes explains the work of *exscription*, and the relation to which it refers, via Merleau-Ponty: "Every inscription *exscribes* . . . latent content, all that is made present as absent, such as the inscribing gesture and the systems of meaning that support it. . . . For Merleau-Ponty, it is speech that *exscribes* silence, the visible that *exscribes* the invisible, the surface that *exscribes* depth, and the spacing of every expressive gesture that *exscribes* Being itself." Landes, *Merleau-Ponty*, 9.

55. "Language presupposes the nonlinguistic as that with which it must maintain itself in a virtual relation . . . so that it may later denote it in actual speech." Agamben, *Homo Sacer*, 20.

56. Donald A. Landes, "Expressive Body, Exscriptive Corpus: The Tracing of the Body from Maurice Merleau-Ponty to Jean-Luc Nancy," *Chiasmi International* 9 (2007): 250.

57. Nancy, *Corpus II*, 88.

58. Ibid., 88 (emphasis added). Phenomenologically, demotion of the ego to a constituted ego by way of assimilative apperception also demotes the body as constituted. According to Henry, "the body is no longer the radically subjective and immanent 'I can' that I am and that is identical to my ego. It is still less what originally turns it into a body in its pure corporeality, as ipseity originally turns the ego into an ego. Instead, it is precisely a constituted body inherent to the sphere of ownness. *It is shown in ownness but not in itself.*" Henry, *Material Phenomenology*, 110.

59. Dr. Rebecca Levine, MD, offered the phrase "precisely choreographed involuntary operations." Levine, personal conversation, February 2017.

60. Perpich, "*Corpus Meum*," 81–82. See Phillip Sarasin, "The Body as Medium: Nineteenth-Century European Hygiene Discourse," *Grey Room* 29 (2007): 48–65, a fascinating discussion of hygiene discourse in the nineteenth century, which taught the subject to read itself as a sign, to know itself and its health by way of understanding the symptoms communicated to it by the body.

61. Nancy, *Corpus II*, 129. It is worth noting the coincidence of illness and the body. Illness, which may be brought about by viruses, is inside the body, not external to it, as are common viruses that lay dormant inside a body for several years. Identifying one as separate from the other ("I am not my disease") is a strategy of disavowal, easing the subject's experience of the interruption of his or her self-sense as whole and unified, which has been brought by intrusions from within.

62. "A body is the withdrawal from self that relates a self to itself as it exposes the world. My body is not just my skin turned toward the outside: it is already itself my outside, the outside in me and for me—opposed by me to myself in order to distinguish me from unity. A stranger to others and first of all to this other that I become thanks to it." Ibid., 87.

63. Ibid., 88.

64. Friedrich Kittler, *Literature, Media, Information Systems*, ed. John Johnston (New York: Routledge, 1997), 91.

65. See Henk Oosterling and Ewa Plonowska Ziarek, eds., *Intermedialities: Philosophy, Arts, Politics* (Lanham, MD: Lexington Books, 2011).

66. David Farrell Krell, "*Das Unheimliche*, Architectural Sections of Heidegger

and Freud," *Research in Phenomenology* 22, no. 1 (1992): 43–61.

67. Krell suggests that the uncanniest part of a human body are the feet, which sometimes, especially when neglected, can announce their forgotten presence in the most unpleasant way.

68. On the relation between psyche and life in *Corpus*, see Jacques Derrida, *On Touching—Jean-Luc Nancy*, trans. Christine Irizarry (Stanford, CA: Stanford University Press, 2005), 49–52.

69. Lanigan, personal correspondence, July 24, 2014.

70. Nancy, *Corpus*, 133.

71. Perpich, "*Corpus Meum*," 81.

72. Nancy, *Corpus*, 15.

73. Michel Foucault, "Of Other Spaces," *Diacritics* 16, no. 1 (Spring 1986): 25. He continues, "The cemetery begins with this strange heterochrony, the loss of life, and with this quasi-eternity in which her permanent lot is dissolution and disappearance." Ibid., 26.

74. Garnet C. Butchart, "The Communicology of Roland Barthes' *Camera Lucida*: Reflections on the Sign-Body Experience of Visual Communication," *Visual Communication* 15, no. 2 (2016): 199–219.

75. Garrido explains,

> The naked presence of the dead body is "naked" because it does not stand as the presence *of* something absent (as its sign or symbol). It does not stand, for instance, as "remains" reminding us of the "full" presence of the Virgin now gone, nor as the singular "phenomenon" of the universal idea of Death. On the contrary, the nakedness of the body consists in referring to nothing but to its own exposition, and thus presenting its own presenting or presentation as such. This presence, here, is therefore the "presence of presence" or presence exposed by the absence or the retreating of any *other* (absent) presence. (Juan Manuel Garrido, "Jean-Luc Nancy's Concept of Body," *Epoché: A Journal for the History of Philosophy* 14, no. 1 [2009]: 192)

76. Nancy, *Corpus*, 55.

77. Garrido, "Nancy's Concept," 193.

78. Pascal David, "Dasein/Existence," in *Dictionary of Untranslatables: A Philosophical Lexicon*, ed. Barbara Cassin, Emily Apter, Jacques Lezra, and Michael Wood (Princeton, NJ: Princeton University Press, 2014), 195.

79. Ibid., 198. According to David, the Heideggerian sense of *Dasein* as movement or coming to presence—directedness toward, which is what the accusative means—is precipitated by the thought of Hegel: "The being-there of *Dasein* is where it is only because it has not yet reached the stage where what can be known through it awaits it." Ibid.

80. Richard Lanigan, "Review of *A Body*, by John Coplans," *American Journal of Semiotics* 17, no. 4 (2003): 372. See also chapter 5 of the present volume on the *with* of being.

81. Regarding the consumption of Christ's body—"a monster that cannot be swallowed," as Nancy puts it—Garrido offers insight: "If what is given to the mouth shows itself as *not being* the Spirit given to faith; if the digestion of bread and wine is not the incorporation of Love, but a materiality or exteriority that, while dissolving in the mouth, *resists* its spiritual meaning; if what is in correlation with this, the 'decaying body' of Jesus that disciples will grieve, *is not* the image of a redeemed humanity, *all this is due to the fact that body exposes itself as body, in its nudity and weight of body*. Body is: what one cannot incorporate, decorporate, what *exscripts* itself at the very moment of being eaten and digested, or understood and signified. Body, or the weight of body,

exscripts itself—body *is* this exscription—from 'Incarnation' in all the senses that we may confer to this concept." Garrido, "Nancy's Concept," 206.

82. Angus, *Primal Scenes*, 158–60.

83. "There is a juridiction proper to each body: 'hoc est enim. . . .'" Nancy, *Corpus*, 53.

84. Ibid., 143. *World* for Nancy has a meaning similar to *lifeworld* for Husserl, the intersubjective and intercorporeal sum of all culture, traditions, people that we encounter on a daily basis. Nancy writes, "A world is a totality of extended emotion and moving extension: in other words, a totality of exposition, which we can also name 'sense' in the sense that 'sense' is the sharing of the ex: that which is in itself refers to the self as outside the self—but this outside is precisely the inside of the world, which consists only in this exposition . . . Ex-ist, being ex, is to be exposed according to corporeal exteriority, it is to be in the world, and in a more radical fashion, is being world." Ibid. In other words, a person represents the world, both in speech about it as well as in material comportment, in life, but does so "only because he or she is already exposed to the world" as a body. Perpich, "*Corpus Meum*," 79.

85. Raffoul, "Logic," 47.

86. "We encounter [people] as embodied beings, beings with a body that expresses a particular meaning in the context of community." Sarah Sorial, "Heidegger, Jean-Luc Nancy, and the Question of Dasein's Embodiment: An Ethics of Touch and Spacing," *Philosophy Today* 48, no. 2 (2004): 227.

87. Perpich, "*Corpus Meum*," 79. She continues, "We are precisely people, human beings with such and such common attributes. But at the same time, this kind does not exist in the sense that some one person or each person could be said to be the whole of what it is to be a person." Ibid., 80.

88. "Of the body, there's always *a lot*. There's always a *crowd* of bodies, there's never a *mass* of bodies. Where there's a mass of bodies, there's no more body, and where there's a mass of bodies, there's a mass grave." Nancy, *Corpus*, 124.

89. Jean-Luc Nancy, *After Fukushima: The Equivalence of Catastrophes*, trans. Charlotte Mandell (New York: Fordham University Press, 2015), 41.

90. "For estimation—or valuation—belongs to the series of calculations of general equivalence, whether it be of money or its substitutes, which are the equivalences of forces, capacities, individuals, risks, speeds and so on. Esteem on the contrary summons the singular and its singular way to come into presence—flower, face, or tone." Ibid., 39.

91. Relevant here is Henry's critical comment about transcendental phenomenology: "For Husserl, the principle and model of our access to being, whether it is a question of our own ego or that of the other, is not the laws of desire and accomplishment, of suffering and enjoyment, of feeling and resentment, of love and hate, but once again, the laws of perception. In what is its ownmost (and, I would add, its most horrendous), it is a phenomenology of perception applied to the other." Henry, *Material Phenomenology*, 114.

92. Perpich, "*Corpus Meum*," 82.

93. Nancy, *Corpus*, 35.

94. Jacques Derrida, "Le toucher: Touch/to touch him," *Paragraph* 16, no. 2 (1993): 147. O'Byrne argues, "*A body is only approached or seen or touched by other bodies*. There is no way to talk about being and being-with in the third person, no way to say that 'it is' or 'there is . . .' or indeed 'I am.' Instead, the only term for the being of bodies together in the world is 'we are.'" O'Byrne, *Natality*, 137.

95. Esposito, *Bíos*, 63.

96. Sharing (F. *partage*) has multiple senses, several of which Nancy lists as follows: "partition, repartition, part,

participation, separation, communication, discord, split, devolution, destination." Nancy, quoted in Raffoul, "Logic," 42. Raffoul expands, "For instance, when used in the expression '*notre partage,*' the term indicates something like 'our common lot,' that is, the lot that *each* of us has in common, i.e., our share. *Partage* thus designates the paradoxical concept of a sharing of what cannot be shared." Raffoul, "Logic," 43.

97. "The being of community is the interval of difference, the spacing that brings us into relation with others in a common non-belonging, in this loss of what is proper that never adds up to a common good." Esposito, *Communitas*, 139. See chapter 3 of the present volume.

98. "The singular is primarily *each* one and, therefore, also *with* and *among* all the others. The singular is a plural." Nancy, *Being Singular Plural*, 32. Morin explains this concept, "The singular plural means that there are singularities whose identity or selfhood can only be found in their 'relation' to other singularities: what exists finds itself in being exposed to or being in contact with other singularities in such a way that nothing exists or makes sense on its own." Morin, *Nancy*, 2.

99. Perpich, "*Corpus Meum,*" 89.
100. Ibid., 88.
101. Nancy, *Corpus*, 65.

Chapter 5

1. Henry, *Material Phenomenology*, 133.
2. Zygmunt Bauman, *Community: Seeking Safety in an Insecure World* (Malden, MA: Polity, 2001), 3.
3. For an overview of the theme of community in modern communication scholarship, see Erin Daina Underwood and Lawrence R. Frey, "Communication and Community: Clarifying the Connection across the Communication Community," *Annals of the International Communication Association* 31, no. 1 (2007): 370–418.
4. Jean-Luc Nancy, "Conloquium," *Minnesota Review*, no. 75 (Fall 2010): 102.
5. Ibid.
6. Ibid. According to Nancy, an analysis of the structure of the "failure" of community (it is what *there is*, and it is impossible to realize) may give rise to what he calls "an ontology of the being-in-common" that could offer insight into our commonality, the *inter* that is between us:

> The *inter* of the in-common, in short, should be thought beyond any logic of subjectivity. It is a *third term* between the I and its other, between you and me, and between us; it installs itself as this "third" between us, and in doing so, decenters our subjectivity. Its *"oeuvre"* is precisely this *"disoeuvrement,"* performed on and as the empty topos of the interval. For if the *inter* is not a subject or substance, if according to the logic of being it can only be a radical "nothing" . . . then it must be thought as a place, a space (topos), an area, however airy, a limit or a borderline. (Nancy and Kate, "'*Cum*' . . . Revisited," 39–41.)

For similar perspective, see Esposito, *Communitas*; Esposito, *Immunitas*; Esposito, *Bíos*; Agamben, *Homo Sacer*; Agamben, *State of Exception*; Jacques Rancière, *Disagreement: Politics and Philosophy*, trans. Julie Rose (Minneapolis: University of Minnesota Press, 1999); Jean-Luc Nancy, *The Disavowed Community*, trans. Philip Armstrong (New York: Fordham University Press, 2016); Nancy, *Inoperative Community*; Nancy, *Being Singular Plural*; Nancy, *Creation of the World*; and Nancy, *After Fukushima*.

7. "A common task, that is to say not at all collective, but a task imposed on *us all*

together . . . to care about the possibility of being, precisely, together and saying 'us' at the moment when this possibility seems to vanish sometimes into a 'one,' sometimes into an 'I' just as anonymous and monstrous as each other, and in truth completely entangled in each other." Nancy, quoted in Watkin, *Phenomenology or Deconstruction?*, 199.

8. Lanigan, *Phenomenology*, 16.

9. James, *Fragmentary Demand*; James, *New French Philosophy*; Ignaas Devisch, *Jean-Luc Nancy and the Question of Community* (London: Bloomsbury, 2013).

10. James, *Fragmentary Demand*, 219. According to James, "Nancy is trying to find a postphenomenological language or idiom to express the way in which, through our bodily senses, the world is always already there for us as that which makes sense prior to theoretical understanding or more abstract forms of cognition." Ibid., 219.

11. Malin Wahlberg, *Documentary Time: Film and Phenomenology* (Minneapolis: University of Minnesota Press, 2008), xii (emphasis added).

12. Lanigan, *Human Science*, 114. For details on semiotic phenomenology as a method, see Lanigan, *Phenomenology*, and *Human Science*.

13. Raffoul, "Logic," 36.

14. "Communities are multiple. The study of them is indispensable if one treats each one of them as being a variation of the *eidos* of community, a variation that would allow hitherto unperceived features to be conferred to this essence." Henry, *Material Phenomenology*, 134.

15. Sean Hand, "Being-in-Common, or the Meaning of Globalization," in *Jean-Luc Nancy: Justice, Legality and World*, ed. Benjamin Hutchens (London: Continuum, 2013), 138.

16. "Reflection on the phenomenal field or *gestalt* as given in lived experience (immediate perception)." Lanigan, *Speaking and Semiology*, 44. Lanigan defines

prereflective awareness as "the naïve realism of our everyday lives," "our normal condition of being and having a world prior to thinking about it and prior to communicating about it." Lanigan, *Human Science*, 29.

17. Richard Lanigan, "Human Embodiment: An Eidetic and Empirical Communicology of Phantom Limb," *Metodo: International Studies in Phenomenology and Philosophy* 3, no. 1 (2013): 261.

18. Prereflective (preobjective) phenomena are those that, as Lanigan explains, "exist in perception for us prior to any conceptualization about their form or presence to us as a unified structure and content." Lanigan, *Speaking and Semiology*, 144.

19. Dermot Moran, *Introduction to Phenomenology* (New York: Routledge, 2000), 418.

20. Lanigan, "Human Embodiment," 261 (emphasis added).

21. As Devisch puts it, for Nancy "there is no *being* that is not already a *social being*." Devisch, *Jean-Luc Nancy*, 84.

22. "As a singular plural entity, man can only comprehend himself from the standpoint of the social." Ibid., 85.

23. Lanigan, "Human Embodiment," 261.

24. "Reflection on the conditions necessary for the perception of the phenomena of the First Reflection." Lanigan, *Speaking and Semiology*, 44.

25. Lanigan, *Phenomenology*, 10.

26. This notion of experience is akin to memory, defined by Ferdinand de Tönnies, as a "shared frame of reference." Ferdinand de Tönnies, *Community and Civil Society*, ed. Jose Harris, trans. Jose Harris and Margaret Hollis (Cambridge, UK: Cambridge University Press, 2001), 24. Tönnies links memory to pleasure and habit, or to custom, what he calls a "common outlook." Ibid., 29. Although I will not draw further on Tönnies's classic sociology of community (*Gemeinschaft*), I do

wish to note a passage on what he calls the "sequence of understanding" the experience of community: "Unity of human wills and the possibility of community is in fact based first and foremost on close blood relationship and mixture of blood, then on spatial proximity, and finally, for human beings, on mental and spiritual closeness." Ibid., 34. As I discuss below, closeness and proximity are presuppositions about the possibility of community.

27. See Macke, *Experience*, especially chapters 5 and 9; Macke, "Intrapersonal Communicology"; Deborah Eicher-Catt, "The Authenticity in Ambiguity: Appreciating Maurice Merleau-Ponty's Abductive Logic as Communicative Practice," *Atlantic Journal of Communication* 13, no. 2 (2005): 113–34; and Lanigan, *Phenomenology*.

28. Lanigan, "Human Embodiment," 262.

29. "The body is the vehicle for perception and expression and it is the agency that allows one to engage in the reversible process of being in public and private existence." Lanigan, *Speaking and Semiology*, 126.

30. Deborah Eicher-Catt and Isaac E. Catt, eds., *Communicology: The New Science of Embodied Discourse* (Lanham, MD: Fairleigh Dickinson University Press, 2010), 17.

31. Frank J. Macke, "Body, Liquidity, and Flesh: Bachelard, Merleau-Ponty, and the Elements of Interpersonal Communication," *Philosophy Today* 51, no. 4 (2007): 401.

32. Anne O'Byrne, "Nancy's Materialist Ontology," in *Jean-Luc Nancy and Plural Thinking: Expositions of World, Ontology, Politics, and Sense*, ed. Peter Gratton and Marie-Eve Morin (Albany: SUNY Press, 2012), 81.

33. Richard Lanigan, "Verbal and Nonverbal Codes of Communicology: The Foundation of Interpersonal Agency and Efficacy," in *Communicology: The New Science of Embodied Discourse*, ed. Deborah Eicher-Catt and Isaac E. Catt (Lanham, MD: Fairleigh Dickinson University Press, 2010), 102–28.

34. Ibid., 114.

35. Nancy, *Listening*, 8.

36. Jean-Luc Nancy, "Beheaded Sun (Soleil cou coupé)," *Qui Parle* 3, no. 2 (1989): 50. Slash marks in the quotation interrupt the stability of the author, reminding us of Nancy's own subjection to language rather than his mastery over it.

37. Lanigan, "Human Embodiment," 277.

38. Henry, *Material Phenomenology*, 108. Henry qualifies the point: "It is only because this perception of the other as a psychic body is presupposed that the necessary apperceptive transfer that will confer this sense of being an organism like mine through the resemblance and analogy can be deduced." Ibid., 109. He continues, "I can perceive only intentionally the body-object of the other. The fact that it is the body of the other, inhabited internally by the other's subjectivity, sensed and moved by it, is only an apresented sense." Ibid., 112.

39. "Communication is the name for the reversible relationship between an *organism* (person) and its *environment* (lived-world), both of which exist in a mutual context or *Environment*. At its most sophisticated level this relationship is one of language." Lanigan, *Phenomenology*, 11. See also Richard Lanigan, "Communicology and Semiotic Hypercodes: The Example of Schizophrenic Discourse" (paper, 36th Annual Meeting of the Semiotic Society of America, Pittsburgh, PA, 2011); and Catt, "Signifying World." Cf. C. S. Peirce on communication: "The recognition by one person of another's personality takes place by means to some extent identical with the means by which he is conscious of his own personality."

Charles S. Peirce, *Collected Papers of Charles Sanders Peirce*, ed. Arthur W. Burks, Charles Hartshorne, and Paul Weiss, 3rd ed. (Cambridge, MA: Belknap Press, 1965): 6:160.

40. Lanigan, *Human Science*, 37.
41. Ibid., 32.
42. Nancy, "Conloquium," 101–8.
43. Ibid., 103.
44. Benveniste, *Problems*, 202.
45. Ibid.
46. Nancy, "Conloquium," 102.
47. Ibid., 104.
48. Angus offers the following in this regard:

> The history of Being, in Heidegger's phrase, is thus the history of these media of connection that open the possibility of, and assign a characteristic form to, the web of meaning that characterizes the world in a given epoch—which includes the constitution of a relation between knower and known. Communication, in this sense, is not a question of the transmission of a priorly articulated thought. It is the form of awareness that shapes the articulation of thought. Thought itself is understood less an "internal" activity than as the multiplicity of connections that is spread out throughout the material forms of social communication. From this perspective, *the media of communication that have been developed throughout human culture are expressions of the socio-historical Being of human life*. They are the embodied rhetorical form that institutes, or establishes, a world. (Angus, *Primal Scenes*, 53 [emphasis added])

49. Lanigan, *Human Science*, 61.
50. The emphasis Nancy places on spacing and distancing, exposition, is characteristic of the postphenomenology of his philosophy.
51. Jean-Luc Nancy, "The Insufficiency of 'Values' and the Necessity of 'Sense,'" *Cultural Values* 1, no. 1 (1997): 130.
52. Nancy, "Conloquium," 104.
53. Ibid., 107.
54. See Lanigan, "Verbal and Nonverbal Codes"; Wilden, *System and Structure*; and Bateson, *Steps*.
55. See Lanigan, "Verbal and Nonverbal Codes."
56. The prepositional genitive *with* indicates a major point of intersection between Nancy's and Esposito's thinking about community. As Esposito explains, "In the concept of 'sharing with' [*condivisione*], the *with* [*con*] is associated with dividing up. . . . Community isn't an entity, nor is it a collective subject, nor a totality of subjects, but rather is the relation that makes them no longer individual subjects because it closes them off from their identity with a line, which traversing them, alters them: it is the 'with,' the 'between,' and the threshold where they meet in a point of contact that brings them into relation with others to the degree to which it separates them from themselves." Esposito, *Communitas*, 139.
57. Cicero's phrase is *conloquium evocare* (L. "community called forth in conversation").
58. Nancy, "Conloquium," 101. On community with the dead, see Michel Henry, *I Am the Truth*, trans. Susan Emanuel (Stanford, CA: Stanford University Press, 2003).
59. The importance of reflexive French verbs in Nancy's philosophy is worth noting. For example, Lanigan (personal conversation) argues that the French expression *Je t'aime et moi* not only means "I love you and I" (I love what we are together) but also calls attention to the act of my love for myself, an ego-libido self-giving that is not simply a self-loss. "I love you and I"—that is, I love myself first and foremost.

60. Laura McMahon, *Cinema and Contact: The Withdrawal of Touch in Nancy, Bresson, Duras and Denis* (London: Legenda, 2012), 2.

61. Nancy, *Birth*, 204.

62. Graham Harman, "On Interface: Nancy's Weights and Measures," in *Jean-Luc Nancy and Plural Thinking: Expositions of World, Ontology, Politics, and Sense*, ed. Peter Gratton and Marie-Eve Morin (Albany: SUNY Press, 2012), 98.

63. Nancy, *Corpus*, 83.

64. Anne O'Byrne, "The Politics of Intrusion," *CR: The New Centennial Review* 2, no. 3 (2002): 177.

65. Wilden, *Rules*, 253.

66. Nancy, *Corpus*, 124.

67. Grossberg's recent writings on culture, power, and embodied being (what he calls "affect") correspond with this task. His work argues persuasively for the task of examining the conjunctions of culture, power, and embodiment in contexts of late-modern capitalism, an argument he develops by way of what he calls an "ontology of mediation": "Such an ontology assumes that reality is always and only relational, and that it can be mapped only as an unpredictable, non-linear, and multiple series of relations—determinations, articulations, mediations, or effectivities. . . . Mediation is the movement of events or bodies from one set of relations to another as they are constantly becoming something other than what they are." Grossberg, *Cultural Studies*, 190–91. Like Grossberg, Nancy's relational ontological task of thinking about *being-with* is political at its core.

68. See Marion's studies of what he calls the "saturated phenomenon" of the flesh: Jean-Luc Marion, *Being Given: Toward a Phenomenology of Givenness*, trans. Jeffery L. Kosky (Stanford, CA: Stanford University Press, 2002); Marion, *In Excess*; and Marion, *Erotic Phenomenon*. Didier Anzieu argues that "the original form of communication, both in reality and even more intensely in phantasy, is direct, unmediated, from skin to skin." Didier Anzieu, *The Skin-Ego*, trans. Chris Turner (New Haven, CT: Yale University Press, 1989), 97.

69. Nancy, *Corpus*, 128.

70. Nancy, *Corpus II*, 88.

71. See Lanigan, *Speaking and Semiology*, 97–159.

72. Parts outside parts. Nancy, *Corpus*, 91.

73. McMahon, *Cinema and Contact*, 8.

74. "There is proximity, but only to the extent that extreme closeness emphasizes the distancing it opens up. All of being is in touch with all of being, but the law of touching is separation." Nancy, *Being Singular Plural*, 5.

75. A productive link could be made between Nancy's philosophy of being-with and Lanigan's semiotic phenomenological analysis of isolation and confrontation polarization (violence) and communication (dialogue) in tensions between what he calls "in-groups" and "out-groups" in urban contexts. See Lanigan, *Phenomenology*, 134–43.

76. See chapter 2 of this volume, as well as Nancy: "Being is not given—or a gift is not given to it—unless a gift, well short of what we imagine and what we practice in its name, is or should be always abandoned. One thinks one hears, one would like to hear, *donner* [to give] in *abandonner*, but the opposite is true. ('Don't give with one hand and wit[h]hold with the other,' says the law; but it is the giving itself as such that must not be withheld.)" Nancy, *Birth*, 45.

77. Jean-Luc Nancy, *The Experience of Freedom*, trans. Bridget McDonald (Stanford, CA: Stanford University Press, 1994); Esposito, *Terms*; Agamben, *Homo Sacer*.

78. Community is "a contact, it is a contagion: a touching, the transmission of a trembling at the edge of being, the communication of a passion that makes us fellow, or the communication of the passion

to be fellow, to be in common." Nancy, *Being Singular Plural*, 61. Sharing generates community, which Nancy defines as "contact, juxtaposition, porosity, osmosis, frictions, attraction and repulsion, etc." Nancy, *Creation of the World*, 110.

79. "We are charged with our *with*, which is to say with *us*. This does not mean that we must rush to understand this as something like 'responsibility of the community,' or 'the town' or 'the people,' etcetera. This means that we have as a charge, as a task—but we might as well say 'to live' or 'to be'—the *with* or the *between* in which we have our existence, which is to say at once our place or milieu and that to which and by which we *exist* in the strongest sense. In other words, we are *exposed*." Nancy, "Conloquium," 105.

80. Ibid. (emphasis added).

81. Lawlor, *Early Twentieth Century*.

82. Claire Colebrook, "Animal," in *The Agamben Dictionary*, ed. Alex Murray and Jessica Whyte (Edinburgh: Edinburgh University Press, 2011), 22.

83. Raffoul, "Logic," 49.

84. Nancy, "Conloquium," 106.

85. "Consequently the *Mitsein* or *Mitdasein* that Heidegger has formulated but avoided to analyze, should not be understood as a 'being there with' . . . but as a 'being-with *da*.' Yes, we are with one another, but this means first of all that we are with the topos of the *inter*, being-with being nothing else than being *on* this topos, than being *da*. Thus this being-with *da* is synonymous with being in the open, being always elsewhere." Nancy and Kate, "'*Cum*' . . . Revisited," 41.

86. Nancy, "Conloquium," 106. Nancy's contribution to Heidegger scholarship is significant. As Lanigan explains "In *Being and Time*, Heidegger distinguishes *Dasein* ('being-there'; ontological usage = philosophy) from *da Sein* usually written as *dasein* ('there-being'; ontic use = psychology)—this is *not* always clear in the English translation. Nancy is using *Mitdasein* to focus on *Dasein* so that the 'ready-to-hand' [*mit*] (conscious experience) is constituted by 'talk' [G. *Rede*] as distinct from 'idle talk' [*Gerede*]. *Rede* is Nancy's *in conloquium* because for him *avec* is *mit*." Lanigan, personal correspondence, March 24, 2014.

87. Raffoul, "Logic," 49. He continues, "This is why the task is to think this relation in terms of the *between* of singularities, the relation/non-relation indicated by the 'with' of Being-with, or the 'in' of being-*in*-common." Ibid., 49.

88. Nancy and Kate, "'*Cum*' . . . Revisited," 40.

89. Nancy, "Conloquium," 107. "Sense" is yet another term in Nancy's vocabulary to address the coexposure of world and being. Sense is what we live in and through, Nancy says: "Following its structure of an *inter*, sense is 'nothing.' But this nothing is by no means nonsense (the simple reverse of epiphanic meaning) . . . This nothing is not 'no thing' but the capacity proper in and by which the passage from us to us, 'between us,' from the world to the world, can take place." Nancy and Kate, "'*Cum*' . . . Revisited," 41.

90. "Still one must distrust here all pious resonances of 'openness,' as well as of the 'community.' Being open such as analyzed above has little to do with generosity, whether ascribed to some individual ethical attitude or to life as a whole. Being open is only the condition for the coexistence of finite singularities; *between* them—on their limit, between 'outside' and 'inside'—circulates the possibility of sense." Ibid., 43.

91. Nancy, *Corpus*, 86.

92. Raffoul, "Abandonment," 65.

93. Nancy and Kate, "'*Cum*' . . . Revisited," 38.

94. The notion of inoperability is central to Nancy's philosophy of community. In contrast to appeals to race and/or ethnicity as the foundation of political identity (nation, state, community, or person),

he emphasizes the fissures, cuts, and separation (the antifoundations) that characterize identity: "It is not a foundation, but more, an opening—a serration, a wound, an open mouth." Nancy, "Beheaded Sun," 45. This wound or opening at the heart of community is precisely inoperable. For example, "America no longer boasts absolute self-knowledge. It is also *beheaded*, a civilization come apart." Ibid., 48.

95. The body is "an extension of the *there*, the site of a breakthrough through which *it can come in from the world*." Nancy, *Corpus*, 25. See also Esposito, *Communitas*.

96. A summary quotation from Nancy indicates the critical, philosophical potential of attending to our *with*: "Thinking intermediality, then, may well lead to new philosophies of the community, of communication, and of media and mediality, all of which gradually come to accept that the old distinction between our 'we' and the world is no longer tenable." Nancy and Kate, "'Cum' . . . Revisited," 43.

97. See Lanigan, *Speaking and Semiology*, 78–81; Lanigan, *Phenomenology*, 157–93; Lanigan, *Human Science*, 81–113; Deborah Eicher-Catt and Isaac E. Catt, "What Can It Mean to Say That Communication Is 'Effective' (and for Whom) in Postmodernity?," *Atlantic Journal of Communication* 16, nos. 3–4 (2008): 119–21; Catt, "Communication Is Not a Skill"; Chang, *Deconstructing*, 33–67; and Wilden, *System and Structure*, 1–30.

98. Derrida, *Monolingualism*, 118.

Epilogue

1. See Chang's analysis of the "subjectivist thesis" of communication theory, what he calls "the ideology of the communicative." Chang, *Deconstructing*, xi, 17, 69–111.

2. Cf. Motely, who reduces the communication/noncommunication theory debate to intentionality: "In short, if all behaviors, intentional or not, are potentially communicative, then one cannot not communicate; but if some behaviors, e.g., unintentional ones, are not potentially communicative, then one can be noncommunicative." Motely, "On Whether," 2.

3. Angus, *Primal Scenes*, 72.

4. O'Neill, *Communicative Body*, 80–81.

5. "Whether implicit or explicit, the *goal* of all human expression is communication." Eicher-Catt, "Communicology," 357. Fritz qualifies that "human beings engaged in communicative interaction with one another are never concerned only with the content of utterances, or only with rational and efficient information exchange, but also with the feelings of others, social harmony, and other goods operative in the situation." Janie Harden Fritz, *Professional Civility: Communicative Virtue at Work* (New York: Peter Lang, 2013), 77.

6. "An utterer is one who makes something outer, and language is just one way of 'outering' what is inner, namely, the thought." Martinich, *Communication*, 18.

7. "Thus, contrary to Husserl, communication is not marked by a subjective intention to communicate through a mark. Rather, communication is a constitutive characteristic of the world we inhabit. Whether it be the tracks of animals or marks on a computer screen, communication is what makes cultural subjects of us. Proximally and for the most part, it calls us, we do not use it, insofar as we dwell within an already-instituted opening." Angus, *Primal Scenes*, 190.

BIBLIOGRAPHY

Agamben, Giorgio. *Homo Sacer: Sovereign Power and Bare Life*. Translated by Daniel Heller-Roazen. Stanford, CA: Stanford University Press, 1998.

———. *Language and Death: The Place of Negativity*. Translated by Karen E. Pinkus with Michael Hardt. Minneapolis: University of Minnesota Press, 1991.

———. *Remnants of Auschwitz: The Witness and the Archive*. Translated by Daniel Heller-Roazen. Brooklyn: Zone Books, 1999.

———. *The Sacrament of Language: An Archaeology of the Oath*. Translated by Adam Kotsko. Stanford, CA: Stanford University Press, 2011.

———. *State of Exception*. Translated by Kevin Attell. Chicago: University of Chicago Press, 2005.

Angus, Ian. *Primal Scenes of Communication: Communication, Consumerism, and Social Movements*. Albany: SUNY Press, 2000.

Anzieu, Didier. *The Skin-Ego*. Translated by Chris Turner. New Haven, CT: Yale University Press, 1989.

Atkin, Albert. "Peirce's Theory of Signs." In *Stanford Encyclopedia of Philosophy*. Stanford University, 1997–. Article published October 13, 2006; last modified April 4, 2013. https://plato.stanford.edu/entries/peirce-semiotics/.

Bartolini, Paolo. "Benveniste, Émile." In *The Agamben Dictionary*, edited by Alex Murray and Jessica Whyte, 35–36. Edinburgh: Edinburgh University Press, 2011.

Bateson, Gregory. "Cybernetic Explanation." In *Steps to an Ecology of Mind: Collected Essays in Anthropology, Psychiatry, Evolution, and Epistemology*, 405–15. Chicago: University of Chicago Press, 1972.

Bauman, Zygmunt. *Community: Seeking Safety in an Insecure World*. Malden, MA: Polity, 2001.

Benjamin, Walter. *Reflections: Essays, Aphorisms, Autobiographical Writings*. Edited by Peter Demetz. New York: Harcourt Brace Jovanovich, 1978.

Benveniste, Émile. *Problems in General Linguistics*. Edited by Mary Elizabeth Meek. Miami: University of Miami Press, 1973.

Berlo, David K. *The Process of Communication: An Introduction to Theory and Practice*. New York: Holt, Rinehart, and Winston, 1960.

Blumler, Jay G., and Elihu Katz. *The Uses of Mass Communications: Current Perspectives on Gratifications Research*. Beverly Hills, CA: SAGE, 1974.

Butchart, Garnet C. "The Communicology of Roland Barthes' *Camera Lucida*: Reflections on the

Sign-Body Experience of Visual Communication." *Visual Communication* 15, no. 2 (2016): 199–219.

Cadava, Eduardo, Peter Connor, and Jean-Luc Nancy, eds. *Who Comes after the Subject?* New York: Routledge, 1991.

Campbell, Timothy C. "*Bíos*, Immunity, Life: The Thought of Roberto Esposito." Translator's introduction to *Bíos: Biopolitics and Philosophy*, by Roberto Esposito. Minneapolis: University of Minnesota Press, 2008.

———. *Improper Life: Technology and Biopolitics from Heidegger to Agamben*. Minneapolis: University of Minnesota Press, 2011.

Carey, James. *Communication as Culture: Essays on Media and Society*. New York: Routledge, 1989.

Catt, Isaac E. "Communication Is Not a Skill: Critique of Communication Pedagogy as Narcissistic Expression." In *Communicology: The New Science of Embodied Discourse*, edited by Deborah Eicher-Catt and Isaac E. Catt, 131–50. Lanham, MD: Fairleigh Dickinson University Press, 2010.

———. "Communicology and Human Conduct: An Essay Dedicated to Max." *Semiotica*, no. 204 (2015): 341–60.

———. *Embodiment in the Semiotic Matrix: Communicology in Peirce, Dewey, Bateson, and Bourdieu*. Lanham, MD: Fairleigh Dickinson University Press, 2017.

———. "Gregory Bateson's 'New Science' in the Context of Communicology." *American Journal of Semiotics* 19, no. 1 (2003): 153–72.

———. "The Signifying World between Ineffability and Intelligibility: Body as Sign in Communicology." *Review of Communication* 11, no. 2 (2011): 122–44.

Chang, Briankle G. "Communication as Communicability." In *Communication As . . . Perspectives on Theory*, edited by Gregory J. Shepherd, Jeffrey St. John, and Ted Striphas, 242–48. Thousand Oaks, CA: SAGE, 2006.

———. *Deconstructing Communication: Representation, Subject, and Economies of Exchange*. Minneapolis: University of Minnesota Press, 1996.

Chang, Briankle G., and Garnet C. Butchart, eds. *Philosophy of Communication*. Cambridge, MA: MIT Press, 2012.

Chiesa, Lorenzo. *Subjectivity and Otherness: A Philosophical Reading of Lacan*. Cambridge, MA: MIT Press, 2007.

Clark, William Lawrence, and William Lawrence Marshall. *A Treatise on the Law of Crimes*. 2nd ed. St. Paul, MN: Keefe-Davidson, 1905.

Cohen, Anthony P. *The Symbolic Construction of Community*. New York: Routledge, 2001.

Colebrook, Claire. "Animal." In *The Agamben Dictionary*, edited by Alex Murray and Jessica Whyte, 22–24. Edinburgh: Edinburgh University Press, 2011.

Connor, Steven. *Dumbstruck: A Cultural History of Ventriloquism*. Oxford: Oxford University Press, 2000.

Cooren, François. "Communication Theory at the Center: Ventriloquism and the Communicative Constitution of Reality." *Journal of Communication* 62, no. 1 (2012): 1–20.

Culler, Jonathan. *Ferdinand de Saussure*. Ithaca, NY: Cornell University Press, 1986.

David, Pascal. "Dasein/Existence." In *Dictionary of Untranslatables: A Philosophical Lexicon*, edited by Barbara Cassin, Emily Apter, Jacques Lezra, and Michael Wood, 195–200. Princeton, NJ: Princeton University Press, 2014.

de la Durantaye, Leland. *Giorgio Agamben: A Critical Introduction*. Stanford, CA: Stanford University Press, 2009.

Delia, Jesse. "Communication Research: A History." In *Handbook of Communication Science*, edited by Charles R. Berger and Steven H. Chaffee, 20–98. Beverly Hills, CA: SAGE, 1987.

Derrida, Jacques. *Monolingualism of the Other; or, The Prosthesis of Origin*. Translated by Patrick Mensah. Stanford, CA: Stanford University Press, 1998.

———. *On Touching—Jean-Luc Nancy*. Translated by Christine Irizarry. Stanford, CA: Stanford University Press, 2005.

———. "'Le toucher': Touch/to touch him." *Paragraph* 16, no. 2 (1993): 122–57.

Devisch, Ignaas. *Jean-Luc Nancy and the Question of Community*. London: Bloomsbury, 2013.

Dues, Michael, and Mary Louise Brown. *Boxing Plato's Shadow: An Introduction to the Study of Human Communication*. New York: McGraw-Hill, 2004.

Eicher-Catt, Deborah. "The Authenticity in Ambiguity: Appreciating Maurice Merleau-Ponty's Abductive Logic as Communicative Practice." *Atlantic Journal of Communication* 13, no. 2 (2005): 113–34.

Eicher-Catt, Deborah, and Isaac E. Catt, eds. *Communicology: The New Science of Embodied Discourse*. Lanham, MD: Fairleigh Dickinson University Press, 2010.

———. "What Can It Mean to Say That Communication Is 'Effective' (and for Whom) in Postmodernity?" *Atlantic Journal of Communication* 16, nos. 3–4 (2008): 119–21.

Esposito, Roberto. *Bíos: Biopolitics and Philosophy*. Translated by Timothy C. Campbell. Minneapolis: University of Minnesota Press, 2008.

———. *Communitas: The Origin and Destiny of Community*. Translated by Timothy C. Campbell. Stanford, CA: Stanford University Press, 2010.

———. *Immunitas: The Protection and Negation of Life*. Cambridge, UK: Polity, 2011.

———. *Living Thought: The Origins and Actuality of Italian Philosophy*. Translated by Zakiya Hanafi. Stanford, CA: Stanford University Press, 2012.

———. *Persons and Things: From the Body's Point of View*. Malden, MA: Polity, 2015.

———. *Terms of the Political: Community, Immunity, Biopolitics*. Translated by Rhiannon Noel Welch. New York: Fordham University Press, 2013.

———. *Third Person: Politics of Life and Philosophy of the Impersonal*. Translated by Zakiya Hanafi. Cambridge, UK: Polity, 2012.

Esposito, Roberto, Jean-Luc Nancy, and Timothy Campbell. "Dialogue on the Philosophy to Come." *Minnesota Review*, no. 75 (Fall 2010): 71–88.

Fink, Bruce. *The Lacanian Subject*. Princeton, NJ: Princeton University Press, 1996.

———. *Lacan to the Letter: Reading "Écrits" Closely*. Minneapolis: University of Minnesota Press, 2004.

Fiske, John. *Introduction to Communication Studies*. London: Routledge, 1990.

Foucault, Michel. *The Birth of Biopolitics: Lectures at the Collège de France, 1978–1979*. Edited by Arnold I. Davidson. Translated by Graham Burchell. New York: Palgrave Macmillan, 2008.

———. "Of Other Spaces." *Diacritics* 16, no. 1 (Spring 1986): 22–27.
Freud, Sigmund. "Psychical (or Mental) Treatment." In *A Case of Hysteria: Three Essays on Sexuality and Other Works*, translated by James Strachey, 281–302. Reprint, London: Hogarth Press, 1975.
Fritz, Janie Harden. *Professional Civility: Communicative Virtue at Work*. New York: Peter Lang, 2013.
Fynsk, Christopher. "A Note on Language and the Body." *Paragraph* 16, no. 2 (1993): 192–201.
Garrido, Juan Manuel. "Jean-Luc Nancy's Concept of Body." *Epoché: A Journal for the History of Philosophy* 14, no. 1 (2009): 189–211.
Gasché, Rodolphe. *Of Minimal Things: Studies on the Notion of Relation*. Stanford, CA: Stanford University Press, 1999.
Genosko, Gary. *Remodeling Communication: From WWII to the WWW*. Toronto: University of Toronto Press, 2012.
Gerbner, George. "Toward a General Model of Communication." *Audio Visual Communication Review* 4, no. 3 (1956): 171–99.
Gilmore, Eugene Allen, and William Charles Wermuth. *Modern American Law: A Systematic and Comprehensive Commentary on the Fundamental Principles of American Law and Procedure*. Vol. 3. Chicago: Blackstone Institute, 1914.
Glendinning, Simon. "What Is Continental Philosophy?" In *The Edinburgh Encyclopedia of Continental Philosophy*, edited by Simon Glendinning, 3–20. Edinburgh: Edinburgh University Press, 1999.
Goh, Irving. *The Reject: Community, Politics, and Religion after the Subject*. New York: Fordham University Press, 2014.
Grossberg, Lawrence. *Cultural Studies in the Future Tense*. Durham, NC: Duke University Press, 2010.
Gunn, Joshua. "Refitting Fantasy: Psychoanalysis, Subjectivity, and Talking to the Dead." *Quarterly Journal of Speech* 90, no. 1 (2004): 1–23.
Gusdorf, Georges. *La parole*. Translated by Paul T. Brockelman. Evanston, IL: Northwestern University Press, 1965.
Habermas, Jürgen. *Theory of Communicative Action, Volume 1: Reason and the Rationalization of Society*. Boston: Beacon Press, 1984.
Hacking, Ian. *Rewriting the Soul: Multiple Personality and the Sciences of Memory*. Princeton, NJ: Princeton University Press, 1998.
Hainge, Greg. "Of Glitch and Men: The Place of the Human in the Successful Integration of Failure and Noise in the Digital Realm." *Communication Theory* 17, no. 1 (2007): 26–42.
Hall, Stuart. "Signification, Representation, Ideology: Althusser and the Post-structuralist Debates." *Critical Studies in Media Communication* 2, no. 2 (1985): 91–114.
Halpern, Orit. *Beautiful Data: A History of Vision and Reason since 1945*. Durham, NC: Duke University Press, 2015.
———. "Dreams for Our Perceptual Present: Temporality, Storage, and Interactivity in Cybernetics." *Configurations* 13, no. 2 (2005): 283–319.
Hamacher, Werner. "Ou, séance, touche de Nancy, ici." *Paragraph* 16, no. 2 (1993): 216–31.
Hand, Sean. "Being-in-Common, or the Meaning of Globalization." In *Jean-Luc Nancy: Justice, Legality and World*, edited by Benjamin Hutchens, 131–45. London: Continuum, 2013.
Hardt, Hanno. *Critical Communication Studies: Essays on*

Communication, History and Theory in America. London: Routledge, 2008.
Hardt, Michael, and Antonio Negri. *Multitude*. New York: Penguin, 2004.
Harman, Graham. "On Interface: Nancy's Weights and Measures." In *Jean-Luc Nancy and Plural Thinking: Expositions of World, Ontology, Politics, and Sense*, edited by Peter Gratton and Marie-Eve Morin, 95–107. Albany: SUNY Press, 2012.
Hawkes, Terence. *Structuralism and Semiotics*. Berkeley, CA: University of California Press, 1977.
Heidegger, Martin. *Being and Time*. Translated by John Macquarrie and Edward Robinson. New York: HarperCollins, 1962.
Henry, Michel. *I Am the Truth*. Translated by Susan Emanuel. Stanford, CA: Stanford University Press, 2003.
———. *Material Phenomenology*. Translated by Scott Davidson. New York: Fordham University Press, 2008.
Heron, Nicholas. "Subject." In *The Agamben Dictionary*, edited by Alex Murray and Jessica Whyte, 187–89. Edinburgh: Edinburgh University Press, 2011.
Hook, Derek. *Six Moments in Lacan: Communication and Identification and Psychoanalysis*. New York: Routledge, 2018.
Hovland, Carl Iver, Arthur A. Lumsdaine, and Fred D. Sheffield. *Experiments on Mass Communication*. Princeton, NJ: Princeton University Press, 1949.
Hutchens, B[enjamin] C., ed. *Jean-Luc Nancy: Justice, Legality and World*. New York: Bloomsbury, 2012.
———. *Jean-Luc Nancy and the Future of Philosophy*. Montreal: McGill-Queen's University Press, 2005.
Hyde, Michael J. "Jacques Lacan's Psychoanalytic Theory of Speech and Language." *Quarterly Journal of Speech* 66, no. 1 (1980): 96–118.
Innis, Harold Adams. *The Bias of Communication*. Toronto: University of Toronto Press, 1999.
———. *Empire and Communications*. Toronto: University of Toronto Press, 2008.
James, Ian. *The Fragmentary Demand: An Introduction to the Philosophy of Jean-Luc Nancy*. Stanford, CA: Stanford University Press, 2006.
———. *The New French Philosophy*. Malden, MA: Polity, 2012.
Katz, Elihu. "The Two-Step Flow of Communication: An Up-to-Date Report on an Hypothesis." *Public Opinion Quarterly* 21, no. 1 (1957): 61–78.
Katz, Elihu, and Paul Felix Lazarsfeld. *Personal Influence: The Part Played by People in the Flow of Mass Communications*. New Brunswick, NJ: Transaction, 2009.
Kearney, Richard. *Modern Movements in European Philosophy: Phenomenology, Critical Theory, Structuralism*. Manchester: Manchester University Press, 1994.
———. "The Wager of Carnal Hermeneutics." In *Carnal Hermeneutics*, edited by Richard Kearney and Brian Treanor, 15–56. New York: Fordham University Press, 2015.
Kearney, Richard, and Brian Treanor, eds. *Carnal Hermeneutics*. New York: Fordham University Press, 2015.
Kittler, Friedrich. *Literature, Media, Information Systems*. Edited by John Johnston. New York: Routledge, 1997.
Klapper, Joseph. *The Effects of Mass Communication*. Glencoe, IL: Free Press, 1960.
Krell, David Farrell. "*Das Unheimliche*, Architectural Sections of Heidegger and Freud." *Research in Phenomenology* 22, no. 1 (1992): 43–61.

Lacan, Jacques. *Écrits: A Selection*. Translated by Alan Sheridan. New York: Norton, 1977.
———. *Écrits: A Selection*. Translated by Bruce Fink. New York: Norton, 2002.
———. *Écrits: The First Complete Edition in English*. Translated by Bruce Fink. New York: Norton, 2007.
———. *The Language of the Self: The Function of Language in Psychoanalysis*. Translated by Anthony Wilden. 2nd ed. Baltimore: Johns Hopkins University Press, 1981.
———. *The Seminar of Jacques Lacan: The Four Fundamental Concepts of Psychoanalysis*. Edited by Jacques-Alain Miller. Translated by Alan Sheridan. New York: Norton, 1998.
———. *The Seminar of Jacques Lacan, Book I: Freud's Papers on Technique, 1953–1954*. Edited by Jacques-Alain Miller. Translated by John Forrester. New York: Norton, 1991.
———. "Seminar on 'The Purloined Letter.'" Translated by Jeffrey Mehlman. *Yale French Studies* 48 (1972): 39–72.
———. *Television: A Challenge to the Psychoanalytic Establishment*. Translated by Denis Hollier, Rosalind Krauss, Annette Michelson, and Jeffrey Mehlman. New York: Norton, 1990.
Lacoue-Labarthe, Philippe, and Jean-Luc Nancy. *The Title of the Letter: A Reading of Lacan*. Albany: SUNY Press, 1992.
Landes, Donald A. "Expressive Body, Exscriptive Corpus: The Tracing of the Body from Maurice Merleau-Ponty to Jean-Luc Nancy." *Chiasmi International* 9 (2007): 237–56.
———. *Merleau-Ponty and the Paradoxes of Expression*. New York: Bloomsbury, 2013.
Langford, Peter. *Roberto Esposito: Law, Community and the Political*. New York: Routledge, 2015.

Lanigan, Richard. "Communicology and Semiotic Hypercodes: The Example of Schizophrenic Discourse." Paper presented at the 36th Annual Meeting of the Semiotic Society of America, Pittsburgh, PA, 2011.
———. "Human Embodiment: An Eidetic and Empirical Communicology of Phantom Limb." *Metodo: International Studies in Phenomenology and Philosophy* 3, no. 1 (2015): 257–87.
———. *The Human Science of Communicology: A Phenomenology of Discourse in Foucault and Merleau-Ponty*. Pittsburgh: Duquesne University Press, 1992.
———. "Information Theories." In *Theories and Models of Communication*, edited by Paul Cobley and Peter Schultz, 58–83. Boston: De Gruyter Mouton, 2013.
———. *Phenomenology of Communication: Merleau-Ponty's Thematics in Communicology and Semiology*. Pittsburgh: Duquesne University Press, 1988.
———. "Review of *A Body*, by John Coplans." *American Journal of Semiotics* 17, no. 2 (2003): 371–73.
———. *Speaking and Semiology: Maurice Merleau-Ponty's Phenomenological Theory of Existential Communication*. The Hague: Mouton, 1972.
———. "Television: The Semiotic Phenomenology of Communication and the Image." In *Semiotics of the Media: State of the Art, Projects, and Perspectives*, edited by Winfried Nöth, 381–91. New York: Walter de Gruyter, 1997.
———. "Verbal and Nonverbal Codes of Communicology: The Foundation of Interpersonal Agency and Efficacy." In *Communicology: The New Science of Embodied Discourse*, edited by Deborah Eicher-Catt and Isaac E. Catt, 102–28. Lanham,

MD: Fairleigh Dickinson University Press, 2010.
Lasswell, Harold D. "The Structure and Function of Communication in Society." *The Communication of Ideas* 37 (1948): 215–28.
Lawlor, Leonard. *Early Twentieth-Century Continental Philosophy*. Bloomington: Indiana University Press, 2012.
Lazarsfeld, Paul Felix, Bernard Berelson, and Hazel Gaudet. *The People's Choice: How the Voter Makes Up His Mind in a Presidential Campaign*. New York: Duell, Sloan, and Pearce, 1944.
Leach, Edmund. *Culture and Communication: The Logic by Which Symbols Are Connected. An Introduction to the Use of Structuralist Analysis in Social Anthropology*. Cambridge, UK: Cambridge University Press, 1976.
Leeds-Hurwitz, Wendy. "Crossing Disciplinary Boundaries: The Macy Conferences on Cybernetics as a Case Study in Multidisciplinary Communication." *Cybernetica* 37, nos. 3–4 (1994): 349–69.
Lemm, Vanessa. "Biopolitics and Community in Roberto Esposito." Introduction to *The Terms of the Political: Community, Immunity, Biopolitics*, by Roberto Esposito, 1–13. New York: Fordham University Press, 2013.
Levy, Ghyslain. "Un patient est remboursé; ou, Variations sur le thème du paiement et de ses diverses alternatives dans la situation analytique." *Psychanalystes: Revue du Collège des Psychanalystes* 20 (1986): 21–33.
Lichtenberg, Joseph D., Frank M. Lachmann, and James L. Fosshage. *A Spirit of Inquiry: Communication in Psychoanalysis*. Hillsdale, NJ: Analytic Press, 2002.
Luhmann, Niklas. *Social Systems*. Translated by John Bednarz Jr. with Dirk Baecker. Stanford, CA: Stanford University Press, 1996.
Lundberg, Christian. "The Royal Road Not Taken: Joshua Gunn's 'Refitting Fantasy: Psychoanalysis, Subjectivity, and Talking to the Dead' and Lacan's Symbolic Order." *Quarterly Journal of Speech* 90, no. 4 (2004): 495–500.
Macke, Frank J. "Body, Liquidity, and Flesh: Bachelard, Merleau-Ponty, and the Elements of Interpersonal Communication." *Philosophy Today* 51, no. 4 (2007): 401–15.
———. *The Experience of Human Communication: Body, Flesh, and Relationship*. Lanham, MD: Fairleigh Dickinson University Press, 2015.
———. "Intrapersonal Communicology: Reflection, Reflexivity, and Relational Consciousness in Embodied Subjectivity." *Atlantic Journal of Communication* 16, nos. 3–4 (2008): 122–48.
Marion, Jean-Luc. *Being Given: Toward a Phenomenology of Givenness*. Translated by Jeffery L. Kosky. Stanford, CA: Stanford University Press, 2002.
———. *The Erotic Phenomenon*. Translated by Stephen E. Lewis. Chicago: University of Chicago Press, 2007.
———. *In Excess: Studies of Saturated Phenomena*. Translated by Robyn Horner and Vincent Berruad. New York: Fordham University Press, 2002.
Martinez, Jacqueline M. *Communicative Sexualities*. Lanham, MD: Lexington Books, 2011.
Martinich, Aloysius P. *Communication and Reference*. Hawthorne, NY: Walter de Gruyter, 1984.
Mattelart, Armand, and Michèle Mattelart. *Theories of Communication: A Short Introduction*. Translated by Susan Gruenheck Taponier and James A. Cohen. London: SAGE, 1998.

McCombs, Maxwell E., and Donald L. Shaw. "The Agenda-Setting Function of Mass Media." *Public Opinion Quarterly* 36, no. 2 (1972): 176–87.

McMahon, Laura. *Cinema and Contact: The Withdrawal of Touch in Nancy, Bresson, Duras and Denis*. London: Legenda, 2012.

McQuail, Dennis. *Mass Communication Theory: An Introduction*. Thousand Oaks, CA: SAGE, 1994.

Mead, George Herbert. "The Problem of Society: How We Become Selves." In *Movements of Thought in the Nineteenth Century*, edited by Merritt H. Moore, 360–85. Chicago: University of Chicago Press, 1972.

Merleau-Ponty, Maurice. *Phenomenology of Perception*. Translated by Colin Smith. New York: Routledge, 2004.

Moran, Dermot. *Introduction to Phenomenology*. New York: Routledge, 2000.

Morin, Marie-Eve. *Jean-Luc Nancy*. Malden, MA: Polity, 2012.

Motely, Michael T. "On Whether One Can(not) Not Communicate: An Examination via Traditional Communication Postulates." *Western Journal of Speech* 54, no. 1 (1990): 1–20.

Muller, John P., and William J. Richardson. *The Purloined Poe: Lacan, Derrida & Psychoanalytic Reading*. Baltimore: Johns Hopkins University Press, 1988.

Murray, Alex, and Jessica Whyte, eds. *The Agamben Dictionary*. Edinburgh: Edinburgh University Press, 2011.

Nancy, Jean-Luc. *After Fukushima: The Equivalence of Catastrophes*. Translated by Charlotte Mandell. New York: Fordham University Press, 2015.

———. "Beheaded Sun (Soleil cou coupé)." *Qui Parle* 3, no. 2 (1989): 41–53.

———. *Being Nude: The Skin of Images*. Translated by Anne O'Byrne and Carlie Anglemire. New York: Fordham University Press, 2014.

———. *Being Singular Plural*. Translated by Robert Richardson and Anne O'Byrne. Stanford, CA: Stanford University Press, 2000.

———. *The Birth to Presence*. Translated by Brian Holmes et al. Stanford, CA: Stanford University Press, 1993.

———. "Conloquium." *Minnesota Review*, no. 75 (Fall 2010): 101–8.

———. *Corpus*. Translated by Richard A. Rand. New York: Fordham University Press, 2008.

———. *Corpus II: Writings on Sexuality*. Translated by Anne O'Byrne. New York: Fordham University Press, 2013.

———. *The Creation of the World or Globalization*. Translated by François Raffoul and David Pettigrew. Albany: SUNY Press, 2007.

———. *The Disavowed Community*. Translated by Philip Armstrong. New York: Fordham University Press, 2016.

———. *The Evidence of Film: Abbas Kiarostami*. Translated by Christine Irizarry and Verena Andermatt Conley. Brussels: Yves Gevaert, 2001.

———. *The Experience of Freedom*. Translated by Bridget McDonald. Stanford, CA: Stanford University Press, 1994.

———. *The Inoperative Community*. Edited by Peter Connor. Translated by Peter Connor, Lisa Garbus, Michael Holland, and Simona Sawhney. Minneapolis: University of Minnesota Press, 1991.

———. "The Insufficiency of 'Values' and the Necessity of 'Sense.'" *Cultural Values* 1, no. 1 (1997): 127–31.

———. *Listening*. Translated by Charlotte Mandell. New York: Fordham University Press, 2007.

———. *The Sense of the World*. Translated by Jeffery S. Librett. Minneapolis: University of Minnesota Press, 1997.

Nancy, Jean-Luc, and Laurens ten Kate. "'Cum' . . . Revisited: Preliminaries to Thinking the Interval." In *Intermedialities: Philosophy, Arts, Politics*, edited by Henk Oosterling and Ewa Plonowska Ziarek, 37–43. Lanham, MD: Lexington Books, 2011.

Nixon, Mignon. "On the Couch." *October* 113 (2005): 39–76.

O'Byrne, Anne. "Nancy's Materialist Ontology." In *Jean-Luc Nancy and Plural Thinking: Expositions of World, Ontology, Politics, and Sense*, edited by Peter Gratton and Marie-Eve Morin, 79–93. Albany: SUNY Press, 2012.

———. *Natality and Finitude*. Bloomington: Indiana University Press, 2010.

———. "The Politics of Intrusion." *CR: The New Centennial Review* 2, no. 3 (2002): 169–87.

O'Neill, John. *The Communicative Body: Studies in Communicative Philosophy, Politics, and Sociology*. Evanston, IL: Northwestern University Press, 1989.

Oosterling, Henk, and Ewa Plonowska Ziarek, eds. *Intermedialities: Philosophy, Arts, Politics*. Lanham, MD: Lexington Books, 2011.

Peirce, Charles S. *Collected Papers of Charles Sanders Peirce*. Edited by Arthur W. Burks, Charles Hartshorne, and Paul Weiss. Vol. 6. Cambridge, MA: Belknap Press, 1965.

Perpich, Diane. "*Corpus Meum*: Disintegrating Bodies and the Ideal of Integrity." *Hypatia* 20, no. 3 (2005): 75–91.

Peters, John Durham. "Democracy and Mass Communication Theory: Dewey, Lippmann, Lazarsfeld." *Communication* 11, no. 3 (1989): 199–220.

Peters, John Durham, and Peter Simonson, eds. *Mass Communication and American Social Thought: Key Texts, 1919–1968*. Oxford: Rowman and Littlefield, 2004.

Petrilli, Susan. "For a Critique of the Subject." *Southern Semiotic Review* 1, no. 1 (2013).

———. *The Self as a Sign, the World, and the Other: Living Semiotics*. New Brunswick, NJ: Transaction, 2013.

Pettegrew, Loyd S. "Psychoanalytic Theory: A Neglected Rhetorical Dimension." *Philosophy & Rhetoric* 10, no. 1 (1977): 46–59.

Putney, Albert H. *Criminal Law, Criminal Procedure, Wills, Administration*. Vol. 10. Popular Law Library. Minneapolis: Cree, 1908.

Raffoul, François. "Abandonment." In *Jean-Luc Nancy: Justice, Legality and World*, edited by B. C. Hutchens, 65–81. New York: Continuum, 2012.

———. "The Logic of the With: On Nancy's *Être singulier pluriel*." *Studies in Practical Philosophy* 1, no. 1 (1999): 36–52.

Ramsey, Ramsey Eric. *The Long Path to Nearness: A Contribution to a Corporeal Philosophy of Communication and the Groundwork for an Ethics of Relief*. Atlantic Highlands, NJ: Humanities Press, 1998.

Rancière, Jacques. *Disagreement: Politics and Philosophy*. Translated by Julie Rose. Minneapolis: University of Minnesota Press, 1999.

Reddy, Michael J. "The Conduit Metaphor: A Case of Frame Conflict in Our Language about Language." In *Metaphor and Thought*, 2nd ed., edited by Andrew Ortony, 164–201. Cambridge, UK: Cambridge University Press, 1993.

Ricoeur, Paul. *On Translation*. London: Routledge, 2006.

Rizzuto, Ana-María. "Speech Events, Language Development, and the

Clinical Situation." *International Journal of Psychoanalysis* 83, no. 6 (2002): 1325–43.

———. "The Talking Cure and the Analyst's Intentions." *Psychoanalytic Review* 95, no. 5 (2008): 729–49.

Rogers, Annie G. *The Unsayable: The Hidden Language of Trauma*. New York: Random House, 2006.

Sapir, Edward. "Communication." In *Encyclopedia of the Social Sciences*, edited by Edwin R. A. Seligman, 4:78–81. New York: Macmillan, 1930.

———. *Selected Writings in Language, Culture and Personality*. Edited by David Goodman Mandelbaum. Berkeley, CA: University of California Press, 1949.

Sarasin, Philipp. "The Body as Medium: Nineteenth-Century European Hygiene Discourse." *Grey Room* 29 (2007): 48–65.

Saussure, Ferdinand de. *Course in General Linguistics*. Edited by Charles Bally, Albert Sechehaye, and Albert Riedlinger. Translated by Wade Baskin. New York: McGraw-Hill, 1966.

Scheb, John M., and John M. Scheb II. *Criminal Law and Procedure*. 5th ed. Belmont, CA: Wadsworth, 2008.

Schiller, Herbert. *Mass Communications and American Empire*. Boulder, CO: Westview Press, 1992.

Schramm, Wilbur. "How Communication Works." In *The Process and Effects of Mass Communication*, by Wilbur Schramm, 3–26. Champaign: University of Illinois Press, 1954.

Schutz, Alfred. *Phenomenology of the Social World*. Translated by George Walsh and Fredrick Lehnert. Evanston, IL: Northwestern University Press, 1967.

Shannon, Claude E., and Warren Weaver. *The Mathematical Theory of Communication*. Champaign: University of Illinois Press, 1949.

Shepherd, Gregory J., Jeffrey St. John, and Theodore G. Striphas, eds. *Communication As . . . Perspectives on Theory*. Thousand Oaks, CA: SAGE, 2006.

Smythe, Dallas Walker. *Dependency Road: Communications, Capitalism, Consciousness, and Canada*. Norwood, NJ: Ablex, 1981.

Sobchack, Vivian. *The Address of the Eye: A Phenomenology of Film Experience*. Princeton, NJ: Princeton University Press, 1992.

Sorial, Sarah. "Heidegger, Jean-Luc Nancy, and the Question of Dasein's Embodiment: An Ethics of Touch and Spacing." *Philosophy Today* 48, no. 2 (2004): 216–30.

Sparrow, Tom. *The End of Phenomenology: Metaphysics and the New Realism*. Edinburgh: Edinburgh University Press, 2014.

Stevens, Alexandre. "Lacanian Interpretation." *Hurly-Burly: The International Lacanian Journal of Psychoanalysis* 1 (2009): 57–59.

Tönnies, Ferdinand de. *Community and Civil Society*. Edited by Jose Harris. Translated by Jose Harris and Margaret Hollis. Cambridge, UK: Cambridge University Press, 2001.

Underwood, Erin Daina, and Lawrence R. Frey. "Communication and Community: Clarifying the Connection across the Communication Community." *Annals of the International Communication Association* 31, no. 1 (2007): 370–418.

Wahlberg, Malin. *Documentary Time: Film and Phenomenology*. Minneapolis: University of Minnesota Press, 2008.

Watkin, Christopher. *Phenomenology or Deconstruction? The Question of Ontology in Maurice Merleau-Ponty, Paul Ricoeur and Jean-Luc Nancy*.

Edinburgh: Edinburgh University Press, 2009.
Watzlawick, Paul, Janet H. Beavin, and Donald D. Jackson. *Pragmatics of Human Communication: A Study of Interactional Patterns, Pathologies and Paradoxes*. New York: Norton, 1967.
West, David. *Continental Philosophy: An Introduction*. Malden, MA: Polity, 2010.
Wilden, Anthony. *The Rules Are No Game: The Strategy of Communication*. New York: Routledge, 1987.
———. *System and Structure: Essays in Communication and Exchange*. 2nd ed. London: Tavistock, 1984.
———. Translator's introduction to *The Language of the Self: The Function of Language in Psychoanalysis*, by Jacques Lacan, vii–xix. Translated by Anthony Wilden. Baltimore: Johns Hopkins University Press, 1981.
Will, George F. "Intellectual Viruses." *Pittsburgh Post Gazette*, January 30, 2017.
Williams, Raymond. "Communications as Cultural Science." *Journal of Communication* 24, no. 3 (1974): 17–25.
———. *Keywords: A Vocabulary of Culture and Society*. New York: Oxford University Press, 2014.
Yalom, Irvin D. *Love's Executioner and Other Tales of Psychotherapy*. New York: Perennial, 2000.
Žižek, Slavoj. *For They Know Not What They Do: Enjoyment as a Political Factor*. 2nd ed. New York: Verso, 2002.
———. *The Plague of Fantasies*. New York: Verso, 1997.

INDEX

abandonment
    abandoned being, 6, 12, 44, 57, 58, 133, 156 n. 49, 156 n. 56, 175 n. 76
    to language, 12, 13, 55–62, 64, 65, 66, 81, 125, 136, 137, 139
    Nancy on law and, 157 n. 59, 157 n. 60
affinity
    charity and, 135
    communication as, 14, 58, 78, 79, 138, 139, 140
    in definition of communication, 4, 14, 62, 77, 81, 131
    inside of communication and, 45, 46
    munus invites thinking of, 89
    opening self to other and, 141
Agamben, Giorgio
    on abandoned being, 6, 12
    on ban of language, 44, 55, 56, 59, 65, 85, 139, 156 n. 49, 156 n. 53
    on biopolitics, 15, 43, 65
    on guilt, 143 n. 6
    on language and the nonlinguistic, 168 n. 55
    on language as ontological condition of being human, 44, 53, 55–56, 57, 61, 62, 65, 66, 156 n. 58, 158 n. 78
    on law, 15, 56, 64, 65, 155 n. 47
    on sovereign power, 6, 11, 48–49, 51, 54
    on sovereignty of language, 11–12, 43, 50–55, 56–57, 59, 62, 137
    on taking place of language, 53, 56, 99
    on voice, 52, 59, 157 n. 61
Angus, Ian, 145 n. 11, 152 n. 68, 153 n. 10, 163 n. 62, 174 n. 48, 177 n. 7

autoimmunization, 18, 74, 85–90, 94, 140, 161 n. 39, 164 n. 67

ban of language
    Agamben on, 44, 55, 56, 59, 65, 85, 139, 156 n. 49, 156 n. 53
    as relation, 44, 56, 57
being-with, 116–36
    consciousness of, 65
    as embodied, 63, 93, 122
    Nancy on, 9, 19–20, 118–21, 123, 126–28, 132–36, 175 n. 75, 176 n. 79, 177 n. 96
    one another, 94, 102, 117, 132, 134, 138
    philosophy of communication and, 133–36
Benveniste, Émile
    on humans as speaking beings, 12, 44, 58, 153 n. 5
    on language and subjectivity, 12, 52, 153 n. 7, 154 n. 29
    on performatives, 54–55
    on pronouns, 52–54, 125–26
    on sign and sign in context, 51
    on speaking and language, 155 n. 40
    subjectivity as defined by, 105
biopolitics, 15–16, 43, 65, 67, 93, 114
body, the
    as agency of psyche, 105, 109
    being-with as embodied, 63, 122
    bodily presence, 6, 96, 98, 99, 100–101, 102, 104, 110, 167 n. 47
    of Christ, 99, 165 n. 3, 165 n. 4, 169 n. 81

body, the (*continued*)
  in communication studies, 111–15
  community of bodies, 113, 128
  discourses about, 96, 98, 112, 114, 115
  dis-integration of, 6, 9, 19, 96, 97–100, 107, 109, 113, 114, 137, 142
  embodied being, 5, 13, 18, 22, 64, 95, 96, 103, 112, 114, 130, 136, 139, 140, 170 n. 86, 175 n. 67
  embodied communication communities, 9, 60
  embodiment of human communication, 3–4, 24, 65, 93, 122
  exposure of, 20, 95, 96, 100–104, 105, 107, 129, 130
  expression and, 106, 115, 122, 138, 157 n. 67, 158 n. 74
  as index, 18, 94–115, 137, 141, 167 n. 46
  as between inside and outside, 103, 104–9, 111, 112, 114, 140
  integrity of, 16, 18–19, 96, 97, 99, 113, 114, 141, 142
  language and, 65, 117, 159 n. 82
  lived body, 93, 98, 105, 110, 111, 130, 158 n. 69
  in mirror phase of identification, 36, 60
  Nancy on "this is my body," 18–19, 95–96, 98, 103–4, 111, 165 n. 4
  self's relation to, 107, 109, 112, 123–24, 167 n. 49, 168 n. 58, 168 n. 62
  semiotic phenomenology and embodiment, 121–25
  spacing-timing of, 96, 100–104, 107, 109–11, 112, 114–15, 130
  touch and, 128–30
  unified, 36, 96, 97, 98, 99, 108, 113, 141
borders (boundaries)
  in biopolitical paradigm, 15
  identity, 18, 67, 68, 70, 74, 75, 80–81, 84, 85, 94, 95, 117, 129, 137, 141, 162 n. 47
  touch as boundary experience, 130

Catt, Isaac E., 121, 150 n. 30
Chang, Briankle G., 23, 146 n. 22, 158 n. 81, 163 n. 55
communication
  affinity and, 4, 14, 58, 62, 78, 79, 138, 139, 140

  antinomy of human, 79–80, 82
  as basis of exposure, 41, 78, 80, 83–84, 88, 92, 93, 138, 139, 140
  being-in-communication, 65, 80, 84, 90, 112, 135–36
  the body in studies of, 111–15
  communities of, 9, 11, 20, 54, 60, 63, 87
  and-as community, 85–90
  community as bound to, 116–17
  as contact, 90, 132, 137, 138, 139, 142
  as contagion, 66, 78, 79, 85, 132, 137, 138, 140
  as contaminating, 81, 83–84, 85, 139
  continental philosophical approach to, 4–5, 8, 9
  defined, 4, 77, 143 n. 8, 163 n. 53
  embodiment of human, 3–4, 24, 65, 93, 122
  Esposito on, 14–18, 21, 76
  exposure to, 13, 65, 66, 92
  having-to-be in, 13, 61, 63, 125, 158 n. 81
  as identity-altering, 89, 92, 93, 139, 140
  as immunization, 6, 17, 65, 66–93, 94, 117, 133, 137, 139–40, 141
  impossibility of human noncommunication, 3, 6, 11–13, 41, 42–65, 66, 68, 79, 81, 82, 120, 131, 137, 138, 139
  inside of, 45–50, 63, 64
  as intentional, 138, 177 n. 2
  Lacan on, 9–10, 21, 23, 24–41
  law of, 58, 59, 62, 65, 85, 137, 156 n. 58
  mass, 4, 83, 85, 140, 163 n. 59
  modern theory of, 4, 78–79, 136, 144 n. 10, 163 n. 55
  munus as origin of, 17, 68, 82, 89, 90, 141
  Nancy on, 19, 21, 160 n. 12
  normative order of, 45–47, 48, 81, 85, 137
  obligation to communicate, 58, 63, 82, 137
  outside of, 45–50, 63, 64
  possibility of, 3, 23, 40, 92, 120, 139
  as protection, 14, 66, 68, 81–82, 92, 94, 116, 139, 140, 141
  psychoanalysis and, 9–10, 23–24, 27–34, 41, 42
  relation and, 92, 96, 127, 139, 165 n. 10

reversibility of, 123–24, 173 n. 39
senses of, 4, 77, 80–85
takes place, 34, 91, 93
as threat, 14, 66, 68, 81, 84, 88, 91–92, 94, 116, 140
as threshold between self and other, 67–68, 78, 79, 81–84, 89, 90, 132, 163 n. 55
as uncertain, 11, 40–41, 42, 116, 137
See also language; noise; philosophy of communication; speaking; utterance
communicology, 118, 146 n. 21, 159 n. 5
community, 116–36
being disqualified from, 14, 147 n. 30
being in, 5, 112, 130–31, 141
building, 70, 119, 131, 136
as coexistence, 73, 91
communication and-as, 85–90
communication as immunization and, 17–18, 66
communication as invitation to, 89, 139, 141
communication communities, 9, 11, 20, 54, 60, 63, 87
discourses of, 63, 117, 135
Esposito on antinomy of, 68–72, 90, 160 n. 12, 161 n. 34
having-to-be in, 58, 71, 125
law and, 2, 70, 73
life and, 15, 147 n. 32
munus as origin of, 17, 68, 74, 90, 141, 160 n. 11, 162 n. 47
Nancy on, 18, 19, 90, 95, 114, 117, 119, 122, 125–28, 160 n. 12, 160 n. 29, 174 n. 56, 175 n. 78
necessity of, 69, 132, 148 n. 36
as nonentity for Esposito, 69, 73, 75, 91, 125, 174 n. 56
problem of, 118, 125, 160 n. 20
protection and, 14, 70, 72, 73, 86
taking place of, 91, 137
threat and, 70, 73
contact
being in, 135–36
bodily, 104, 115, 122, 130
codes that regulate, 130
communication as, 78, 79, 90, 132, 137, 138, 139, 142

munus and, 77, 89
mutual, 74, 75, 135
as phatic function of communication, 127
See also touch
contagion
communication as, 66, 78, 79, 85, 132, 137, 138, 140
munus exposes us to, 77
the outside seen as, 71
overprotection and, 86, 87
semantic, 81, 151 n. 34, 163 n. 56
contamination
communication as contaminating, 81, 83–84, 85, 139
of identity, 74, 77–78, 80, 81
immunization and, 70, 76

Dasein
Heidegger on, 111, 120, 133, 169 n. 79, 176 n. 86
Nancy on, 120, 133, 134
as thrown into existence, 57, 75, 156 n. 57
Derrida, Jacques, 7, 113, 136, 164 n. 67
difference
blurring of distinction with identity, 13
community as experience of, 135
different perspectives, 85, 86, 87, 88, 90
exposure to, 84, 86, 93, 96
self-identity and, 39, 41, 94
touch and, 130, 131
discourses
about the body, 96, 98, 112, 114, 115
of community, 63, 117, 135
cultural, 37, 63
of the Other, 2, 24–27, 29, 32, 35, 38, 40
overprotection against different, 85, 86–87

embodiment. *See* body, the
Esposito, Roberto
on autoimmunization, 18, 74, 85–90, 141
on being of community, 171 n. 97
on communication, 14–18, 21, 76
on communication as immunization, 66–93

Esposito, Roberto (*continued*)
  on community as nonentity, 69, 73, 75, 91, 125, 174 n. 56
  on immunity, 14–17, 67, 70–75
  relevance to philosophy of communication, 16, 68, 85
  on social contract theory, 71, 160 n. 20, 161 n. 44
essentialism, 10, 16, 74, 134, 145 n. 11
exception, 45–50
  relation of, 48, 49, 51, 59
  sovereign, 51, 154 n. 23
  state of, 49, 51, 153 n. 16
exclusive inclusion, 11, 13, 20, 49, 57
exposition, 101–2, 106, 118, 129, 130
exposure, 9
  of being, 94, 102, 112, 134
  of the body, 20, 95, 96, 100–104, 105, 107, 129, 130
  coexposure, 76, 78, 82, 89, 103, 130, 133, 136–38, 140, 141, 142, 176 n. 89
  to communication, 13, 65, 66, 92
  communication as basis of, 41, 78, 80, 83–84, 88, 92, 93, 138, 139, 140
  to difference, 84, 86, 93, 96
  of identity, 74, 81, 87, 94
  immunizing, 84, 85
  Nancy on, 19, 90, 118
  relational, 97, 115
  self-exposure, 20, 134
  touch, 131, 132
expression
  being-with and, 123, 132
  body and, 106, 115, 122, 138, 157 n. 67, 158 n. 74
  capacity for, 62, 102
  communication and, 23, 24, 87, 94, 117
  facial, 36, 107, 139
  group, 82, 138
  language and, 10, 26, 52, 53
  lived body and, 93, 110
  perceptions of others', 13, 60, 63
  in psychoanalysis, 33, 34
  public, 17, 41, 86
  self-expression, 17, 26, 33, 40–41, 80, 102, 115, 119, 124, 130–31
exscription, 9, 105–8, 118, 131–32, 155 n. 34, 168 n. 54

exteriority (outside)
  blurring of distinction with interiority, 13, 49, 63, 75, 107, 138, 139, 140, 154 n. 18
  the body as between inside and, 103, 104–9, 111, 112, 114, 140
  communication as threshold between interiority and, 68, 83–84, 93, 139
  of language, 61, 64, 105, 158 n. 68
  touch and, 129–30

Foucault, Michel, 7, 54, 110, 158 n. 78, 169 n. 73
Freud, Sigmund, 31–32, 35, 108–9

Garrido, Juan Manuel, 169 n. 75, 169 n. 81
Grossberg, Lawrence, 164 n. 77, 175 n. 67

Hacking, Ian, 151 n. 34, 163 n. 56
Hamacher, Werner, 54, 156 n. 52, 167 n. 47
having-to-be
  in communication, 13, 61, 63, 125, 158 n. 81
  for community, 58, 71, 125
  Dasein as, 57, 75, 156 n. 57
  in language, 58, 65, 131
  as obligation, 57, 73
Heidegger, Martin
  on concern, 108–9, 132
  on *Dasein*, 111, 120, 133, 169 n. 79, 176 n. 86
  on *Geheiss*, 153 n. 4
  on humans and language, 12, 31–32, 58, 147 n. 25
  on *Mitsein*, 20, 133, 134, 176 n. 85
  on thrownness, 57, 132
Henry, Michel
  on body and ego, 168 n. 58
  on community, 116, 159 n. 9, 160 n. 11, 160 n. 28, 172 n. 14
  on ego and the other, 123–24, 173 n. 38
  on objective world, 166 n. 37
  on transcendental phenomenology, 170 n. 91
Husserl, Edmund, 109, 120, 123, 170 n. 84, 170 n. 91, 177 n. 7
Hyde, Michael J., 150 n. 29, 152 n. 65

Index

identity
  blurring of distinction with difference, 13
  borders of, 18, 67, 68, 70, 74, 75, 80–81, 84, 94, 95, 117, 129, 137, 141, 162 n. 47
  communication as identity-altering, 89, 92, 93, 139, 140
  contamination and, 74, 77–78, 80, 81
  exposure of, 74, 81, 87, 94
  Lacan on mirror phase of identification, 35–36, 60
  lack in, 42, 79, 112
immunity
  affirmative dimension of, 88–89, 92
  defined, 67
  discourses of, 68
  Esposito on, 14–17, 67, 70–75
  as internal horizon of community, 75, 76
  munus as origin of, 17, 68
  See also immunization
immunization, 15
  autoimmunization, 18, 74, 85–90, 94, 140, 161 n. 39, 164 n. 67
  communication as, 6, 17, 65, 66–93, 94, 117, 133, 137, 139–40, 141
  law's immunizing function, 72, 76, 77, 83, 162 n. 48, 162 n. 50
  inclusive exclusion, 49, 76, 77, 138, 140, 156 n. 47
  indices, the body as, 18, 94–115, 137, 141, 167 n. 46
interiority (inside)
  blurring of distinction with exteriority, 13, 49, 63, 75, 107, 138, 139, 140, 154 n. 18
  the body as between outside and, 103, 104–9, 111, 112, 114, 140
  communication as threshold between exteriority and, 68, 83–84, 93, 139
intersubjectivity
  communication as condition of, 78, 139
  human existence as intersubjective, 61, 75
  signifier "I" in nexus of, 126
  subjectivity as, 130, 139

Jakobson, Roman, 8, 52, 127
James, Ian, 8, 118, 145 n. 17, 172 n. 10

Kearney, Richard, 28, 158 n. 74

Lacan, Jacques
  Benveniste's response to, 12
  on communication, 9–10, 21, 23, 24–41
  on language, 9–10, 11, 23, 24–41, 50
  on order of culture, 25, 54
  psychoanalysis of, 8, 9–10, 11, 23–24, 30–41, 42, 146 n. 20
  on signifiers, 36–37, 60
Landes, Donald A., 106–7, 154 n. 20, 157 n. 67, 168 n. 54
language
  abandonment to, 12, 13, 55–62, 64, 65, 66, 81, 125, 136, 137, 139
  Agamben on sovereignty of, 11–12, 43, 50–55, 56–57, 59, 62, 137
  authority of, 42–43, 44, 49, 52, 59
  being in, 58, 62, 65, 131
  as contract, 50–52, 55, 59, 155 n. 45
  human communication and, 5, 21
  Lacan on, 9–10, 11, 23, 24–41, 50
  law and, 11, 56, 59, 64, 155 n. 47
  Nancy on, 123, 131–32, 159 n. 82
  as nonrelational, 55, 56–57, 58
  as ontological condition of being human, 44, 53, 55–56, 57, 61, 62, 65, 66, 156 n. 58, 158 n. 78
  outside of, 51, 53, 59, 99–100, 106
  perception and, 10, 25, 62, 107, 126
  psychoanalysis on, 24, 26–27, 60
  speaking transcended by, 64–65
  subjectivity and, 12, 41, 52, 53, 59, 63, 68, 117, 138, 153 n. 7, 154 n. 29, 155 n. 37
  taking place of, 53, 56, 57, 62, 99–100
  See also ban of language; discourses; pronouns
langue, 51, 52, 106, 155 n. 31
Lanigan, Richard
  on embodiment, 103, 105, 121, 123, 173 n. 29
  on language in speaking, 157 n. 62
  on reversibility of communication, 173 n. 39

Lanigan, Richard (*continued*)
    on semiotic phenomenology, 146 n. 21
    on semiotic systems, 122–23
    on signifier "I," 126
law
    Agamben on banning and, 156 n. 53
    ban of language experienced as, 44
    of communication, 58, 59, 62, 65, 85, 137, 156 n. 58
    communication function of, 77, 139
    immunizing function of, 72, 76, 77, 83, 162 n. 48, 162 n. 50
    Lacan on self and, 157 n. 65
    language and, 11, 56, 59, 64, 155 n. 47
    munus appropriated by, 76–77
    Nancy on abandonment and, 157 n. 59, 157 n. 60
Lundberg, Christian, 36, 150 n. 27

Macke, Frank J., 121, 152 n. 55, 164 n. 66
Martinez, Jacqueline, 61, 158 n. 71
Mead, George Herbert, 60, 157 n. 66
Merleau-Ponty, Maurice, 7, 103, 168 n. 54
misunderstanding
    communication experienced as, 9, 66
    communication in threat of, 81, 84, 140
    contagions of, 94
    outside of communication and, 45, 46, 48
    overprotection and risk of, 87
    threat of being misunderstood, 14, 83, 141
Mitdasein, 20, 75, 133, 134, 176 n. 85, 176 n. 86
Mitsein, 20, 120, 133, 134, 176 n. 85
munus, 72–77
    co-munus, 73, 75, 77–80, 136
    as gift and debt, 72–74, 75, 77, 82, 89, 91, 160 n. 30
    law's appropriation of, 76–77
    as origin of immunity, community, and communication, 17, 68, 74, 82, 89, 90, 141, 160 n. 11, 162 n. 47

Nancy, Jean-Luc
    on abandoned being, 6, 44, 57, 58, 156 n. 49, 175 n. 76
    on being as becoming, 166 n. 14
    on being-in-common, 117, 119, 121, 164 n. 74, 171 n. 6
    on being-with, 9, 19–20, 118–21, 123, 126–28, 132–36, 142, 175 n. 68, 176 n. 79, 176 n. 96
    on body as corpus, 97–100, 105
    on body as index, 18, 94–115, 167 n. 46
    on body as open, 101, 166 n. 29
    on community, 18, 19, 90, 95, 117, 119, 122, 125–28, 160 n. 12, 160 n. 29, 174 n. 56, 175 n. 78
    on *Dasein*, 120, 133, 134
    on embodied being, 18–19, 95, 96, 97, 112
    on exposure, 19, 90, 118
    on exscription, 9, 105–8, 118, 155 n. 34
    on language, 8–9, 123, 131–32, 159 n. 82
    on law, 15, 156 n. 56, 157 n. 59
    on *Mitdasein*, 20, 133, 134, 176 n. 85
    on openness, 18, 133–36, 176 n. 89
    as philosopher of relation, 5–6, 19, 96, 120
    on possession of the body, 95–96, 105, 106, 113
    on sensing, 123, 176 n. 89
    on sharing, 170 n. 96
    on "this is my body," 18–19, 95–96, 98, 103–4, 111, 165 n. 4
    on touch, 19, 20, 118, 128–31, 175 n. 74
    on a world, 170 n. 84
noise
    as communication outcome, 81, 90
    outside of communication and, 45, 47, 48
    overprotection against, 86
    potential for communication in, 12
    reduction of, 78
    in transfer models, 46, 153 n. 10

O'Byrne, Anne, 121–22, 129, 165 n. 9, 167 n. 42, 170 n. 94
Other, the
    being-with one another, 94, 102, 117, 132, 134, 138
    blurring of distinction with self, 13, 138
    communication as threshold between self and, 67–68, 78, 79, 81–84, 89, 90, 132, 163 n. 55

discourse of, 2, 24–27, 29, 32, 35, 38, 40
having-to-be with others, 58, 139
Henry on ego and, 123–24, 173 n. 38
other-perception, 17, 41, 80, 102, 115, 119, 131
presence of others, 102, 140
touch and, 130, 131
outside. *See* exteriority (outside)

parole, 51, 52, 106, 155 n. 31
perception
  body's capacity for, 102, 105
  embodiment and, 100, 122
  in human communication, 62, 84, 87, 93
  language and, 10, 25, 62, 107, 126
  of others, 17, 41, 80, 102, 115, 119, 131
  self-perception, 22, 27, 30, 32, 37, 39, 124
performatives, 54–55, 155 n. 40
Perpich, Diane, 105, 113, 112, 158 n. 77, 166 n. 21, 170 n. 87
Petrilli, Susan, 61, 158 n. 74
phenomenology
  on body-psyche relation, 105
  defined, 67
  Lacan and Heideggerian, 31–32
  Nancy and, 96, 101, 105, 118
  phenomenological reduction, 121, 124
  See also semiotic phenomenology
philosophy of communication
  on authority of language, 42–43
  ban, law, and, 62–65
  being-with and, 133–36
  the body and, 111–15
  definition of, 21–22
  Esposito's relevance to, 16, 68, 85
  exemplars of, 148 n. 40
  Nancy's relational philosophy as, 19, 96
  psychoanalysis and, 5, 23, 39–41
poststructuralism, 8, 54, 105, 142
presence
  bodily, 6, 96, 98, 99, 100–101, 102, 104, 110, 167 n. 47
  co-presence, 103
  metaphysics of, 18, 127, 128
  Nancy on, 95
  of others, 102, 140

pronouns
  Benveniste on, 52–54, 125–26
  child's use of, 36, 60
  "I," 36, 60, 105, 107, 125–26
  subjectivity indicated by, 59
protection
  in biopolitical paradigm, 15
  communication as, 14, 17, 66, 81–82, 92, 94, 116, 139, 140, 141
  community and, 70, 72, 73
  of identity borders, 67, 68, 75, 80–81, 84, 85
  immunity as, 67, 75
  immunization for, 70, 71, 76, 84, 93
  law as, 77
  overprotection, 17–18, 85–90, 92, 94, 133, 141
psychoanalysis
  on communication, 9–10, 23–24, 41, 42
  communication in, 27–34
  on discourse of the Other, 2, 24–27, 29, 32, 35, 38, 40
  of Lacan, 8, 9–10, 11, 23–24, 30–41, 42, 146 n. 20
  on language, 24, 26–27, 60
  on nonintentional communication, 10, 139
  philosophy of communication and, 5, 23, 39–41

Raffoul, François, 57–58, 112, 118–19, 134, 156 n. 57, 166 n. 35, 176 n. 87
relation
  ban of language as, 44, 56, 57
  being-with as, 117, 120
  the body as multiple in its relations, 99, 112, 129
  communication and, 92, 96, 127, 139, 165 n. 10
  embodied, 63, 134
  experience of, 93, 96
  identity as relational, 69, 75
  language as nonrelational, 56–57, 58
  Nancy on, 5–6, 118, 119
  relational exposure, 97, 115
  relational ontology, 19, 120, 136, 175 n. 67
Rizzuto, Ana-María, 37, 150 n. 20, 151 n. 45

Saussure, Ferdinand de
  on contractual nature of language, 50, 154 n. 21, 155 n. 45
  Lacan and structural linguistics of, 8, 32
  on *langue* and *parole*, 51
  on words as felt, 33
Schutz, Alfred, 2, 60–61, 163 n. 62
self
  blurring of distinction with other, 13, 138
  body's relation to, 96, 101, 107, 109, 112, 123–24, 130, 167 n. 49, 168 n. 58, 168 n. 62
  communication as threshold between other and, 67–68, 78, 79, 81–84, 89, 90, 132, 163 n. 55
  differences within, 39
  lack inherent to, 16, 147 n. 36
  self-expression, 17, 26, 33, 41, 80, 102, 115, 119, 124, 131
  touch and, 130, 131
semiotic phenomenology
  defined, 118
  communicology and, 118, 146 n. 21
  embodiment and, 121–25
  of Nancy, 19, 118, 119–21, 124–25, 126, 132, 146 n. 21, 172 n. 10
semiotics
  defined, 67
  in communicology, 146 n. 21, 159 n. 5
  humans as semiotic beings, 58
  Lanigan on semiotic systems, 122–23
  See also semiotic phenomenology
signifiers
  boundaries as, 48
  of expression, 31
  "I" as, 36, 60, 105, 107, 125–26
  Lacan on, 36–37, 60
speaking
  Agamben on language and, 51, 55
  Benveniste on humans as speaking beings, 12, 44, 58, 153 n. 5
  language takes place in speech, 57, 59
  language transcends, 64–65
  Lanigan on language and, 157 n. 62
  meaningful speech, 51, 52
  not speaking out, 86, 88

in psychoanalysis, 27–31, 34–37
  See also utterance
speech acts, 11, 53, 54–55, 59
structuralism, 8, 50, 105, 118, 146 n. 20
subjectivity
  body-subject, 105
  community as threat to, 73
  disfiguration of the subject, 10, 36, 81
  exposure to communication in constituting, 93, 140
  language and, 12, 41, 52, 53, 59, 63, 68, 117, 138, 153 n. 7, 154 n. 29, 155 n. 37
  subject-object dualism, 114, 140
  See also intersubjectivity; self
symbolic interaction, 60–61, 67, 123–24

threat
  communication as, 14, 66, 68, 81, 84, 88, 91–92, 94, 116, 140
  community and, 70, 73
  of identity border violation, 67, 68, 137
  immunization against, 70, 76, 82
  law as protection from, 77
  of too much immunizing, 85–86
  of violence, 76, 161 n. 44
touch
  bodies of others, 104, 129–30
  communication as, 142
  community as touching, 175 n. 78
  exposed to and in, 132
  giving oneself and, 131
  in haptics, 122–23
  Nancy on, 19, 20, 118, 128–31, 175 n. 74

uncertainty
  of human communication, 11, 40–41, 42, 84, 116, 137
  opening up to, 89, 141
  overprotection and risk of, 87
understanding
  communication defined in terms of, 62, 63, 131
  as effect of communication, 92
  inside of communication and, 45, 46, 48
  mutual, 5, 17, 66, 141

self-understanding, 28, 129
shared, 45, 80
See also misunderstanding
utterance
    Agamben on, 53, 54, 59, 157 n. 61
    in forgery, 1–3, 11, 65
    as making things outer, 177 n. 6
    in performatives, 155 n. 40

    in psychoanalysis, 32
See also speaking

voice, 10, 31–34, 52, 59, 139, 157 n. 61

Watkin, Christopher, 89, 166 n. 28
Wilden, Anthony, 24–25, 48, 127
Williams, Raymond, 4, 91